THE FOREST AND BIRD
BOOK OF
NATURE WALKS

THE FOREST AND BIRD BOOK OF
NATURE WALKS

David Collingwood and E.V. Sale
REVISED BY
Joanna Wright

REED

Published by Reed Books,
a division of Reed Publishing (NZ) Ltd,
39 Rawene Road, Birkenhead, Auckland.
Associated companies, branches and representatives
throughout the world.

ISBN 0 7900 0236 1
© 1992 Reed Publishing (NZ) Ltd

First published 1985
Revised edition 1992

Design by Richard King
Cartography by Sandra Parkkali
Typeset by Computype Services Ltd, Auckland
Printed in Singapore

CONTENTS

PREFACE

Walking is still the best and easiest way to appreciate the natural world. Walking can take you to places you can't get to by car, canoe or ski, and the pace of walking gives you time to take in the sights, sounds and smells of the living world. Even a short stroll away from the car and into a forest can reveal some of the many small wondrous things that go to make up New Zealand's unique natural environment – the song of the grey warbler, a native orchid beside the track, the scent of mahoe blossoms in summer. For seventy years members of the Royal Forest and Bird Protection Society have been exploring this country's trails. Their enthusiasm and knowledge led to the first edition of this book in 1985. This edition, ably revised by Joanna Wright, continues the wide coverage and attention to local detail. For many people, an interest in walking in the bush leads them to question why natural places have become fewer, and smaller and more degraded, a concern about wider environmental issues and a realisation that the footprint of human industrial society rests uneasily with the other forms of life on this planet.

Forest and Bird has long been New Zealand's largest and most effective conservation pressure group. It is now an organisation of 60,000 members and fifty-five branches, from Northland to Stewart Island. Its main aim is to protect New Zealand's natural heritage, but it aims also to foster an *appreciation* of that heritage. Without a popular understanding and appreciation of the special qualities of this country's wildlife and natural places, achieving their protection would be that much harder.

Ian Close
Editor, *Forest and Bird*

PUBLISHERS' NOTE

The information supplied in the track descriptions and maps has been checked and updated as far as possible. However, the constantly changing nature of many walks means that facts can quickly become outdated. The publishers welcome comments and new information, and invite readers to write to: Reed Publishing (NZ) Ltd, Private Bag, Birkenhead, Auckland 10.

INTRODUCTION

Everywhere you go in New Zealand, there is likely to be a selection of walks in the vicinity, whether you are in a city or small town, or closer to the wilderness. The nature of these walks is diverse and their administration varies. The Department of Conservation, regional and city councils, and private bodies like the Royal Forest and Bird Protection Society all take a part in the development and maintenance of walks. Since this book was first published in 1985, the scope of walks throughout the country has greatly increased. This book was originally written as a selection of favourite walks of the Forest and Bird members around the country. These descriptions have been updated and revised, some have been deleted and quite a number of new walks added, but the original style of the book remains. The maps have been redrawn with more current information. Several of the more arduous tracks and tramps have been taken out to give more room for shorter nature walks. Details of these longer tracks are readily available in other books and publications.

It would not be possible to write one book describing all walks available throughout New Zealand: what we have here is a starting point – a selection of over 150 walks from Cape Reinga to Stewart Island. Once you have discovered these, you may wish to find others. Local visitor centres and Department of Conservation offices can supply you with a wealth of information, pamphlets, maps and publications.

I would like to thank all those people who helped with the revision of this book, particularly Nick Smart and numerous staff of the Department of Conservation.

Joanna Wright

LOCATION OF WALKS

Boundaries are based on
Department of Conservation conservancies

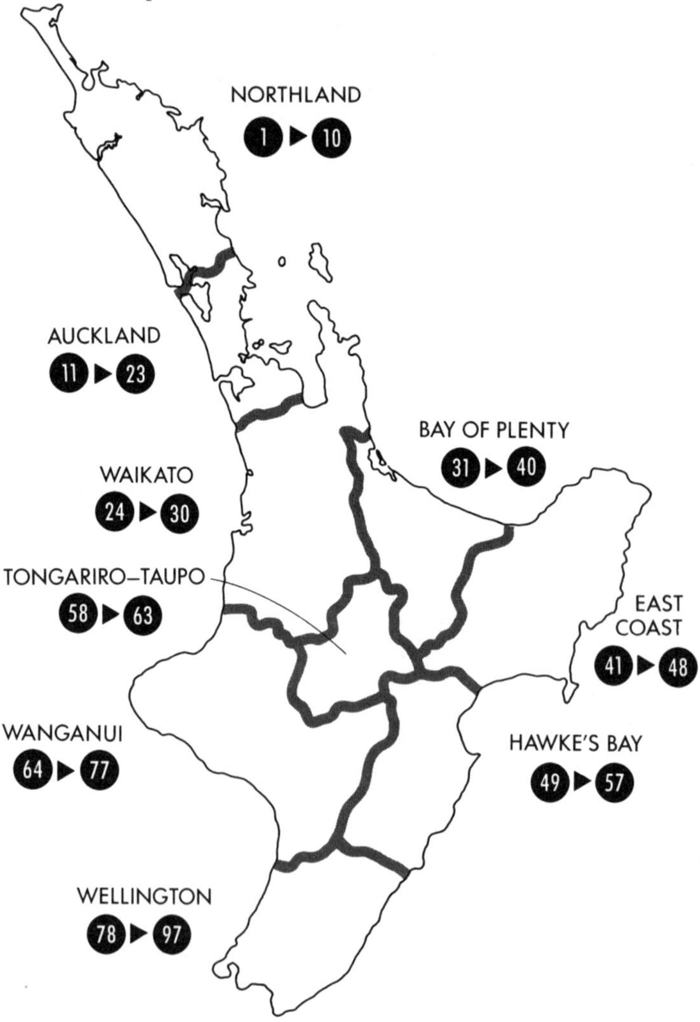

NORTHLAND
1 ▶ 10

AUCKLAND
11 ▶ 23

BAY OF PLENTY
31 ▶ 40

WAIKATO
24 ▶ 30

TONGARIRO–TAUPO
58 ▶ 63

EAST
COAST
41 ▶ 48

WANGANUI
64 ▶ 77

HAWKE'S BAY
49 ▶ 57

WELLINGTON
78 ▶ 97

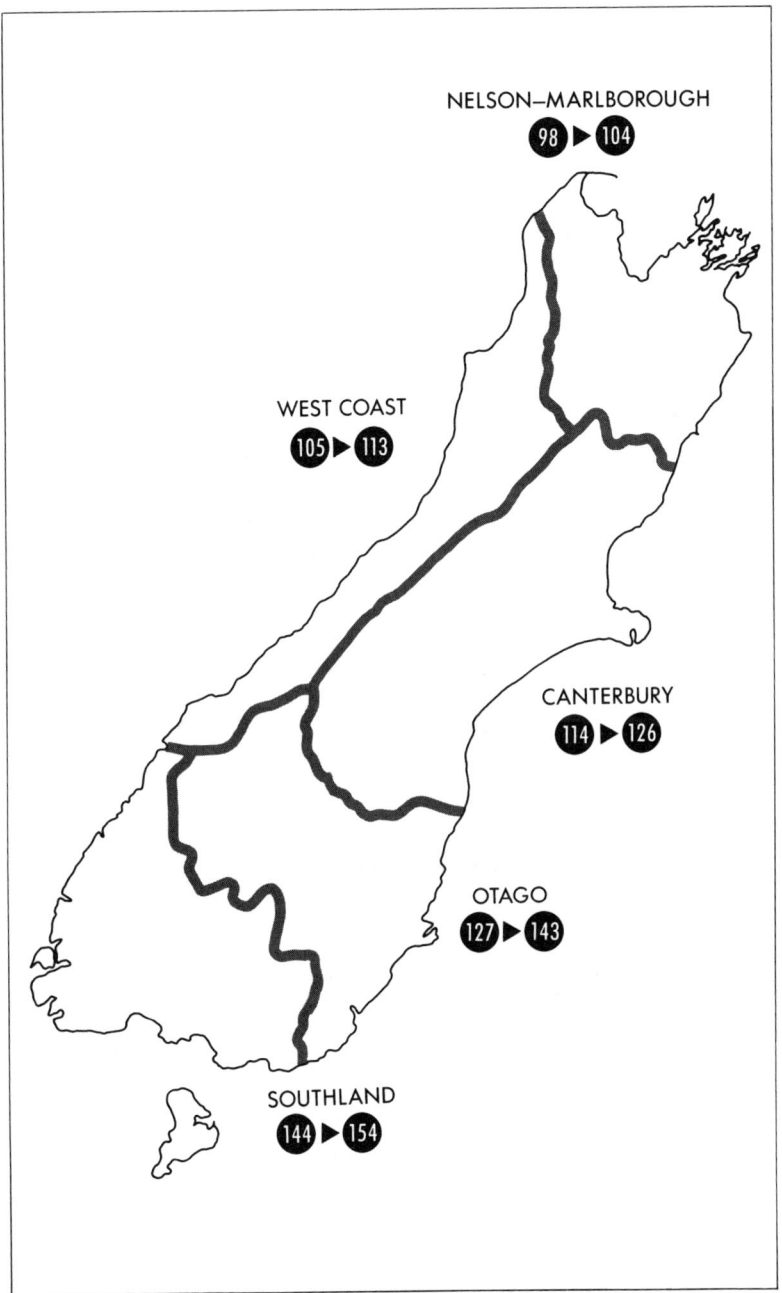

NELSON–MARLBOROUGH
98 ▶ 104

WEST COAST
105 ▶ 113

CANTERBURY
114 ▶ 126

OTAGO
127 ▶ 143

SOUTHLAND
144 ▶ 154

KEY TO MAPS

•••••• Track

Camping area

Picnic facilities

⌂ Hut

State highway

Ⓟ Parking area

Ⓣ Toilets

△ Trig

Waterfall

Viewpoint

North (where map is not aligned north)

Notable tree(s)

⊢ Bridge

Pa site

NORTHLAND

Cape Reinga

Length: Various
Time taken: Up to full day
Grading: Easy to demanding
Code: Year-round, plants, birds, sand dunes, views, camping, picnic areas

Points of note: Although much of the Cape Reinga area has scanty vegetation, there are areas of kauri bush around Te Paki Trig, and even the sand-dune wastes once carried heavy forest during Ice Age periods of lowered sea level.

There are quite a number of walks available in the area. If you are going on any extended walks, don't forget to carry drinking water and sun protection. For more information, contact the Department of Conservation at Kaitaia, the information centre at Waitiki Landing or the store near the lighthouse.

Access: State Highways 1 and 10 both lead to the base of the Aupouri Peninsula at Awanui, near Kaitaia, and from there the road to Cape Reinga runs for about 110 kilometres up the peninsula. There is access for much of the way up Ninety Mile Beach from Waipapakauri to Te Paki Stream for those who do not worry about what the sand and salt are doing to their vehicles.

Apart from some coastal pohutukawa trees and areas of scrub, the vegetation of the area is mainly flax, rushes and sand grasses, where the landform is not pure sand, piled and rippled by the wind into an attractive wilderness landscape. Sea and swamp birds abound, and parts of the area are thick with the shells of flax snails, which are now rarely seen alive and should not be disturbed.

Walks from Cape Reinga: A short track leads past the store to the lighthouse. Everybody who is able does this walk. From the hill just before the road heads down to the store, a track leads down to Sandy Bay (about 20 minutes down and 35 minutes up) and around the cliffs with spectacular views to Tapotupotu Bay (about 1 hour). From here a track continues to Te Paki Trig and on to Pandora Beach, where, if the tide permits, you can walk along Spirits Bay. There is camping at both Tapotupotu and Spirits Bays.

To the south of Cape Reinga, a track heads down to Te Werahi Beach and on to Cape Maria van Diemen, either returning the same way or continuing to Te Werahi gate. The return walk from Cape Reinga to Maria van Diemen takes about 3 hours, but a full day should be allowed for exploring and relaxing.

Walks from Te Werahi gate: The gate is 5 kilometres before Cape Reinga on the main road. If the weather is dry, you can take your car through the gate for about 1 kilometre to the start of the signposted tracks. The shorter walk bears right over the stile, through manuka to a boardwalk, on to an area of sandhills and eventually to the south end of Te Werahi Beach (1 hour), which stretches north-east toward Cape Reinga and south-west toward Cape Maria van Diemen. From here you can return to the starting point by circuits taking in Cape Maria van Diemen and/or Twilight Beach (3–5 hours). With transport arranged at the end, walks can be made to Cape Reinga (2–3 hours), or down the coast over Scott Point to the northern end of Ninety Mile Beach to Te Paki Stream (6 hours).

Te Paki Stream (1½ hours return): The road to Te Paki is off to the left about 5 kilometres north of the information centre at Waitiki Landing. The

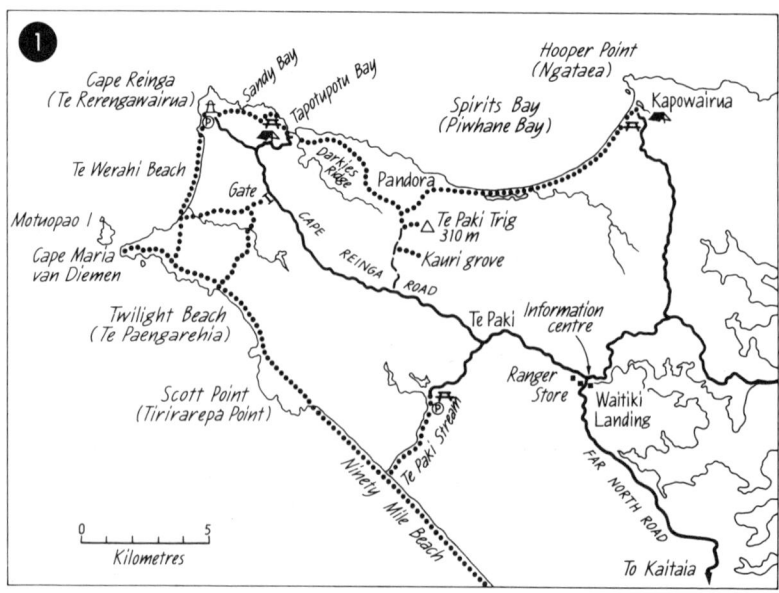

carpark and picnic area is about 3 kilometres down the side road. This is the route taken by the buses that return to Kaitaia via Ninety Mile Beach. On the walk to the coast the sand dunes make an interesting diversion, with evidence of midden sites, but can be rather hot underfoot (wear sandshoes).

Te Paki Trig and Pandora: A four-wheel-drive access road turns off Cape Reinga Road to the right about 5 kilometres past Te Paki. It's about 2½ hours return to the trig from here. A side track, on the right before reaching the trig, leads to a kauri grove. From the junction of the trig track, another track continues north-west along Darkies Ridge to Tapotupotu Bay and another turns off this to the north-east and heads down to Pandora at the western end of Spirits Bay.

Mangonui

Length: Various
Time taken: Up to 1 hour
Grading: Easy
Apparel: Casual
Code: Year-round, trees, birds, panoramas, swimming

Points of note: Mangonui, important in Maori tradition and with an historic European township, offers a number of short coastal walks, with a variety of bird life, chiefly birds of the shoreline.

Access: On Highway 10, about halfway between Kaeo and Kaitaia.

The starting point for several easy walks is at a rest area on Highway 10 about 1 kilometre beyond Mangonui township. Walk from here along Rangikapiti Road and turn right across the cattle stop up to the steps leading to the trig station on the site of Rangikapiti, built by the people of the *Ruakaramea* canoe, who were direct ancestors of the Ngatikahu tribe.

The view includes the full sweep of Coopers Beach, lined with pohutukawa and with a smaller pa at the other end; the entrance to Mangonui Harbour with Rangitoto Pa on the opposite headland near Butlers Point; and, directly below, Mill Bay, where sailing ships visited a kauri mill until early this century and which is now a safe anchorage for the fishing fleet and pleasure craft based at Mangonui. Along the coast are the outlines of Mt Puheke and, on a clear day, Mt Camel.

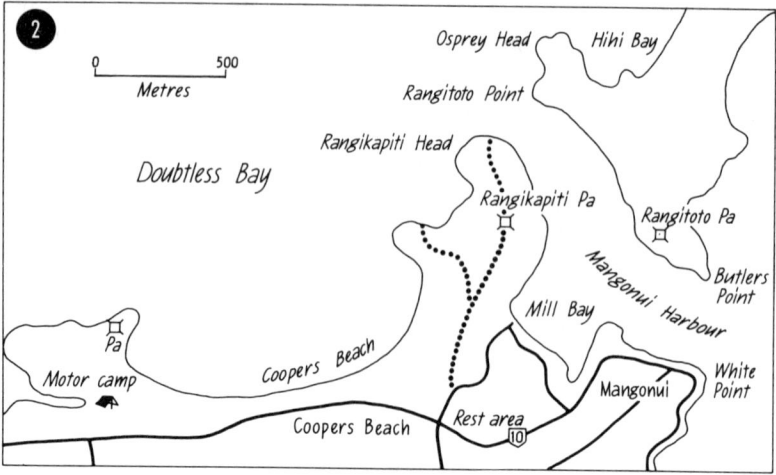

Follow the track leading out to the point and the automatic beacon that guides boats into the narrow harbour entrance (10 minutes). On the way back, walk over the cattle stop and turn right. The road ends at the bush. Take the mown track leading down the ridge to the point. A short, steep track leads down on the left to Coopers Beach. Down to the right is a small beach of golden sand with a backdrop of huge old pohutukawa. This is an ideal spot for a picnic lunch. On the way back, look for regenerating native trees: kohekohe, whau, kawakawa, ponga and coprosma.

For a walk along Coopers Beach, about 30 minutes each way, turn right on to a loop road near the rest area. About 10 metres along this road, just before the second house, a grassy track leads down to the beach past a small parking area. If there has been a recent storm, look in this corner for small fossilised coconuts. Golden oyster shells are sometimes plentiful. At the far end of the beach, past a motor camp, another track leads over the hill to a small shelly beach.

Omahuta Forest

Length: Various
Time taken: Up to 1½ hours
Grading: Easy

Apparel: Casual
Code: Year-round, trees, plants, flowers, birds

Points of note: Seven giant kauri stand in the natural bush setting of a small sanctuary, and there are two fallen giants.

Access: Turn off from State Highway 1 along Omahuta Valley Road, which leaves the highway 1 kilometre south of Mangamuka Bridge. The turnoff is reached from Okaihau in the south over rolling countryside, or from Kaitaia in the north over the bush-clad Maungataniwha Range. The signposted side road into the forest sanctuary is about 6 kilometres along Omahuta Valley Road, on the right, leading past the old forest headquarters.

The road into the sanctuary area winds through areas of cut-over bush, some replanted, some regenerating. Then kauri begin to rise beside the road, and a massive stump (signposted) shows the size of other felled giants.

About 10 minutes' drive into the forest, to the left of and below the road, is a picnic area beside the still waters of Apple Tree Dam, with tables and toilets. The kilometre to the sanctuary itself can be covered by car, but is best walked, either by the road or by a signposted track that starts across the road from the entrance to the picnic area. The road and track lead through high mixed bush, with some fine kauri towering overhead, plentiful bird life and flowering native shrubs. Small bush orchids abound, and in late summer the air is full of the rich scent of the Easter orchid.

The sanctuary walk itself is a circuit, with small off-shoots, through an area of 6 hectares. The area has been preserved as a sanctuary since 1951 because of the cluster of giant kauri miraculously found still standing in a small corner of an area that had suffered almost a century of logging.

Characteristically, the undergrowth of kauri is so thick that the giant trees, some of them more than 1,000, some perhaps 2,000, years old, are not seen until a turn in the path brings them into view. So it is usually one by one that Tokoiwa, Ngapuhi, Hokianga (the largest still standing in the sanctuary, at more than 53 metres high), Rakaunui, Ngatuahine (the twins) and Taniwha are sighted. On the way around them you can view from a platform the fallen giant Kopi, which, at 56 metres, was the third largest kauri to be measured, and another fallen giant, Whakamekere.

In the quiet of the bush you can see and hear a variety of birds – pigeons, tui, kaka, fantails, grey warblers and brightly coloured Australian rosellas. From the boardwalks and viewing platforms, constructed to protect the roots of the giant kauri, you see the trees of the typical Far North forest – rimu, totara, miro, kahikatea, taraire, pukatea and their attendant shrubs and creepers.

There are other kauri amid dense bush in the Omahuta Forest, but this is very rugged country and it is inadvisable to stray out of sight of the road.

You can return to the picnic area by either track or road to complete a circuit. Instead of turning back here, however, it is possible to continue to the Pukekohe Stream Track. From the end of the road, the track leads down to the stream under taraire and rimu forest and then climbs up to a ridge where a 10-minute side track leads to a stand of hard beech, which is uncommon in Northland. The main track descends once more to the stream, where an old kauri dam is still visible. The track then sidles out of the gully and continues through hardwood forest to another track junction. The left branch heads down to the old forest headquarters. The right branch leads through regenerating hardwood/podocarp forest to the sanctuary road, opposite the short track to the giant stump. It is about 15 minutes' walk back along the road to the picnic area.

Puketi Forest

Length: Various
Time taken: 3–4 hours
Grading: Easy to moderate
Apparel: Short walks, casual; longer, full tramping gear
Code: Year-round (except in parts after heavy rain), trees, birds, flowers, plants, sanctuaries, panoramas, waterfalls, swimming

Points of note: Puketi is a 8,061-hectare conservation park, some of which has been cut. Logging continued until 1979, when a substantial kokako population was identified. Substantial areas of untouched native bush remain heavy in kauri. The forest is on easy to steep country, sloping into the Waipapa River, which has some wide stretches and deep pools. There are a number of areas suitable for picnicking, camping and swimming.

Access: Puketi Forest can be reached by road from the east by turning off State Highway 10 north of Waipapa or south of Kaeo; from the south and west by turning off State Highway 1 near Okaihau or south of Rangiahua. Access to the forest is possible from Puketi, Forest and Waiare Roads.

Waihoanga Gorge Kauri Walk (2–2½ hours): One of the most popular routes in the forest, this is within the capabilities of school-age children. Signposted access is by foot from Puketi Road across open country into the forest above a waterfall on the Waihoanga Stream. The marked track then plunges into the

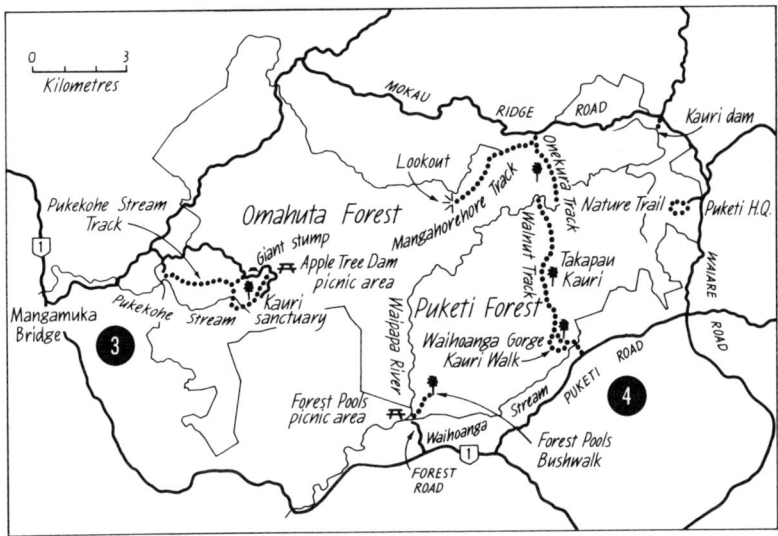

bush, soon reaching a large kauri about 600 years old. This tree shows the scars where it was bled for gum and has the fallen bark and litter of centuries piled up around the base of its trunk. It is surrounded by subsidiary bush – pole kauri, totara, toru, spiderwood, towai, taraire, rata vine, hinau, kiekie and tawa, with kauri grass and fern around the base.

Further on, through an area where forest trees are regenerating along the track, a large kauri was blown down in the hurricane of March 1959, when winds reached more than 100 knots, and one-tenth of the mature kauri trees in the forest fell in one night. Amid kauri grass, new forest trees are filling the gaps.

From here the track loops into a fine stand of mature kauri. These trees have a limited understorey compared with the lusher rimu and kahikatea areas that follow, where the predominant timber trees are joined by kohekohe (the New Zealand mahogany) and puriri, where a karaka sheds its berries and a rata strangles a rimu.

Bird life, as elsewhere in these forests, is most noticeable in early morning and evening. (Morning is preferable for those who want to linger, because of the danger of being caught overnight in the bush.) It includes kaka, kiwi, tui, pigeons, moreporks, tits, warblers and the rare kokako.

There are numerous other tracks in the forest; a selection of these are briefly described below:

Kauri Dam (15–20 minutes): A good track leads down from Waiare Road through regenerating forest, to the remains of an old kauri dam used at the turn of the century.

Puketi Nature Trail (2 hours): This starts by the Puketi Forest visitor centre and leads through a wide range of forest types from scrub to kauri forest, with interpretation signs along the way.

Forest Pools Bushwalk (1–2 hours): A climb up the ridge above the camping area at the end of Forest Road.

Takapau Kauri (3–4 hours return from Puketi Road): A track continues from the end of the Waihoanga Gorge Kauri Walk to the three giant Takapau kauri, one of which is the fourth largest in New Zealand.

Onekura Track (30 minutes): A short, steep track from Mokau Road to the Waipapa River Track. There is a magnificent stand of kauri on the Onekura Bluff.

Walnut Track (30–45 minutes): Another steep track, connecting Waipapa River Track to the end of the old logging road on Pirau Ridge, in the heart of kokako country.

Mangahorehore Track (1 hour 40 minutes): This track gives access from Mokau Road to the Mangahorehore viewpoint.

Manginangina Scenic Reserve (10–20 minutes): Manginangina Scenic Reserve, adjacent to Puketi Forest, provides the easiest way of seeing typical kauri bush, with most of the features present that make this a unique forest association.

Access is easiest from State Highway 10, along a side road signposted just north of Waipapa, but the reserve can also be reached via Puketi Road from the south, from the west off State Highway 1 and from the north off the Waiare Road, south of Kaeo.

You enter the reserve straight from the road, which at this point is lined on both sides by dense bush, including some fine kauri. The walk leads into established bush, unchanged except for a track system. The convenient shortness of the circuit, the variety of the trees and the quality of the kauri make this a popular place in which to enjoy the bush, with long pauses to listen for the birds in the tops of the tall trees. Most birds of the Northland bush are found here.

5

Waitangi Reserve and Haruru Falls

Length: 5 kilometres
Time taken: 2 hours
Grading: Easy
Apparel: Casual
Code: Year-round, trees, birds, fish, waterfall

Points of note: The unique feature of this family walk is a boardwalk through mature mangrove forest. The track traverses the Waitangi National Trust Reserve and generally follows the northern bank of the Waitangi River through areas of regenerating bush. It is signposted at each end, and information leaflets are obtainable from the Waitangi visitor centre.

Access: If walking from Haruru Falls, turn off Highway 10 at Puketona and follow the Paihia Road to the Haruru Falls turn-off. There is a parking area beside the falls and the track leads off just to the left. If approaching from Waitangi, follow the markers from the Treaty House grounds down past the golf course clubhouse. The track description follows the direction from this point.

After skirting the golf course, the track enters bush and follows along the Waitangi Inlet. The bush here is mainly a mixture of tanekaha, kohekohe and ferns. After a 30-minute walk over easy grades, the track crosses a bridge over the Hutia Creek. The boardwalk then winds through the mangroves for about 250 metres.

The Waitangi estuary is the feeding ground for many fish and birds. At low tide come banded rails, pied stilts, dotterels and white-faced herons. Full

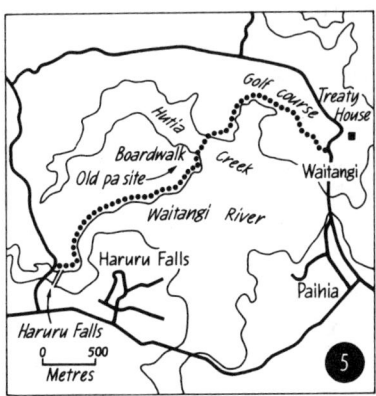

tide brings pied and little black shags, and red-billed and black-backed gulls. Also seen often are fantails, tui, kingfishers and welcome swallows. The most common of the thirty species of fish known to inhabit the inlet are yellow-eyed mullet, flounder, parore and eels, and at high tide snapper, trevalli, tarakihi and kingfish have been observed.

At the far end of the boardwalk a shell midden is evidence of past Maori occupation. The path skirts the inlet, passing through an area with lichen-hung fruit trees and other exotic trees, shrubs and bulbs, obviously the site of a homestead years ago.

At Haruru Falls the Waitangi River leaps quite spectacularly to the estuary below. After rain there is a big volume of water, and occasionally a rainbow may be seen.

6

Bay of Islands

Length: Various
Time taken: Up to full day
Grading: Easy
Apparel: Casual
Code: Year-round, trees, views, swimming

For further information, contact the Department of Conservation, Bay of Islands Maritime and Historic Park, Russell.

Moturua Island: This scenic reserve is notable botanically for its lush and healthy regeneration, and historically for its link with early British and French explorers. An accidental fire several years ago burned over part of the island but left the walk area largely untouched.

At the time of writing, tourist boats do not land passengers on the island. Access is therefore by private or hired boat.

The walk is designed to be walked in an anti-clockwise direction starting from Waipao Bay and crossing a saddle to Otupoho Bay and on to Wai-whapuku Bay. The name Moturua means Double Island, and there is a second, smaller Moturoa off the northern tip, near Hikurangi Pa. The track is good all round the circuit of the island and should be kept to, as there are several cliffs. Moturua has four good bathing beaches and a number of pleasant picnic areas.

Motukiekie Island (½ hour): The walk traverses the length of the island, most of which is in regenerating native bush, with an area planted in exotics where Norfolk Island pines are flourishing.

Cape Brett (8–9 hours): A walk for experienced trampers that can only be done with prior permission from Maori landowners. Note that there may be no water on this track.

Whangamumu (1 hour each way): This walk over a ridge through regenerating bush to a former whaling station site has fine views from the ridge of bush and coast. The entrance to the track is signposted on the Parekura–Rawhiti Road.

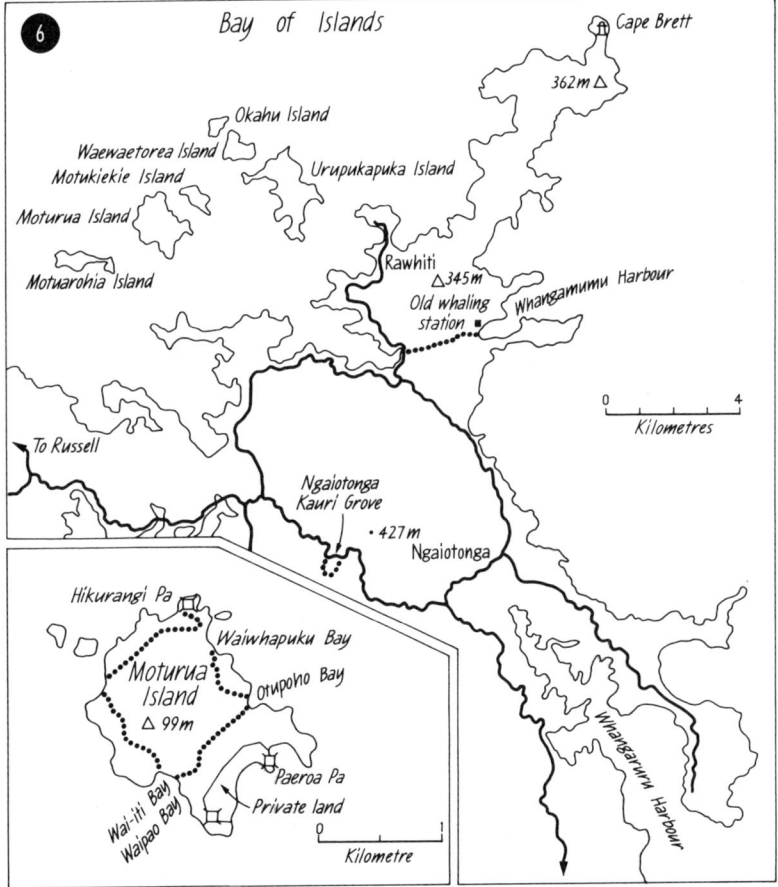

Whangaruru, North Head: Further down the coast from Whangamumu and accessible by road, this area offers several walks, ranging from a few minutes to 2 hours. Puriri, pohutukawa and kowhai give shelter to ferns and orchids, and there are many native birds.

Ngaiotonga Kauri Grove (20 minutes): This nature walk is signposted on a hill section of the coast road south of Russell. Trees and shrubs are labelled along the well-formed loop track.

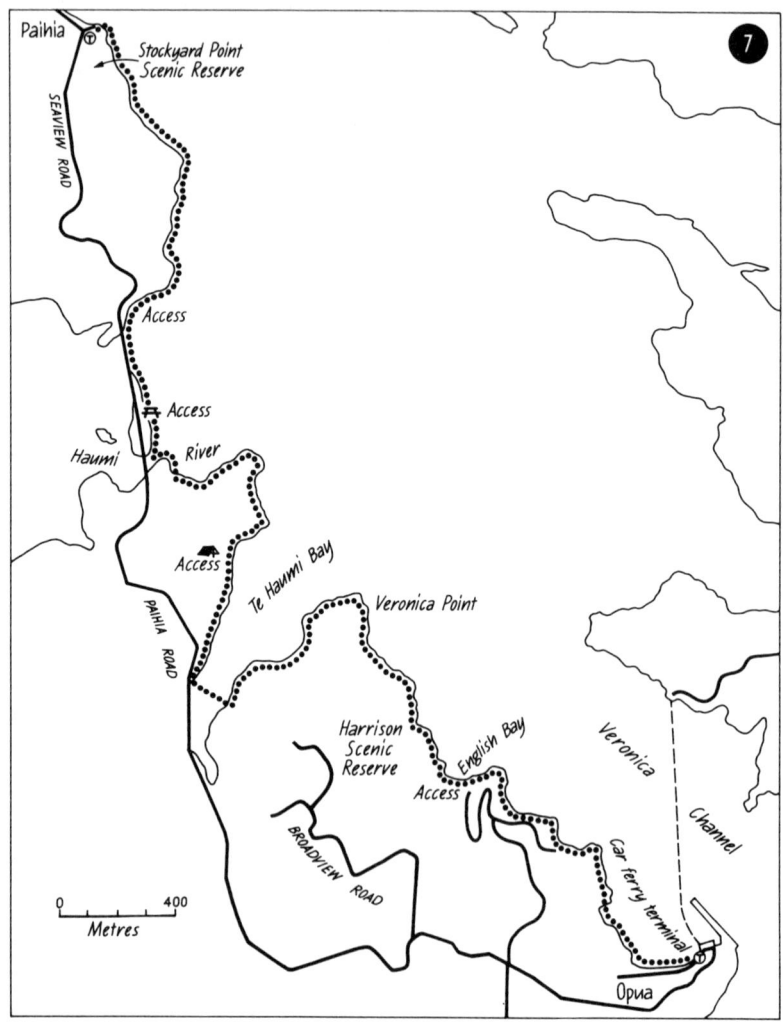

Opua–Paihia Walkway

Length: 8 kilometres
Time taken: 3-4 hours
Grading: Easy
Apparel: Casual
Code: Year-round, trees, birds, estuary, views

Points of note: This extremely popular walk follows the shoreline between Opua and Paihia. It passes through a remnant of coastal broadleaf forest in the Harrison Scenic Reserve, clearings and a boardwalk track through mangrove swamp. If you are planning to do the full walk, it is necessary to arrange transport at either end, but it can also be walked in three shorter sections. Time your walk to avoid high tide on the last section from the causeway to Stockyard Point.

Access: There are four access points to the walk, which starts at the Opua Wharf and ends at the Stockyard Point Scenic Reserve on Seaview Road in Paihia. There are additional access points at English Bay, Te Haumi Bay, and from Paihia Road.

From Opua, the track follows the shore platform, alternating between eroded greywacke and sandy beaches, past English Bay to the Harrison Scenic Reserve, where a side track leads to Broadview Road. The reserve comprises 12.5 hectares of native forest, with kohekohe, puriri, karaka and other species. The main track continues around the shore, climbing slightly to a navigation beacon at Veronica Point, where a short side track goes to a viewpoint, and on to Te Haumi Bay, where a boardwalk passes through mangroves – habitat for the banded rail.

Past the motor camp, the track heads around the next point and along the causeway. It is another 1.25 kilometres around the shore to the Stockyard Point Scenic Reserve.

Opua Forest

Length: Various
Time taken: Up to 3 hours
Grading: Easy to moderate

NATURE WALKS

Apparel: Casual

Code: Year-round, trees, birds

Points of note: Being close to one of the earliest European settlements in New Zealand, the Opua Forest was extensively cut over for all types of timber, and much of it was later burned, but this was long enough ago for extensive regeneration to have taken place. A few good kauri remain from the original forest.

Access: Access is from School Road, which runs from Paihia beside the village green, or from the Opua–Oromahoe Road.

The longest of the recommended tracks starts at the end of School Road and, after about a 20-minute walk, reaches a good lookout point where there is a fine view of the Bay of Islands. Those who do not wish to go further can retrace their steps by a loop with more fine views to the School Road entrance, where there is a picnic table. The continuing track leads on through regenerating bush to reach the Opua–Oromahoe Road after about 3 hours.

Kauri Loop Walk (about 45 minutes) starts about 1 kilometre further west along the Opua–Oromahoe Road from this outlet, and has a picnic area at the start. For those going directly to this walk, the Opua–Oromahoe Road begins near the Kawakawa turn-off from the Paihia–Opua Road, and the Opua recreation area is 3 kilometres along its winding route. The track,

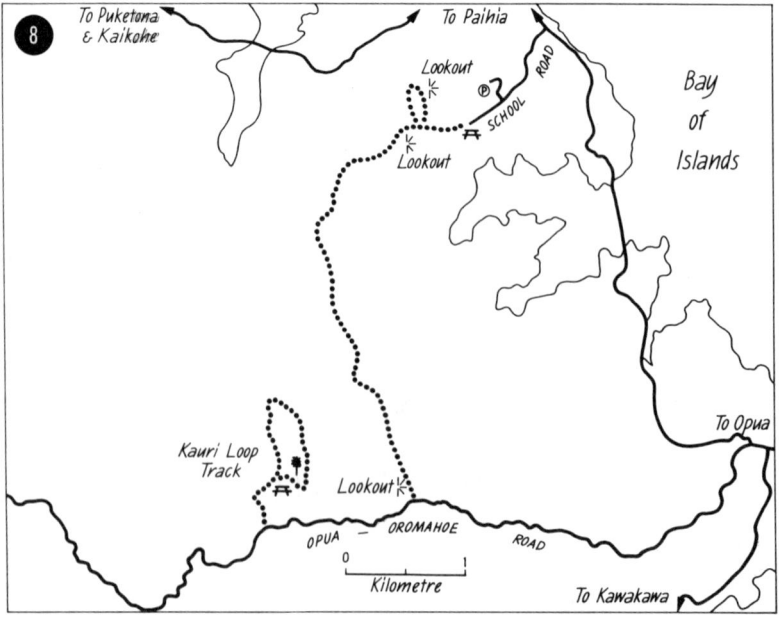

stepped in places, leads into an area of bush, and a short side path takes you to a viewing platform. Some good kauri that escaped the almost total felling in much of the rest of the area include Tane Whakapiripiri (400 years old) and Tane Waonui (500 years old). The stag heads of the big trees stand out above the rest of the bush. Many of the native trees along the track are labelled.

The forest ridges are mainly in manuka and kanuka, with podocarps and broad-leaved species regenerating on the lower ridges and in the valleys. Bird life includes tui, native pigeons, fantails and silvereyes.

Russell Forest

Length: Various
Time taken: Up to full day
Code: Year-round, forest, views, birds

Points of note: The Russell Forest comprises a number of forest areas, extending from the Waikino Inlet in the eastern Bay of Islands, south to Whananaki Inlet, totalling 10,000 hectares of low-altitude regenerating native forest. The primary recreation area is the Punaruku Valley, where there are a number of short walks, and the start of the longer Ngaiotonga Walkway. For further information, contact the Department of Conservation, Whangarei.

Access: Turn off State Highway 1 at Whakapapa onto the coastal route to Russell. A forest road turns off this road 3 kilometres north of Oakura and runs 4 kilometres up the Punaruku Valley. The start of each track is marked on this road.

Hori Wehi Wehi (1–2 hours return): Suitable for family groups, this track is signposted on the right, about two kilometres up the Punaruku Road and finishes about 1 kilometre further along. It passes through stands of kauri and features the particular giant after which the track is named.

Lookout (1–2 hours return): This steep walk to a lookout near Puke-moremore (390 metres) offers views of the forest, Whangaruru Harbour and out to the Poor Knights Islands in the distance. The track starts a short way up the road from Hori Wehi Wehi, on the left.

Monoa Trig (4–6 hours return): Starting by a picnic area about 1 kilometre up the Punaruku Road, this track follows the stream for a distance then climbs a spur to the leading ridge to the trig (399 metres). There are a number

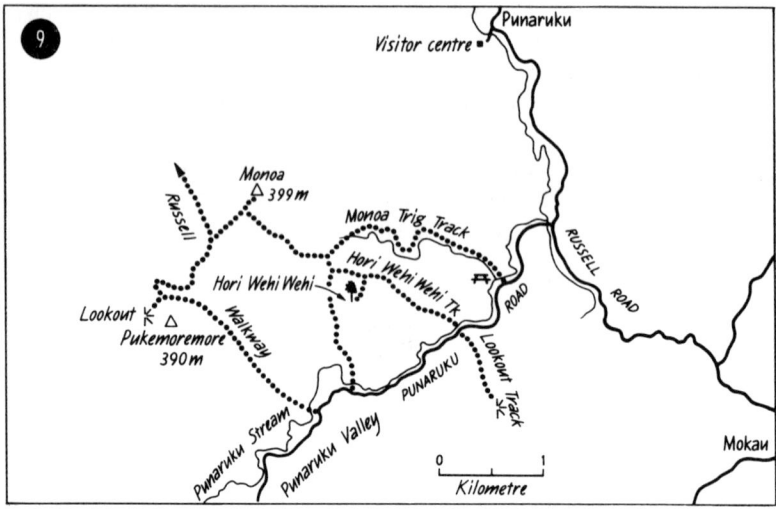

of options for the return trip. A side track from the trig track leads to the Russell Walkway, where a left turn leads to Pukemoremore and back to Punaruku Road about 2.5 kilometres up from the start (2 hours).

Waipoua Forest

Length: Various
Time taken: Various
Grading: Easy (suitable for wheelchairs) to moderate
Apparel: Casual; good footwear for longer walks
Code: Year-round, trees, plants, flowers, birds

Points of note: Kauri forest was once found throughout Northland, Auckland, the Coromandel Peninsula and in northern Waikato. Its popularity for ship-building and general construction, along with commercial use of kauri gum, led to its rapid decline with the arrival of Europeans in the country, and only a few tracts remain. Waipoua Forest is part of the proposed Kauri National Park, which will include more than thirty separate areas scattered throughout Northland.

Waipoua is particularly renowned for its giant trees, but the forest is also extremely rich and varied in different species. It is also home to rare birds such

28

as the North Island kokako and the North Island brown kiwi, with rare appearances of the native forest parrots kakariki and kaka. The carnivorous kauri snail is another notable inhabitant.

There are a number of developed walks in the forest and also in the Waima Forest further to the north. For further information, contact the Department of Conservation, Dargaville.

Access: State Highway 12 runs through the forest, which lies between Dargaville and Opononi. The walks are generally well signposted from this road.

Tane Mahuta is the largest living kauri in New Zealand, with a girth of 14 metres and a height of 51 metres. A short track (3 minutes), suitable for wheelchairs, leaves the highway from a carpark in the northern area of the forest.

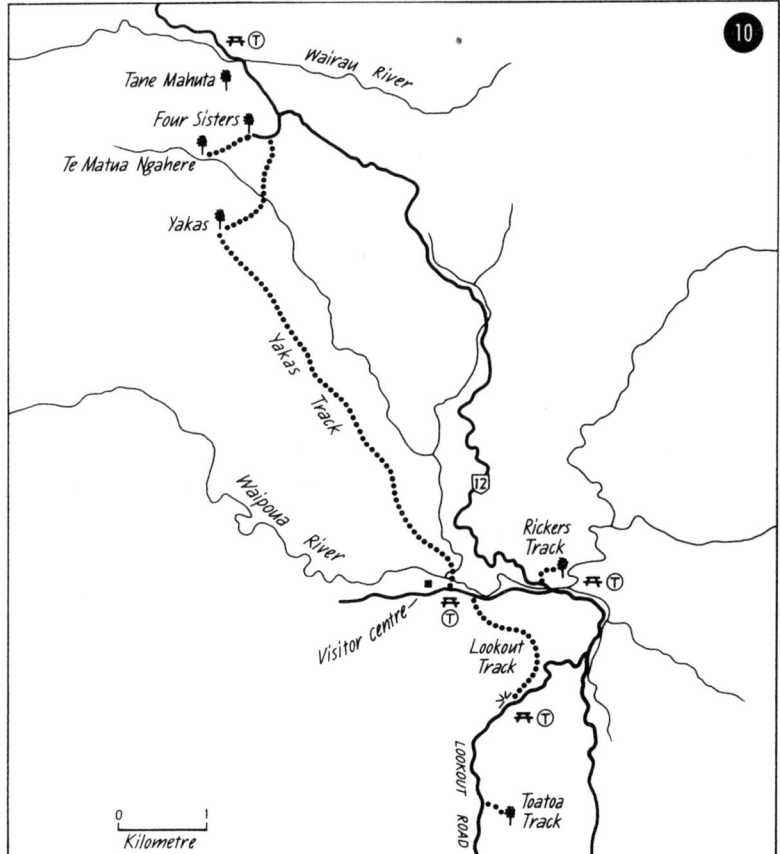

Te Matua Ngahere, the second-largest kauri, is an easy 15-minute walk on a good track. Although it has a smaller volume of timber than Tane Mahuta, it is thicker through the trunk.

The Four Sisters is an impressive stand of four trees growing close together, and is reached on a 100-metre track, suitable for wheelchairs.

Yakas Kauri is a 30-minute walk from the carpark on a track that can be muddy after rain. The Yakas is the largest tree in the Cathedral Grove.

Yakas Track (3 hours): The track continues from the kauri to the Waipoua River and village on the other side of the river. A track also leads along the riverbank to the highway.

Rickers Track (10 minutes): From the carpark on the north side of the Waipoua Bridge, a short track climbs through a stand of young kauri rickers to a viewpoint overlooking the river.

Lookout Track (1 hour): The road to the forest lookout turns off the main highway to the west and is well signposted. The lookout tower, about 1.5 kilometres up the road, is open to the public and gives an expansive view of the forest. A good track leads down from the lookout to the Waipoua Forest village.

Toatoa Track (10 minutes): A couple of kilometres south from the lookout is a short walk with labelled plants.

Waiotemarama Bush Walk (3 hours): This walk in the Waima Forest starts on the Waiotemarama Gorge Road, which turns off the main highway at Waiotemarama or Pakanae. The walk makes a loop at the upper end and is very attractive, with waterfalls, gorges and a variety of forest types.

AUCKLAND

Leigh Walkway

Length: 2 kilometres
Time taken: 1 hour
Grading: Easy to moderate
Apparel: Casual
Code: Year-round, trees, birds, flowers, plants, scenery

Points of note: The track gives extensive views over the outer Hauraki Gulf and down the cliffs to steep rocky shores. It passes through rough grassland for most of the way, but also through patches of coastal forest. The cliffs have been grazed by sheep and cattle in the past, but are now fenced off, and a planting programme of local coastal trees and plants has been initiated in the hope of regenerating the vegetation. Seats are provided at intervals.

The waters surrounding Goat Island are a marine reserve – New Zealand's first, created in 1975. All marine life is protected in the reserve and no fishing is allowed.

Access: The walkway can be reached from the Leigh–Pakiri Road by taking the signposted turn-off to Goat Island Beach. There is a carpark by the beach.

From the carpark the track follows the access road to a private farm and the University of Auckland's Marine Research Laboratory (available for inspection by interested groups who have made prior arrangements with the director).

The track bears right from the access road across a stile and follows a line of white marker posts across farmland to the cliff edge. From here it follows the cliff edge and fenceline for most of the way until it meets private property. You must return along the same track. The walk itself lies entirely on private property, and the farming activities must be respected. The main break from the coast occurs after 1 kilometre, where the track veers inland a little way into a gully with coastal forest containing tall kahikatea, karaka, puriri and taraire trees.

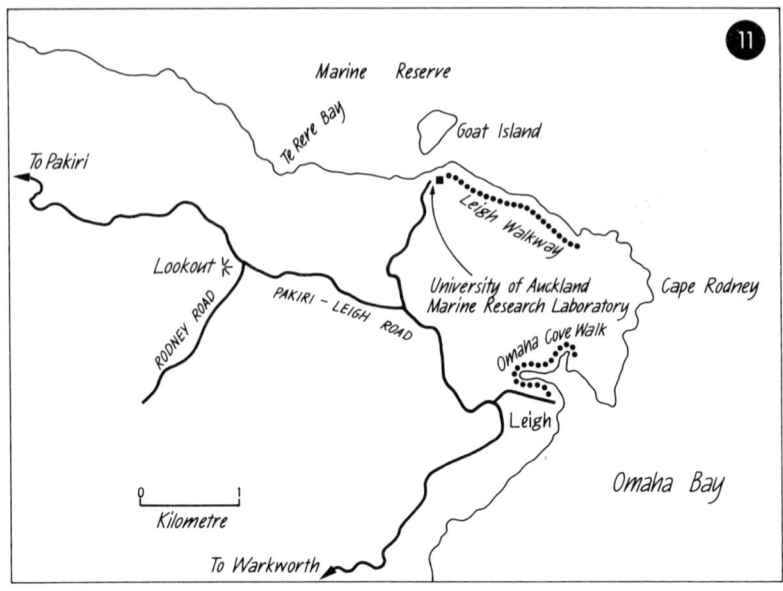

Seabirds can be seen to advantage from the walk, and include petrels, shearwaters, gannets, little blue penguins, black-backed and red-billed gulls, Caspian and white-fronted terns, and reef and white-faced herons. Harriers, welcome swallows, kingfishers, New Zealand pipits, fantails, grey warblers, silvereyes, tui and magpies also frequent the walkway.

Omaha Cove Walk (30 minutes): This pleasant, level walk begins from the Leigh Wharf boat ramp and follows the margins of the harbour, with pleasant views of this fishing harbour and gulf area.

There is a carpark near the wharf, but when this is full, another entrance is available from the Leigh–Wellsford Road, on the town side of the fish factory.

From the boat ramp the track follows the edges of the harbour, initially on a concrete path and over a small footbridge, where the stepped track from the Wellsford Road joins the main track. It continues along a grassed area, in front of private property for 200 metres, then over another footbridge and on through coastal forest and scrub. The track ends at a small beach and private property. Return the same way.

Dome Forest

Length: Various
Time taken: Up to 3½ hours
Grading: Moderate with some steep sections
Apparel: Casual, depending on season
Code: Year-round, trees, flowers, plants, birds, views

Points of note: The first 500 metres of this ridge track, with fine views and a kauri grove at the end, follow a narrow road reserve to the state forest boundary. Visitors should not stray in this area because there is private property on either side.

Access: The track is reached from a parking area on the eastern side of State Highway 1 opposite Kraacks Road, 7 kilometres north of Warkworth or 12 kilometres south of Wellsford.

The path follows a ridge running in a northerly direction, enclosed by secondary growth, and is of easy gradient, apart from two sets of steps. The second set, alongside a fence on the right and encountered within 200 metres, is quite steep and can be slippery after rain. At about 500 metres, the track makes an abrupt turn eastwards and enters the reserve proper. Although well defined, the track also has yellow marker blazes attached to trees.

Beside the track, in season, you can see hooded orchids, kidney ferns, libertias and dianellas under a broadleaf-podocarp mixture of secondary

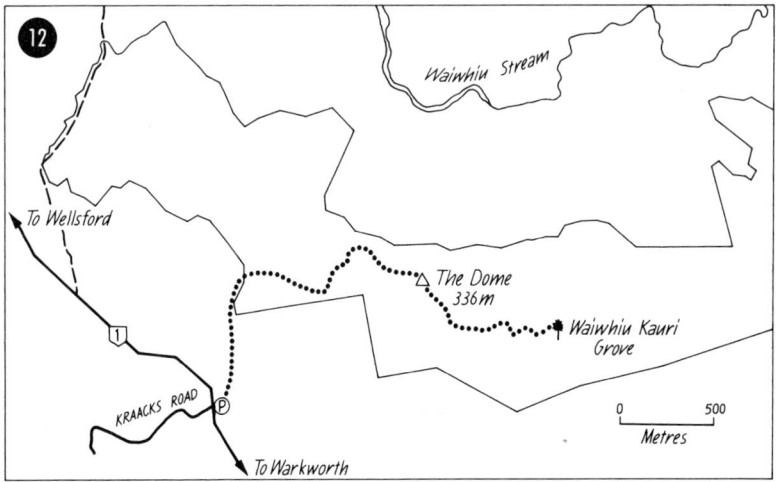

species in cut-over forest. These include mapau, nikau, ponga, rewarewa, rangiora and mingimingi. Scattered through this thick cover are rimu, totara, miro, kahikatea, puriri, tawa and kauri.

There has been some erosion, exposing tree roots, on the track, which ascends and descends many times with very little level walking, until a large overhanging rock is reached, which has to be surmounted to reach the summit. The path detours down and to the left under the overhang and then mounts up and hard around to the right and steeply up over the rock. Care must be taken, as there are no real supports or handholds.

The path then proceeds through clumps of flax (slippery when wet) and thence to the summit of the Dome (336 metres), reached after about an hour from the road. With easier grades for 800 metres, the track continues past several large boulders on the western (right) flank and reaches the reward at the end – the Waiwhiu Kauri Grove, a mature stand of twenty trees.

Native pigeons, warblers, kiwi, harriers, pheasants, Californian quail, rosella parakeets, shining cuckoos, moreporks, kingfishers, fantails, silver-eyes, tui and magpies are seen and heard on the track.

Walks about Warkworth

Length: Various
Time taken: Up to 2 hours
Grading: Easy
Apparel: Casual; good footwear in wet weather
Code: Year-round, trees, plants, flowers, birds

Points of note: Warkworth, at the head of the tidal water of the Mahurangi River, is the centre of a farming district settled soon after 1850. Much timber and kauri gum was sent to Auckland in the early days, but numerous small patches of bush remain, and several contrasting examples are easily accessible to a day visitor.

Access: The walks begin on or near State Highway 1, 67 kilometres north of Auckland.

Riverside walks: The carpark (with picnic tables) behind the main business area of the town faces across the river to a reserve of second-growth forest with much totara and some fine old kowhai trees. Downstream from the wharf, a grassy path shows the successful planting of flax along the river bank and of a variety of native trees on the slope above. Upstream, planted kowhai complement those opposite. Where the riverbed becomes more rocky, white-baiters may be seen in season. Fresh water flows over the weir or dam built originally so that water could be piped some 2 kilometres down to the cement works, one of whose founders, Nathaniel Wilson, is commemorated in a plaque on the steps leading to the double bridge. A flower garden on the deck of the older bridge is maintained by the local beautifying society.

Birds to be seen along this walk include black-backed and red-billed gulls, Caspian terns, white-faced and reef herons, mallard ducks, harriers, welcome swallows, kingfishers, fantails, grey warblers, silvereyes and tui.

Kowhai Park, established in 1933, is a bush reserve of some 4 hectares bordering the main highway as it leaves Warkworth for the north. The walk is approached from the roundabout where the traffic turns off to Leigh and the Mahurangi Peninsula. The gravelled track runs parallel to Mill Stream, then climbs over a drier spur (with picnic table) and descends rather steeply as it passes disused lime kilns.

Medium-sized trees predominate, including many old kowhai. Notable among larger trees (labelled) are some good matai and kahikatea, several kauri and at least one big totara.

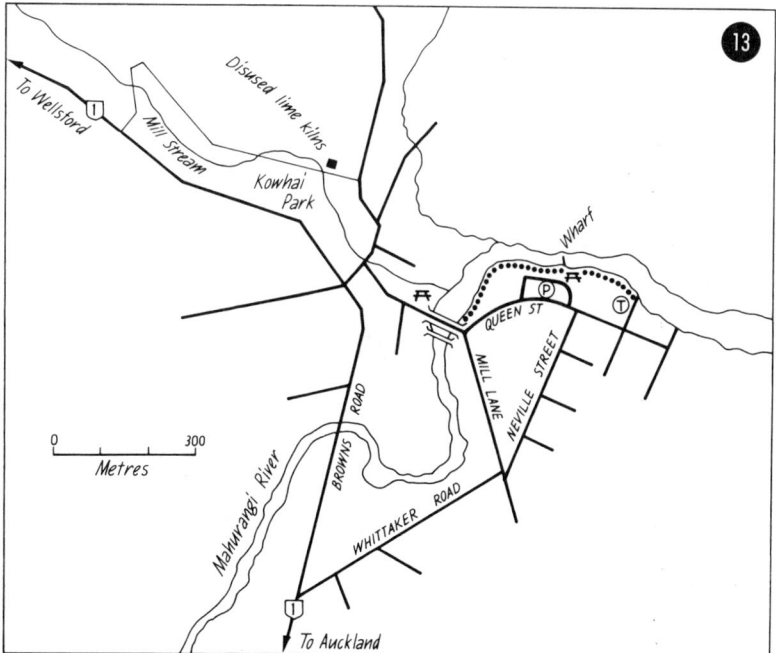

Parry Kauri Park is on a loop road, south of the main highway between the Satellite Station and Warkworth. The park is signposted at McKinney Road and Palmer Street. The gate is padlocked against vehicles at night.

Tudor Collins Drive into the park leads to the Warkworth and District Museum. There are picnic tables nearby. In the 8-hectare park, partly in pasture, there is a short bush walk worth half an hour's browsing. Two fine kauri trees, named McKinney and Simpson, are ideally situated for photographing. Between them young native conifers of six species – kahikatea, tanekaha, miro, rimu, totara and kauri – make an attractive edge to the bush.

Behind the McKinney Kauri a path leads over a stile and through a stand of young kauri where ground orchids abound in spring. Groves of taraire and some gnarled old puriri loaded with epiphytes alternate with massed tall treeferns occupying areas recovering from more recent clearing. Young nikau palms are a feature of the forest floor, and by the stream the purplish-green leaves of parataniwha (begonia fern) form a colourful mosaic. More than sixty species of native plants can be seen before the track emerges through a small gate below the Simpson Kauri.

Woodcocks Kawaka Reserve: From State Highway 1 take Woodcocks Road, 1 kilometre south of Warkworth, and then drive 5 kilometres to the reserve.

This short bush walk, with a single track, ends on a ponga knoll. As the area is underdeveloped at the time of writing, visitors are asked to assist in the preservation of young native regrowth by not leaving the track.

The bush consists mainly of mature and immature kawaka, with a subsidiary mingling of tanekaha, rewarewa, matipo and kahikatea. There is some regeneration of kauri in isolated pockets. Large numbers of fern species are present, and during August and September several extensive areas of the green-hooded ground orchid can be observed.

Mt Auckland Walkway

Length: 6.5 kilometres
Time taken: Airstrip to trig, 2 hours; trig to Glorit Farm, 1½ hours
Grading: Moderate to steep
Apparel: Seasonal tramping gear
Code: Year-round, trees, birds, flowers, plants, views

Points of note: The track traverses a podocarp-kauri-hardwood forest in which rimu, kauri, kahikatea and totara thrive in different areas. Associated with this is a dense mosaic of hardwood species including taraire, karaka, puriri, kohekohe, hinau and kowhai. There are many epiphytes and lianes and a rare orchid, *Yoania australis*, to be found beneath the taraire.

The name of the peak, Atuanui, has a mystical significance (atua – god; nui – great). Maori use is evident by the large pa site on the summit. It has been a state forest since 1887 and before that was milled in accessible areas.

Access: The approach to this walkway is via the Glorit–Kaipara Hills Road, 22 kilometres north of Kaukapakapa, or a steep climb from the Glorit Farm settlement, on Highway 16, where there are parking and toilet facilities.

From the Kaipara Hills Road entrance a driveway leads up to an airstrip and the route then leads along the left-hand fenceline (white markers) toward the Atuanui State Forest. The walkway follows a ridge through native forest, with three opportunities for signposted side trips to see groups of mature kauri.

Though not level, the terrain is not at all difficult. At the summit of Atuanui/Mt Auckland (305 metres), there are panoramic views. In the north foreground winds the Hoteo River, and to the west and north spreads the Kaipara Harbour. In clear conditions the Hen and Chicken Islands, Great Barrier Island and Coromandel Peninsula can be seen to the east.

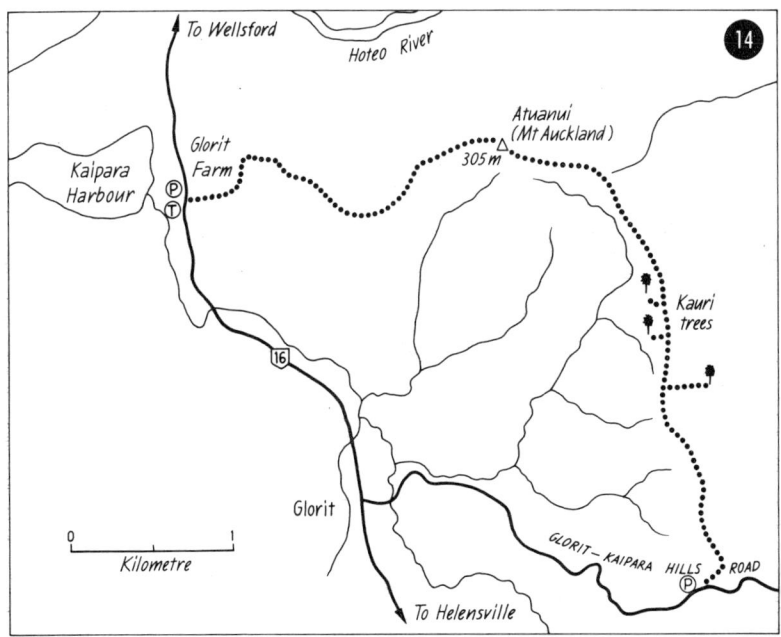

From the trig the track descends steeply out of the bush to the Glorit Farm settlement and State Highway 16.

Birds you may see include New Zealand pipits, fantails, grey warblers, silvereyes, tui, magpies, white-faced herons, pheasants, Californian quail, rosella parakeets, shining cuckoos, moreporks, welcome swallows and kingfishers. Petrels and shearwaters have previously nested near the summit.

Shakespear Heritage Trail

Length: 3.8 kilometres
Time taken: 1³/₄ hours
Grading: Easy
Apparel: Casual
Code: Picnic and camping areas, beaches, swimming, boating, views

Points of note: Shakespear Regional Park covers 376 hectares at the tip of the Whangaparaoa Peninsula. There is a variety of vegetation, with bush, scrub, wetlands and swamp contrasting with pasture. Army, Okoromai and Te Haruhi Bays provide excellent swimming and picnicking. Historically, the park is also interesting, with evidence of two Maori pa, at Army and Te Haruhi Bays, and European defence structures.

The gates to the park are closed overnight; the closing time is displayed on the gate. There are information boards at all the bays, and a ranger is on duty.

As well as the Heritage Trail, there are other walks that are colour-coded and easy to follow. For more information, contact the Auckland Regional Council.

Access: The reserve is about an hour's drive north of Auckland. Take the Whangaparaoa Peninsula turn-off from State Highway 1 and follow the main road to the park.

The Heritage Trail has numbered points along the way, which are explained in an Auckland Regional Parks pamphlet, usually available by the information boards for a small fee.

The walk starts at Army Bay and leads up the stream in Waterfall Gully, through mature native forest. Puriri and karaka are common species, along with kohekohe, taraire, kowhai and whau. The track crosses the stream and passes the waterfall. After crossing the stream a couple more times, it leads out onto pasture and climbs a ridge to the lookout. A plane table identifies the islands of the Hauraki Gulf that can be seen from this magnificent vantage point.

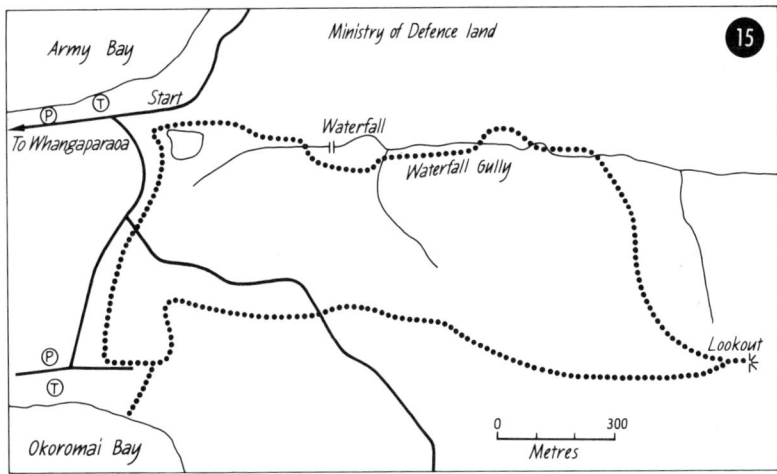

The track now heads west along an open ridge to the gun emplacement. From here it continues across farmland, crosses the road and leads to Okoromai Bay. Finally, the track follows a raised bank through the swamp, back to the start by the duck pond at Army Bay. Pukeko and spotless crake may be seen in this area.

Okura Bush

Length: 9 kilometres
Time taken: 2–3 hours each way
Grading: Average
Apparel: Casual; good footwear in wet weather
Code: Year-round, trees, birds, views, historic cottage

Points of note: This walk leads through the Okura Scenic Reserve, which contains 116 hectares of native bush, along the shores of the Okura and Weiti River estuaries and Karepiro Bay. This is the best example of regenerating lowland, coastal, podocarp-hardwood forest on the east coast, near Auckland. There are some large kauri, and some thirty other recorded tree species.

The walk can be made one way, with transport arranged at the other end, or return, with a possible alternative via the foreshore at low tide. Many people walk from Haigh Access Road to Dacre Cottage and return (about 2½ hours). Beyond here the track is less well formed.

39

Access: The southern end of the track is reached at the end of Haigh Access Road, which turns off the East Coast Road past Redvale. A footbridge spans the Okura River here. At low tide, however, it is also possible to cross the tidal flats from Okura to a sandspit on the northern shore. The northern end of the track is at Stillwater. There is a camping ground by this access point.

At the bridge the track heads into the bush. After about 20 minutes it

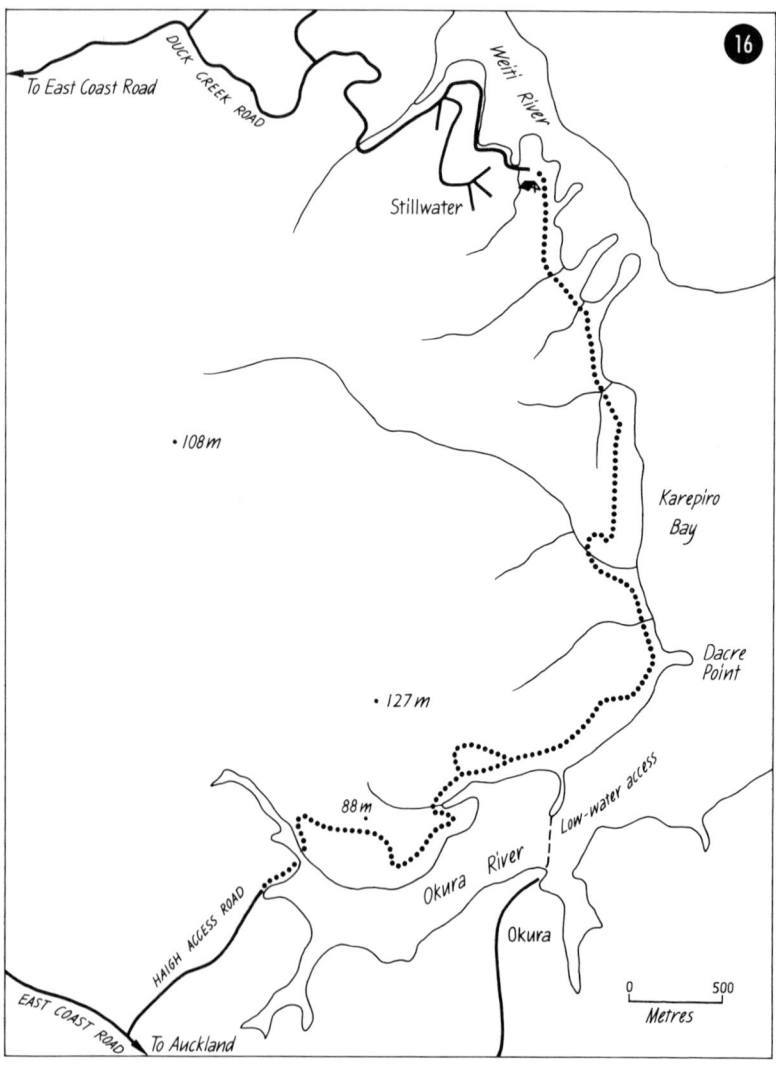

descends closer to the shore and passes the sandspit opposite Okura, before heading back into the bush and continuing to Dacre Point. Here it leads down to Karepiro Bay and along to Dacre Cottage, owned by the Historic Places Trust.

Across the stream the track climbs up to the top of a bluff, where it continues, with good views of the Hauraki Gulf, until it drops down to the Weiti estuary and continues to the track end. Fantails are the most commonly seen bird in the bush. The sandspit, mudflats and estuaries are good places for observing seabirds, particularly oystercatchers and dotterels.

Round the Bays

Length: 6–8 kilometres
Time taken: 2–3 hours
Grading: Easy
Apparel: Casual
Code: Year-round, birds, trees

Points of note: A city walk that offers native bush, waterways and wetlands, this excursion allows you to see a surprising number of birds within half a day. It connects with Tamaki Drive bus routes, and there are refreshments and toilets at Mission Bay and other beaches.

Access: A good place to start is near Parnell Baths on the Waitemata Harbour waterfront. The baths occupy a corner of Judges Bay adjacent to the Rose Gardens at Parnell.

Set out eastward along Tamaki Drive. Look inland across Hobson Bay to the large pohutukawa growing precariously from low cliffs, prone to slipping in places. Watch for seabirds, for besides gulls, gannets and Caspian terns, the white-fronted tern (tara) is usually present, especially around the dinghy sheds or heading across the harbour towards the wave screen, the posts of which form a safe refuge for nesting terns and gulls during early summer. If the tide is out, pied stilts, white-faced herons and several kingfishers will be feeding on the mudflats and red-billed gulls may be paddling vigorously in the shallows, a trick they use to stir up small crustaceans.

After 1 kilometre turn inland on Ngapipi Road. The headland here, below Paritai Drive, carries a dense cover of mixed native and adventive vegetation, and the path climbs, giving views of Mt Hobson, Mt Eden and

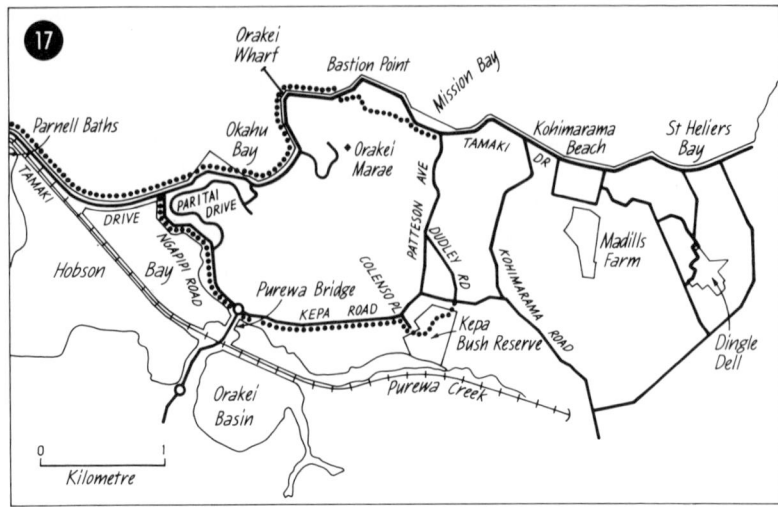

the city before descending to the stone Purewa Bridge, where several pohutukawa have established a tenuous hold. The Orakei Basin, a volcanic explosion crater, is the next landmark, seen on the right-hand side while ascending Kepa Road.

Paddocks at this point are grazed by cattle and ponies, but there are also spinneys with sufficient undergrowth to shelter pheasant and Californian quail and to provide cover for the nesting of introduced finches and yellow-hammers. Ducks and pukeko find food and shelter along the water's edge.

Except in very wet conditions, the next stage is a detour by way of Colenso Place to follow the sheltered track through Kepa Bush Reserve, an important remnant of the original coastal forest of the Auckland isthmus. Kohekohe, rewarewa and rata are dominant trees, with kanuka on the ridges and a protective screen of hawthorn and other exotics around the fringe. The Auckland branch of the Forest and Bird Society has co-operated with the local community committee to ensure protection of this 12-hectare reserve and to plant karo, kowhai and other natives at the picnic area entrance opposite Dudley Road.

Rejoining Kepa Road just short of the intersection with Kohimarama Road, you can choose to return to Tamaki Drive by Kohimarama Road or via Dudley Road and Patteson Avenue, or through the reserve known as Madills Farm.

Buses are frequent along the waterfront, but if you are walking back to the city, you should climb the steps from Mission Bay over Bastion Point to see splendid views of the Hauraki Gulf and Rangitoto Island. An easy descent to Tamaki Drive past Orakei Wharf, another likely spot for terns and welcome swallows, brings you to Okahu Bay, a popular swimming beach from November to February. It is 2 kilometres back to the Judges Bay starting point or, if your legs are weary, the bus service into the city will come in handy to complete the circuit of the bays.

For a longer ramble, from Kepa Road follow Kohimarama Road to the beach of that name and thence stride out eastwards along Tamaki Drive to St Heliers Bay, a short way inland and Dingle Dell, a peaceful reserve of streams and native trees to which has been added a memorial grove of kauri in honour of King George VI.

During the waterfront leg it is worth looking out for pied oystercatchers, white-faced herons, and possibly a blue reef heron, which, with common birds, should bring the day's tally to more than twenty species. Refreshment stops are plentiful along this part of the route, and there are regular buses to Parnell Baths or into the city Downtown Terminal.

Tahuna-Torea Nature Reserve

Length: Various
Time taken: Up to 2 hours
Grading: Easy
Apparel: Casual
Code: Year-round, birds, plants, seashore, observation shelter, sanctuaries

Points of note: Tahuna-Torea (the gathering place of the oystercatcher) is a nature reserve in the city area where the visitor can see comparatively unmodified coastal vegetation, and the patient birdwatcher can discover a surprisingly wide range of species. There is an observation shelter and hide, and a system of all-weather tracks. Members of the Auckland branch of the Forest and Bird Society take part in caring for this City Council domain.

Access: The reserve, also known as Glendowie Sandspit, lies between West Tamaki and Riddell Roads, in the Auckland suburb of Glendowie, and juts into the Tamaki Estuary. Buses from the city Downtown Terminal for Glendowie to its Riddell Road terminus or for Glen Innes to the Taniwha Street-West Tamaki Road corner, take you within a few minutes' walk of the reserve. Entry points are from West Tamaki Road, by steps from Vista Crescent or by a coastal footpath from Riddell Road.

The observation shelter off West Tamaki Road gives a wide view over several

43

ponds. Pied stilts and white-faced herons feed in the shallows, with mallards, grey ducks and pukeko, frequently accompanied by chicks in the summer months. This is an excellent vantage point for photography.

Along the foreshore, Arbor Day plantings of flax and pohutukawa provide shelter and are well established among the predominant cover of fennel and tall grass. This track turns inland to skirt the marshy part of the reserve and allows a quiet approach to the mangrove-fringed tidal inlet.

Flocks of shore birds, oystercatchers, stilts, godwits and Caspian terns take refuge in this part of the sanctuary. The oystercatchers are at their most numerous from March to August, while godwits, accompanied by knots, predominate in the summer months, especially during March as they gather, in breeding plumage, just prior to migration. For the best views of these wading birds, time the walk for high tide or an hour or so later.

A feature of the northern side of the reserve is the brackish pond, originally a series of Maori fish traps and now a good place to see shags, kingfishers, herons and welcome swallows, which are encouraged to breed within the reserve by the provision of nest boxes.

From here at least three courses are open. On a fine day the choice could be a stroll eastward exploring the mudflats or following the shelly beach to reach the tip of the sandspit, a roosting place of pied shags and black-backed gulls, near the main channel of the Tamaki Estuary and close to passing yachts.

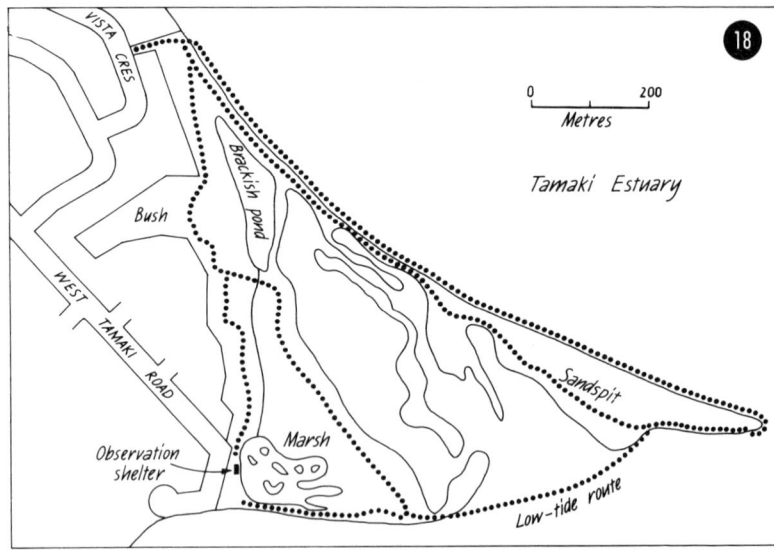

The coastal route in the opposite direction from the pond leads via a tarsealed cliff path to a large grassed reserve, which is an alternative haunt of the shore-bird flocks should they not have been found in the sanctuary itself.

A bush path, with side tracks to several raised vantage points, traverses the last of the habitats to be explored during the Tahuna-Torea walks.

Onetangi Bush Reserve

Length: Various
Time taken: Day trip from Auckland to Waiheke Island; bush walks, 1–2 hours
Grading: Easy
Apparel: Casual
Code: Year-round, trees, birds, flowers, swimming

Points of note: The walk is in the Onetangi Bush Reserve, a 45-hectare area purchased by the Forest and Bird Society in 1961 to preserve one of the few remaining stands of native forest on Waiheke Island. A visit to the reserve by boat and bus from Auckland makes an excellent day's outing, with a choice of bush or beach walks and good swimming in summer.

Access: Ferries to Waiheke leave from the Auckland downtown ferry terminal, and a combined boat and bus return ticket to Onetangi is recommended. (Check times and fares in advance.) It can be chilly on the boat, so have extra clothing even in summer, and take binoculars to watch for seabirds during the crossing.

From Auckland to Matiatia Wharf on Waiheke is a 35-minute boat trip that passes Rangitoto, Motutapu and Motuihe Islands. Rocks on Motuihe are a likely place to spot shags and white-fronted terns. The terns (kahawai birds, or tara) may also be seen feeding in large flocks. These often attract the attention of a migratory pirate, the Arctic skua, a brownish bird with pointed tail, not to be confused with the young of the black-backed gull. Gannets, little blue penguins and fluttering shearwaters are also encountered on inner gulf waters.

At Matiatia, board an Onetangi bus, which proceeds via Oneroa and Ostend to the beach front at Onetangi, where toilets and refreshments are available. Here the store will provide directions to the reserve, which is a 1-kilometre walk inland via Victoria Road and Scotts Terrace.

Opposite the Scotts Terrace entrance to the reserve is a cottage belonging to the society, which is popular for weekends and members' short holidays.

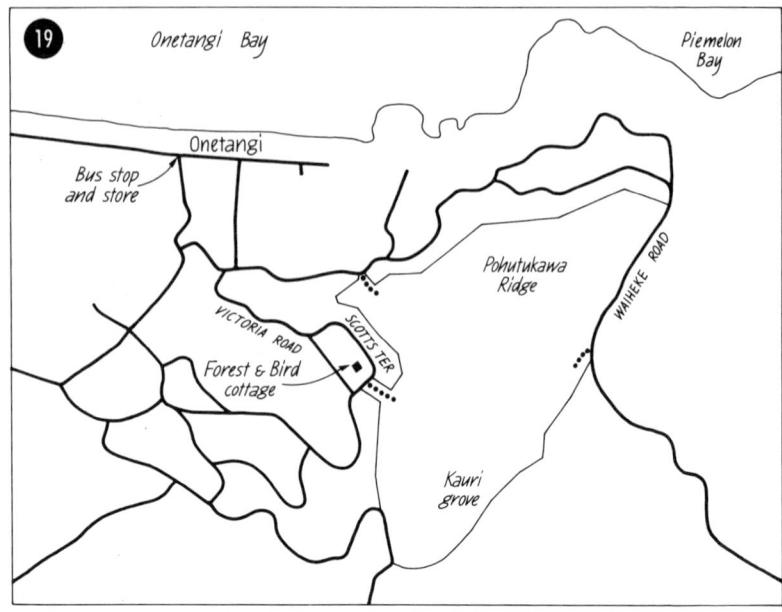

For bookings, write to D. McLean, 55a Queens Drive, Oneroa, Waiheke Island, or phone Waiheke 6494.

Signs at this gate and route markers within the reserve invite visitors to walk through the bush but ask that all care be taken and that animals be excluded.

Botanical features of the reserve include several impressive nikau palm groves, some large trees (notably kauri and matai) and a wealth of seedlings by which the understorey is regenerating. Some replanting has been encouraged, using species that occur naturally on the island, and the good state of the bush bears witness to the absence of harmful opossums.

A stream and its tributaries run through the bush, and in summer the damp places will be the best to find native birds. Bellbirds are absent, but tui are plentiful and should be easily seen and heard; and fantails, grey warblers and silvereyes are well-established residents. Native pigeons are always a feature, and kaka are sometimes to be seen over the reserve, being a resident species in bush on more remote parts of the island.

As well as the Scotts Terrace gate there are two access points from Waiheke Road. The higher reaches of the reserve afford fine views of the bush and over Onetangi Bay and the Hauraki Gulf. Allow extra time if you wish to make a beach walk or to have a swim before catching the bus to the wharf.

20

Waitakere Ranges Centennial Memorial Park

The Waitakere Ranges offer a superb opportunity for walking in close proximity to Auckland. Below is a brief selection of all-weather loop tracks of about an hour's duration, suitable for all walkers.

Auckland City Walk: From Swanson, in West Auckland, follow the Scenic Drive to Te Henga Road, which leads to Bethells Beach. A short distance down this, turn left onto Falls Road, which leads to the park (about 7 kilometres from Swanson).

This track is in the Cascade/Kauri area, one of the few stands of virgin kauri forest remaining in the Waitakere Ranges. For security, vehicle access is restricted at night and the gates are usually closed about sunset. Check at the Arataki Park Information Centre on the Scenic Drive or by signs at the entrance. An Auckland Regional Parks pamphlet explains a number of marked stations along this walk.

The track heads through native bush with some large kauri trees. It starts at the lower end of the picnic area and leads up Waitakere Stream to its junction with Cascade Stream. The falls are a short distance up this side

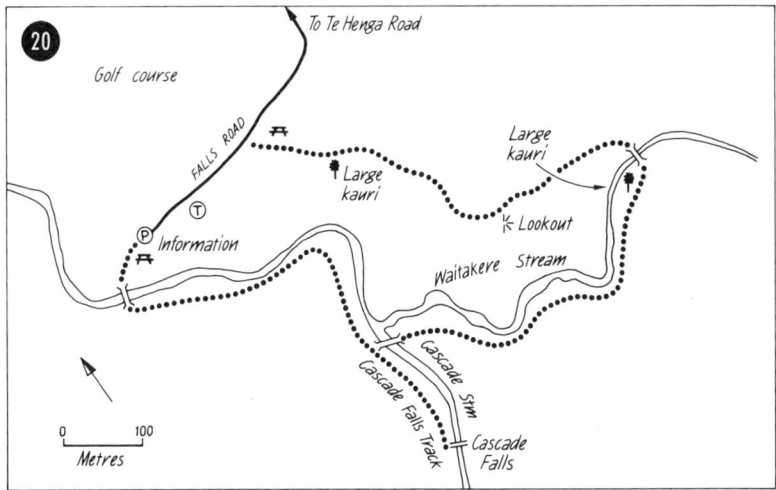

stream. The main track crosses a bridge and continues along the stream to a second bridge, where it climbs back up to the picnic area. There are a number of longer tracks in the area.

Fairy Falls–Old Coach Road Track: The Fairy Falls Track starts opposite the carpark on the east of the Scenic Drive, about halfway between the information centre and Swanson.

This enjoyable walk of 2–3 hours takes in a spectacular waterfall and returns to the Scenic Drive via the Old Coach Road Track, which passes some large kauri and rimu. It is also possible to be picked up by car at the end of the Fairy Falls Track on Mountain Road (1–2 hours).

The track begins on the level, but then descends steeply to the top of the falls (45 minutes). A very steep track leads down to the base of the falls and continues downstream a short way before climbing to Mountain Road. The Old Coach Track continues to the left here. A side path to the left from this, Goodfellow Track, offers an alternative route back to the Fairy Falls Track (30 minutes). The coach road heads up to the Scenic Drive and a walking track leads close to the road, back to the start (2–3 hours).

Arataki Nature Trail: Starting opposite the information centre on Scenic Drive, 5 kilometres from Titirangi, this nature walk is divided into three loops of varying length, so visitors can choose a suitable walking time (20 minutes to 1½ hours). A pamphlet available at the centre aids in interpretation.

The shortest loop is the plant identification trail, with over fifty labelled native plants. The upper loop leads through regenerating forest, and can be a little steeper in places. The lower loop leads through mature rain forest to a grove of magnificent kauri at the far end. There are some steep sections and a few stairs on this track, with a number of seats along the way.

Jubilee Walk: Take the Huia Road from Titirangi and after about 13 kilometres turn left on to Pine Avenue and the Cornwallis Beach carpark. The walk begins 2 minutes from the lower carpark, back up the road on the right.

From the entrance, the track loops through coastal bush to a lookout over Mill Bay, then returns to the road. Across the road it re-enters the bush and winds downhill through regenerating scrub typical of gumland. The sundew plant, *Drosera*, and native orchids grow well in this habitat. There are regenerating kauri trees and an area of planted pines. A section of boardwalk crosses a wetland area dominated by sedge, before the track heads back to exit at the upper carpark (1¼ hours).

This walk commemorates the golden jubilee of the Auckland Centennial

Memorial Park and is of particular interest because it passes through one of the last areas of gumland in the Auckland region. There are a number of interpretation points explained by a Regional Parks pamphlet.

Karamatura Loop Track: From Titirangi, take the Huia Road to the Huia settlement (about 14 kilometres) and continue toward Little Huia. Enter the

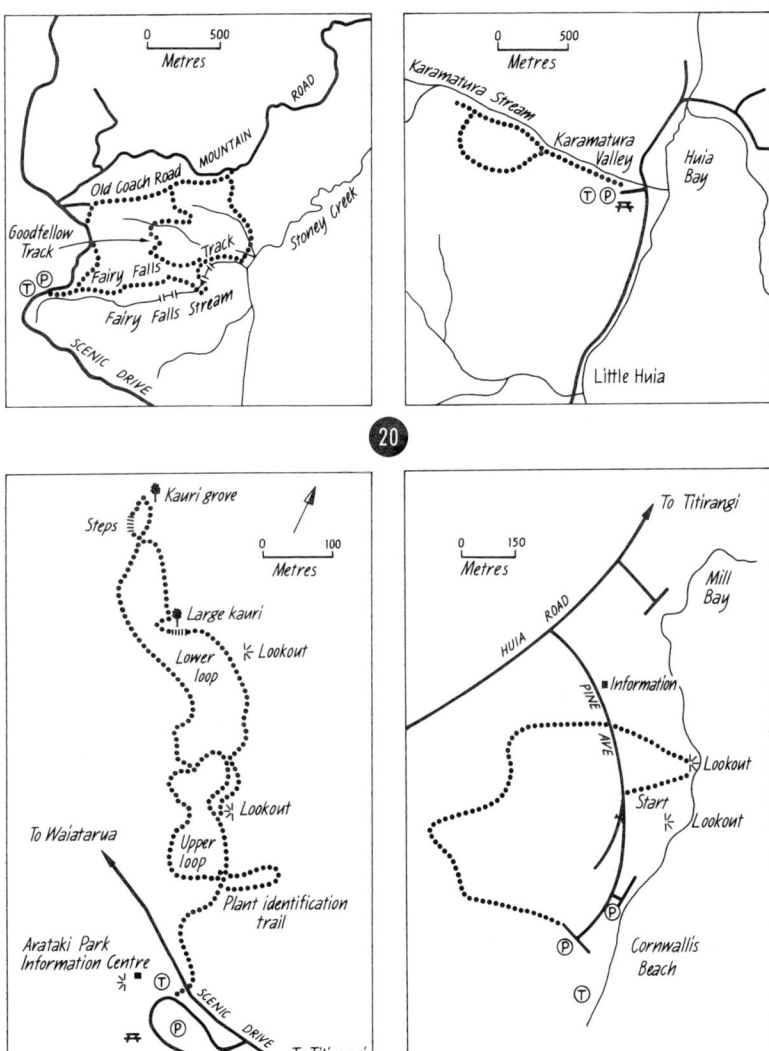

49

Karamatura picnic area, which is well marked on the right.

The track leads up the Karamatura Stream, through attractive bush alongside an old tramline to a good swimming hole in a rock pool. The loop track climbs the hillside a short distance and provides excellent views across the valley. Magnificent rata trees grow in the area. The track then leads back down to the stream and returns to the picnic area (30 minutes–1 hour).

Murphys Bush

Length: Various
Time taken: 20–30 minutes
Grading: Easy
Apparel: Casual; good footwear in wet weather
Code: Year-round, trees, birds

Points of note: The reserve, which was opened in July 1977, is the largest stand of mature flatland bush consisting mainly of kahikatea near to Auckland city.

Access: The reserve lies within Manukau City and is owned and administered by the city council. To reach it from Auckland City, drive south along the Southern Motorway, turning left at the Otara off-ramp through Otara to Ormiston Road (following the signposting toward Whitford). Turn right at Murphys Road and just past the intersection with Flat Bush School Road there is a signpost to Murphys Bush Reserve on the right. The reserve is 24 kilometres from the centre of Auckland.

A circular drive inside the main gates leads to a grass parking area, play areas and a toilet block. There is a slope down to the track entrance where posts with red arrows mark the trails. The eastern end of the reserve is the only part tracked – as a preservation policy – with trails looping back to the carpark.

The more common trees among about seventy species recorded in the bush (some are identified with labels) include titoki, tawa, karaka, kohekohe, taraire, rewarewa, puriri, rimu, totara and matai as well as kahikatea. There are numerous tui in and around the reserve as well as pigeons, fantails, kingfishers, silvereyes, harriers and moreporks.

Grassed areas for picnics are set aside on the outside fringes of the reserve, which is open to the public from sunrise to sunset.

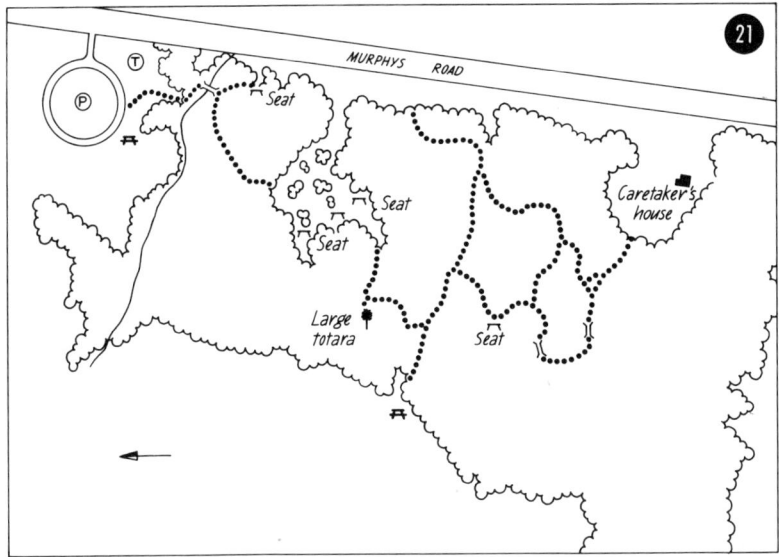

22

Mt William Walkway

Length: 6.5 kilometres
Time taken: 3 hours one way
Grading: Average
Apparel: Casual; good footwear in wet weather
Code: Year-round (farmland north of the reserve may be closed for lambing in spring), trees, views

Points of note: There are magnificent views from this hill walk. The scenic reserve at the southern end is extremely rich in plant species and notable for an uncommon association of kauri, hard beech and king fern.

Access: To reach the northern end of the walk, turn off State Highway 1 on the first left turn past the Bombay traffic lights, into Beaver Road. From here turn right into Razorback Road, then left to Puketutu Road. The walk starts over the stile at the end of this road.

To reach the southern end, take the Thames turn-off (State Highway 2). An AA sign indicates a left turn up Irish Road (past the sawmill) and then left into McMillan Road. Mt William is approximately 50 kilometres from the Auckland city centre. It is advisable to arrange transport for the end of the walk.

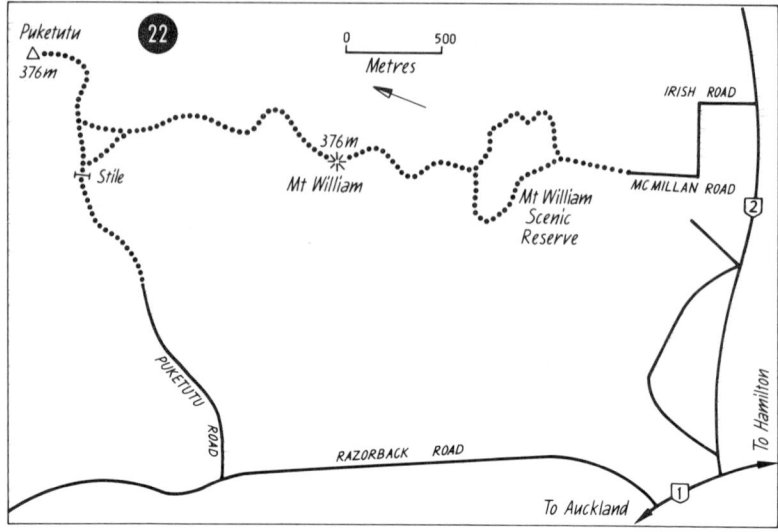

From the stile at the northern end, the track climbs through open pasture to the short side track for the Puketutu Trig (376 metres) from which there is a superb 360-degree view. Return to the main track, which leads to Mt William (376 metres), with excellent views all the way along. From here the track descends to the Mt William Scenic Reserve, where it splits in two: the eastern track leads through mixed forest, and the western track leads through kauri, beech and king ferns. Lemonwood and kaimako, also found in the reserve, are not common in the Auckland area. Other tree species include taraire, karaka, puriri, pukatea, kohekohe, tanekaha, totara, rimu, mahoe, rewarewa, heketara and kaikomako. There are over forty species of fern identified in the Valley of Ferns. Streams in the reserve are bridged. Both tracks rejoin near the boundary of the reserve. Posts indicate the route across farmland to the end of McMillan Road.

Waharau Regional Park

Length: Various
Time taken: Up to 4½ hours
Grading: Easy to strenuous

Apparel: Good footwear

Code: Year-round, trees, birds, views

Points of note: The Waharau Regional Park covers 238 hectares from the eastern Hunua Ranges to the shore of the Firth of Thames. Camping is available, and the Waharau Outdoor Education Camp caters for school and community groups.

Access: The park is 84 kilometres south-east from Auckland City. The entrance is reached on the Kaiaua–Clevedon Road, between Orere Point and Kaiaua, about 38 kilometres from Clevedon.

The main track system operates as a series of loops which get progressively longer, and higher on the slopes of the Hunua Ranges, allowing for varying levels of fitness and time. These are all suitable for family groups.

Bush Walk (30 minutes): This short walk, marked by green arrows, leads through regenerating bush and tree-fern groves.

Lower Link Track Loop (1 hour): Yellow arrows mark this walk, which leads through pockets of native forest, fringed with manuka, and occasional grassy clearings, which offer excellent views.

Upper Link Track Loop (1½ hours): Orange arrows mark this walk, which follows along former logging tracks and is lined by kauri rickers.

Waharau Ridge Track Loop (4½ hours): This more strenuous tramp, marked by red arrows, climbs to the ridge and offers expansive views of the Coromandel Peninsula and Firth of Thames.

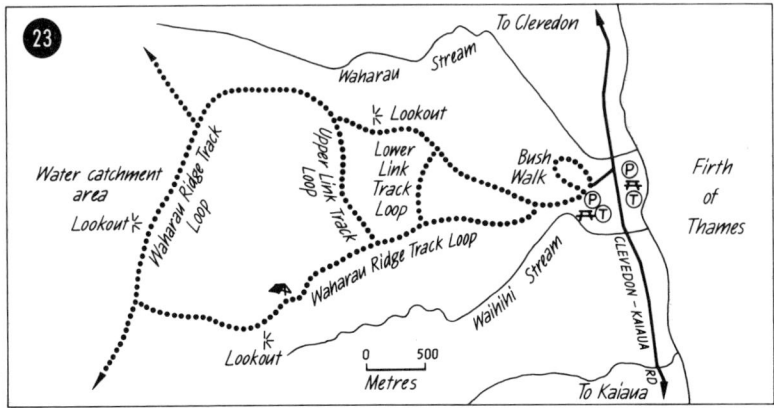

WAIKATO

Waiomu Kauri Grove

Length: 5 kilometres
Time taken: 2 hours return
Grading: Average
Apparel: Casual; good footwear in wet weather
Code: Year-round, trees, birds, views

Points of note: This walk in the Coromandel State Forest Park passes through bush, sometimes regenerating, sometimes mature, the highlight of which is a grove of fine kauri.

Access: Waiomu is about 13 kilometres north of Thames on the highway to Coromandel. At the north end of the settlement, cross the bridge and turn right up Waiomu Valley Road. There is good parking at the end of the road, and the track is marked from this point.

The track, which as far as the kauri grove involves little climbing, begins on legal road access. Entry to the forest park is about 5 minutes from the carpark area.

About 5 minutes' walk beyond a disused turn-off is a side track across the stream to the Monowai mine site, and it is worthwhile crossing the stream to see the remains of a cyanide tank used in the previous working of the mine.

On the main track, manuka regrowth is gradually replaced by areas of fine tree-ferns and some broadleaf regeneration. The track crosses the Paroquet Stream to some of the old workings of another mine, with some pieces of crystal still in the loose stone at the edge of the track. Further up the valley, increasing bush regeneration includes young rimu and kauri, and soon the first tall trees. Totara stand out here because of the extensive possum damage they have suffered.

Less than an hour from the start, at a steady walking pace, you make the last stream crossing. The track ascends a ridge to the first kauri of an impressive grove. It is worth pushing on for yet another 15 minutes to see

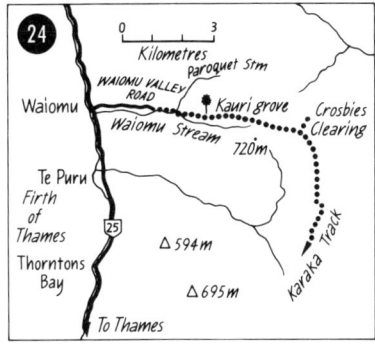
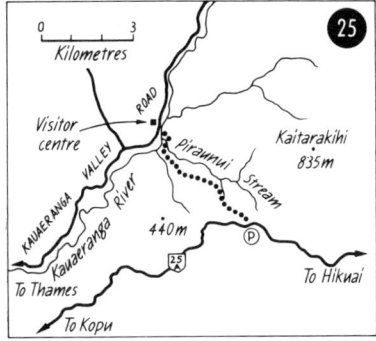

some fine specimen trees in the valleys below, and to reach a bluff where you can look back west to the Waiomu settlement and across the Hauraki Gulf to Kaiaua on the far shore. In this area all the common bush birds are present – pigeon, kaka, shining cuckoo, fantail, tomtit, robin, tui and bellbird. Kokako have been seen and heard in this valley.

The walk on to Crosbies Clearing is strenuous but very worthwhile. The track is not well maintained and may be slippery or muddy in parts; it is certainly at times very steep. Crosbies was once farmed, and the bush is now advancing up the valleys and on to tops formerly in pasture, to the eventual loss of some magnificent views.

Piraunui Pack Track

Length: 8 kilometres
Time taken: About 3¼ hours
Grading: Moderate
Apparel: Good footwear and parka
Code: Year-round, trees, plants, birds, views

Points of note: The route follows the old pack track that used to be a main supply route from the Kauaeranga Valley up to the kauri camps in the Neavesville (Measletown) areas in the early days. As a result the gradient is easy.

Access: The Piraunui Track begins from a large parking area on the left of the Kopu–Hikuai Road just below its summit.

The track runs from the highway down to the Kauaeranga Valley floor. It winds easily and steadily downhill, through fairly profuse undergrowth at first, and then through more open places with large hard ferns, bracken and remnants of old forest trees. Mature mamaku show damage by possums. Extensive views open to the right, including the steep, gouged peak of Kaitarakihi (835 metres), the highest peak in this area of the Coromandel Ranges, and offering a very rewarding climb.

The track continues with the occasional scramble over streams or washouts. The deep valley on the right reveals a few small stands of mature rata towering above thick second-growth bush. Well down the track large areas of young kauri can be seen on the far side of the valley, with a bird's eye view of a mass of tree-ferns.

The track emerges on to farmland, continuing to a large hayshed. The Kauaeranga River is 10 minutes ahead, across a ford over the Piraunui Stream. Care needs to be taken in crossing both the stream and the river, to reach the main forest road and Park Headquarters.

If the weather has been bad and the river is up (even a rise of 2 or 3 centimetres can make the flow much faster), there is an alternative route through the farm and across a private ford. To take this route, bear left at the barn through a small grove of pines and gums, and a gate, on to a farm road past an old smithy, a store and other buildings of a bygone era. Thames township is 11 kilometres down the road, and transport should be arranged at the lower end of the walk.

Hakarimata Trig

Length: Various
Time taken: Up to 6 hours
Grading: Easy on flat; moderate on steeper sections
Apparel: Short walks, casual; longer, tramping gear
Code: Year-round, trees, plants, birds

Points of note: The track system follows the Hakarimata Range across the Waipa and Waikato Rivers from Ngaruawahia. The 1,602 hectares of public land traversed are almost entirely bush-covered, with scattered kauri.

Access: Turn off State Highway 1 in the middle of Ngaruawahia, across the railway line, and follow Waingaro signs across the Waipa River bridge.

The Hakarimata Trig Walk (3 hours return) starts 100 metres right from the bridge at the end of Brownlee Street. It begins as a pleasant streamside walk (25 minutes) suitable for all ages, and gets steeper above a dam. It leads through bush with scattered kauri to the main track along the ridge, and then right for 5 minutes to the Hakarimata Trig (371 metres), with views over the Waikato.

From the same starting point a walk goes to the Waingaro Road end of the range. It proceeds down-ridge to the south from the summit, past the access from the trig walk and along the undulating ridge to a steep descent into a streambed. This end of the walk is, like the start, easy and pleasant, past waterfalls and small rapids. The total walk time to the exit at Waingaro Road is 4 hours.

Alternatively, the walk from the summit can be continued north to an exit on Parker Road, which exits on to Huntly West Road. This takes 6 hours and, like the Waingaro track, is more suited to trampers than afternoon strollers. A feature of this route is the branch track to two large kauri, about an hour before the exit is reached. The track down to the river level is steep.

Apart from the kauri, the tops and ridges along the Hakarimata Range have some large rimu and rata, with pockets of miro, Hall's totara and tanekaha among other native species.

Unless a return walk is made, you should arrange to be picked up at the chosen track exit.

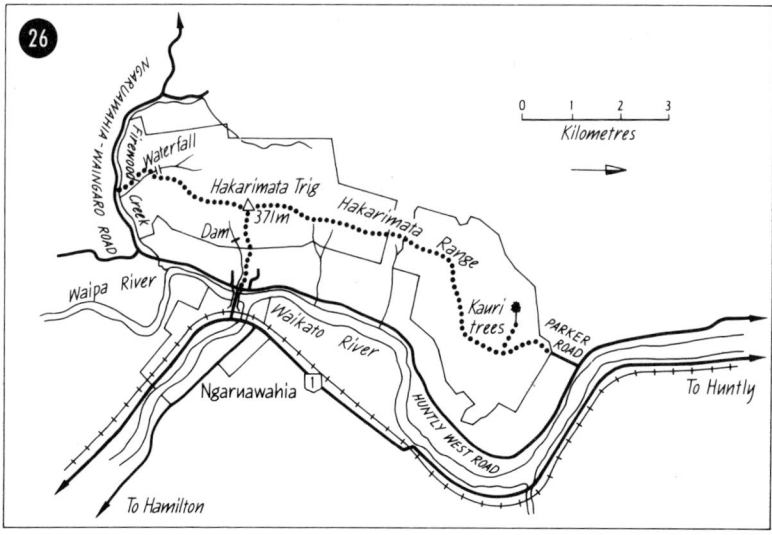

27

Te Tapui Scenic Reserve

Length: 6 kilometres
Time taken: 3 hours return
Grading: Moderate
Apparel: Good footwear
Code: Year-round, birds, trees, flowers

Points of note: This walk in the Te Tapui Scenic Reserve, a heavily forested area typical of the original Waikato hill country, goes to the top of Maungakawa, one of the two volcanic cones in the 2,370-hectare reserve.

Access: From Hamilton drive east via Tauwhare, Kiwitahi and Walton, turning off on to Paratu Loop and Link Roads to Piakonui Road, 4.5 kilometres along which is the track entrance, with parking and a bush-surrounded picnic area. The track entrance is 21 kilometres from Matamata.

A marked track leads up the hill through native bush to the top of Maungakawa (495 metres). The high forest is mainly of tawa, kohekohe, rewarewa and pukatea, with some rimu and northern rata. There are nikau palms around the margins, where most of the bird life is also encountered – harriers, pigeons, bellbirds and tui among others, as well as introduced birds including quail, pheasants and finches. The walk up takes about 1½–2 hours, with the return downhill somewhat faster. A platform on the summit offers fine views, particularly to the north.

28

Sanatorium Hill

Length: 3 kilometres
Time taken: 1 hour
Grading: Easy
Apparel: Casual
Code: Year-round, trees

Points of note: This hilltop walk is through another Maungakawa – Maungakawa Scenic Reserve – only a few kilometres from Te Tapui and its Maungakawa Hill. The area gains its popular name from a sanatorium run there for twenty years in the

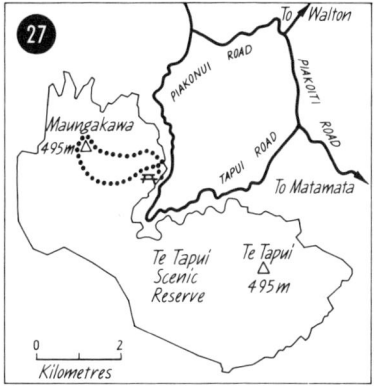

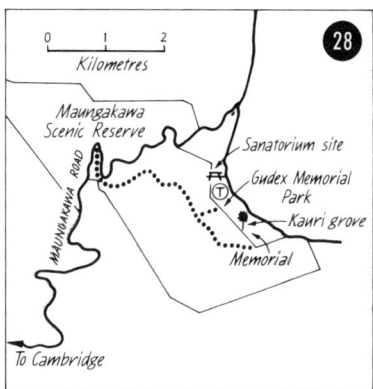

early part of this century, centred on a lavish residence built in 1890 by the widow of Daniel Thornton, a wealthy industrialist from Russia. Only a few foundations of this building remain.

Access: The reserve is 8 kilometres west of Cambridge on Maungakawa Road, reached by a winding road to the top of the hill.

There is a good grassed picnic area with some fine individual trees around the site of the old buildings, which enjoyed magnificent views over the Waikato plains. There is also a small area of bush. The reserve is notable for including the 3-hectare Gudex Memorial Park, established as a tribute to M. C. Gudex, a much-respected writer, broadcaster and leader in local horticulture and nature conservation who planted a small grove of kauri there in 1960.

Walter Scott Reserve

Length: 3 kilometres
Time taken: 1 hour
Grading: Easy
Apparel: Casual; good footwear in wet weather
Code: Year-round, trees, plants, flowers, birds

Points of note: An easy and enjoyable bush walk, on the northern foothills of Mt Pirongia, popular with families and school parties because of its grade, distance, well-formed track and varied botany.

Access: From the Te Awamutu–Kawhia Road take the Pekanui Road at Ngutunui, and turn into Scott Road, at the end of which is a well-formed carpark, with picnic tables and tap water.

The track, which circles the reserve and is owned by the Forest and Bird Society, begins and ends at the carpark. Entering the bush, take the right-hand track and travel in an anti-clockwise direction. The track rises slightly, well formed and stepped where necessary, through a canopy of kamahi and tawa forest. You soon reach a short side track to the right, signposted 'Rimu Grove'. Take this short walk to a small rimu stand planted as a memorial to Athol Caldwell.

Back on the main track you are walking on historic ground, for here is a section of one of the Maori walking tracks from Kawhia to the interior of the King Country and Waikato. Te Rauparaha was born and grew up at Kawhia, and it is reasonable to assume that he walked this track.

After 200 metres, note the large totara stump on the left – the only sign of the logging of former years and still sound as a bell. Further on, a gap in the canopy where a large tawa has fallen lets in light to encourage ferns and seedlings, providing a good place for entomologists to fossick.

At the boundary fence there is a view of Ruapehu and Ngauruhoe. Here the track leaves the historic Maori trail and passes large nikau and tawa, festooned with several kinds of lianes. The track here to the left, the Valder Walk, is a shortcut back to the carpark.

After another kilometre, along a moss-bordered track skirting areas of bracken fern and dodging gullies, the tramper comes to a natural bridge over the stream. At the approaches king ferns have been planted, secluded elsewhere in dense cover.

Take a 50-metre diversion downstream to see, growing in mid-stream, a large kahikatea estimated to be 600 years old. Further on, pass under

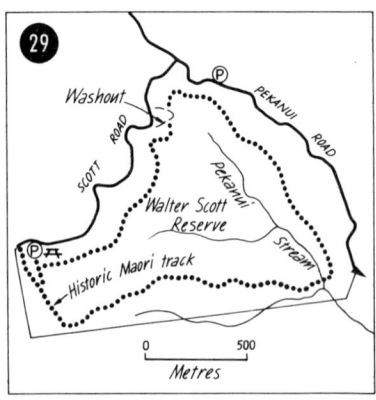

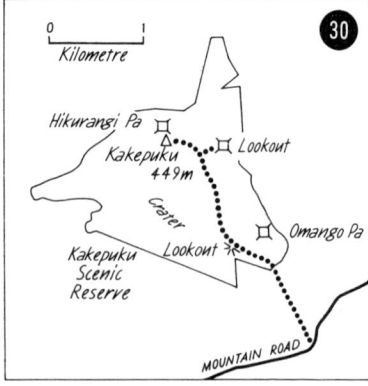

kohekohe, rewarewa and pukatea in great profusion, observing the stand of pukatea saplings and the buttresses at the base of the derelict mature trees.

On the left is a mamaku fern with a massive 10-metre base and further on, in a washout now rapidly healing, are sun-loving plants such as makomako and toetoe. Unusual plants on the sides of the track, looking like young pine trees, are in fact *Dawsonia superba*, the world's tallest moss.

On the approach to the carpark, you can glimpse the massive trunk of a rimu along the Valder Track through the entangled mass of supplejack and ferns.

Birds to listen for are tui, bellbirds, pigeons, fantails, grey warblers and shining cuckoos and, on an evening stroll, moreporks and kiwi.

Kakepuku

Length: 5 kilometres
Time taken: 2 hours return
Grading: Average, steep in parts
Apparel: Good footwear
Code: Year-round, trees, plants, birds, views

Points of note: On this walk you climb to the top of an old volcano, now bush-clad, in an 85-hectare reserve administered by the Department of Conservation.

Access: From Te Awamutu drive west toward Pokuru, turning left after 7 kilometres and then right after 1 kilometre into Mountain Road. The signposted track entrance is 3.5 kilometres along this road.

The well-marked track starts through farmland, continuing through bush to an open area with fine views to the south. The track follows a ridge and leads through a remnant of original forest in the old crater. The forest contains large rimu and rata, with many tawa, kohekohe, hinau, rewarewa, mangeao, pukatea and puriri.

You can enjoy splendid views from the summit of Kakepuku (449 metres), which has a good platform incorporating the trig.

BAY OF PLENTY

Orokawa Bay and
William Wright Falls

Length: 4.5 kilometres
Time taken: 2½ hours return
Grading: Easy
Apparel: Casual
Code: Year-round, trees, coastal views, waterfall

Points of note: Pleasant coastal and bush walks, offering the extra reward of many pohutukawa in bloom at Christmas.

Access: Access is from the north end of Waihi Beach, which is signposted off State Highway 2 just south of Waihi.

Orokawa Bay lies a short distance north of Waihi Beach. Because of intervening hills, it is not possible to walk along the coast there. Just 100 metres past the northernmost parking area, as the beach runs out, a track leads up the cliff face, the foot of which can be awash at high tide for a short distance. A short distance up, the track forks and that to Orokawa Bay leads off to the left.

The well-graded track leads through scattered puriri, pohutukawa, bush-fringe shrubs and manuka. At no point is the elevation much greater than 100 metres. The route crosses two small ridges and bypasses two headlands. There is a short branch track to a lookout on the first headland. Excellent views up and down the coast and to offshore islands, including the Aldermen Islands, are also obtained from vantage points along the track to the bay.

The track drops steeply after about 2 kilometres to the pohutukawa-fringed southern end of Orokawa Bay. The bay is about 1 kilometre long and shelves fairly steeply. Swimming can be dangerous, but a stream entering the bay near the north end makes a good picnic spot, and children can bathe there. Soft sand may make for slow walking on the beach.

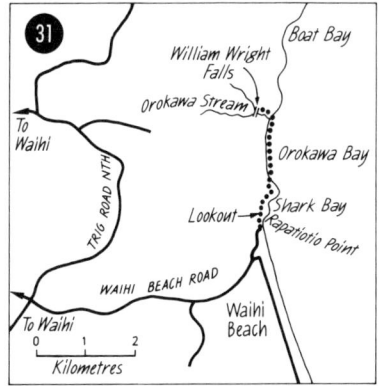

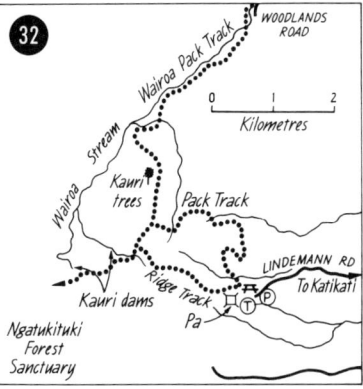

The track to William Wright Falls starts up the northern bank of the stream. It keeps to the stream nearly all the way, crossing it many times, until the falls are reached. Comparatively little climbing is involved and the going is easy unless there has been heavy rain, although this enables the falls to be seen to best advantage. The valley is filled with regenerating native forest in which nikau palms are frequent.

Kaimai Kauri Dams

Length: Various
Time taken: Up to 5 hours
Grading: Easy
Apparel: Light tramping gear
Code: Year-round, bush, birds

Points of note: An area of predominantly young forest, well advanced in recovery from earlier logging, it includes remains of two of the dams used for driving out the kauri. Although the dams are now in ruins, evidence of old water races can be seen.

Access: Travel westward along Lindemann Road, a short distance north of the town of Katikati, to the foothills of the Kaimai Range. The road ends in a grassed area suitable for parking, just below the bushline.

Three tracks lead off from this point, the centre one providing a meandering, easy ascent to the first of two kauri dams, a casual climb taking about 3 hours.

Apart from a few relatively easy obstacles, the travelling is not strenuous and the scenery is typical of the region, with glimpses of a coastal panorama from Whangamata to Maketu, and Mayor Island to Motiti. Considerable areas of healthy beech and kauri clothe the fairly rugged slopes, with scattered podocarps and plentiful tawa. About 4 kilometres up is the junction with the Wairoa Pack track, which leads off to the right and continues 5 kilometres (1½–2 hours) to the Woodlands Road end.

Toward the top of this winding track, at the bottom of a gully, was the first dam, which spanned a narrow ravine. The top beam, a kauri log, was about 6 metres above the streambed. When sufficient trees had been felled and the logs rolled into the streambed, and enough lake created, the dam would be tripped and the logs sent on their way downstream to the sawmill.

Five minutes' walk further on are the few visible remains of the second dam, which spanned a much wider but shallow basin. Several large kauri stumps are exposed in a clearing above the dam, one measuring nearly 3 metres across the saw-cut, all solid timber.

The return journey may be made by a more direct route, which is fairly steep in parts but takes little more than an hour, down the Ridge Track.

Tuahu and Sentinel Rock Tracks

Length: Various
Time taken: Up to 5 hours
Grading: Easy to moderate
Apparel: Casual; stout shoes
Code: Year-round, bush, birds, views

Points of note: The Tuahu Track is an old Maori trail across the Kaimai Range from Hot Springs Road on the east to Wairakau Road on the west.

Access: Access from the east is from the end of Hot Springs Road, which wends westward from State Highway 2, 4 kilometres south of Katikati. From the west, take a marked route through farmland and a plantation of young pines from Wairakau Road, which runs east off the old Te Aroha–Tauranga Road, 6.5 kilometres south of Te Aroha.

At the end of Hot Springs Road, the formed surface narrows to become the Tuahu Track, which is well cleared and easily followed on a gentle grade right

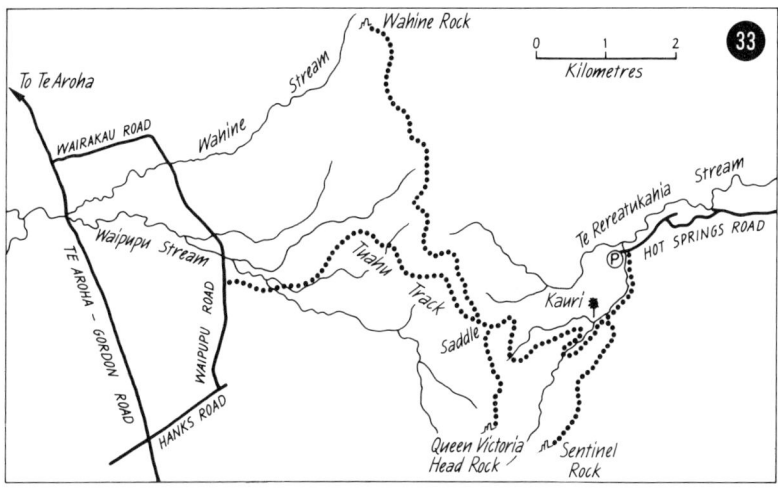

across the range. The track is benched across the slopes above the south fork of the Te Rereatukahia Stream. Approximately 20 minutes' walk from the road end, a signposted track turns uphill and climbs steeply for 100 metres to a large kauri estimated to be more than 1,000 years old. This track carries on to Sentinel Rock.

The Tuahu Track continues, from the fork, up the south arm of the Te Rereatukahia Stream, crosses it below a small pool and then climbs on an easy gradient around the spurs and across several small streams to a saddle on the crest of the range and the junction with the North–South Track; this leads north along the crest to the Te Rereatukahia Hut and on to Wahine Rock, and south to Queen Victoria Head Rock. The Tuahu winds down through bush on the Waikato side of the range, high above a plantation of young pine trees to a point where the track runs alongside a fence adjacent to the pines. The exit is now via a marked track through the pine plantation to Waipupu Road.

The track to Sentinel Rock, which leaves the Tuahu Track near the big kauri, climbs an undulating ridge to the rock, an isolated outcrop east of the main Kaimai ridge. A steep and rough track zig-zags up the southern face of the rock to a vantage point on top.

34

Mt Maunganui

Length: 3 kilometres
Time taken: Circuit, 40 minutes; summit, 1 hour
Grading: Easy
Apparel: Casual
Code: Year-round, trees, birds, views

Points of note: This is a sea-coast walk around, and a climb up, a prominent Bay of Plenty landmark at the entrance to Tauranga Harbour.

Access: A track system starts behind the motor camp at the Mount end of Mt Maunganui beach.

A 40-minute walk around the base of Mt Maunganui leads through pohutukawa for most of the way, at varying distances above high-water mark. The view changes from settled areas to the harbour and the open ocean, with Mayor Island offshore. The walk can be made in either direction.

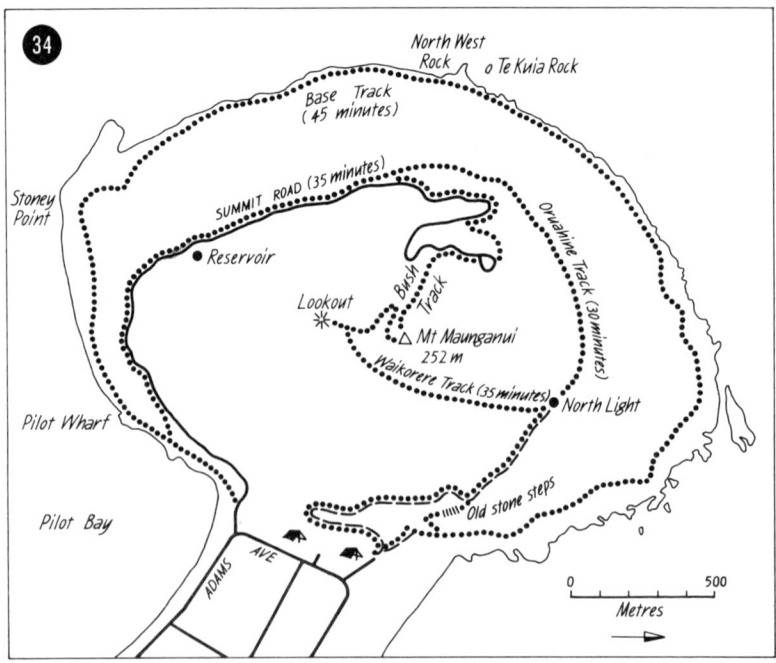

A track to the summit of the Mount (252 metres) is signposted and leads off from the Round the Mountain Track a short distance from the start. The track winds around the mountain in an anti-clockwise direction. Climbing is steady but not too steep, and the views are excellent. A steeper route down is available.

Otanewainuku

Length: Various
Time taken: Rimu Walk, 45 minutes; Loop Track, 1½–2 hours
Grading: Easy and moderate
Apparel: Casual
Code: Year-round, trees, views, parking

Points of note: The summit of Otanewainuku offers panoramic views of the Bay of Plenty and Mamaku Plateau. The forest supports a rich population of birds, including pigeons, kokako, kiwi, whitehead and robins.

Access: The picnic area is a 20-minute drive south from Tauranga, via Oropi Road and Mountain Road to the signposted public shelter and carpark. Alternatively, it can be reached on No. 2 Road, 13 kilometres from Te Puke, or Mangatoi Road via the Tauranga–Rotorua Road.

Rimu Walk starts at the southern end of the parking area and passes through forest with large rimu trees, along with tawa, hinau, rata, pukatea and other species. It rejoins Mountain Road about 100 metres along from the start.

Loop Track starts at the picnic area and climbs gently about 100 metres to the track junction. The western (right) fork climbs gradually at first, then zig-zags more steeply to a ridge, which it follows around a spur to the main Otanewainuku ridge. A short track leads north, to a trig and lookout. The summit track continues south along the undulating main ridge, until it climbs steeply about 50 metres to the summit (640 metres), which offers a commanding view. Otanewainuku is a hard, rhyolite volcanic dome, similar to Mts Minden, Misery and Maunganui. The rock of the Mamaku Plateau surrounding it is ignimbrite.

The Loop Track continues south from the trig and descends steeply off the ridge to a benched track, which follows around the south-eastern side off the mountain, past a large kahikatea, and rejoins the track to the picnic area.

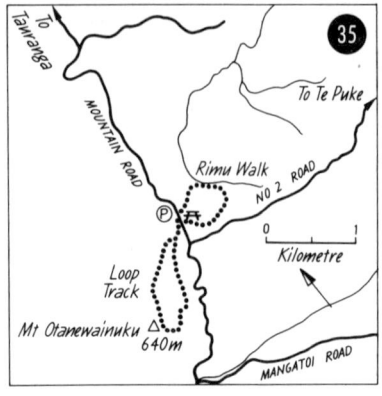

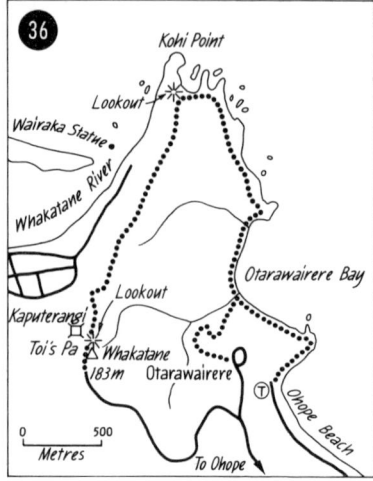

The forest changes somewhat with altitude on this walk, from tawa and kohekohe common in lower altitudes, to miro and tawari common in higher altitudes. *Earina* and *Dendrobium* orchids are present in the forest, and rata and clematis also add colour in the summer months.

Kohi Point and Otarawairere

Length: 7 kilometres
Time taken: 3 hours
Grading: Easy to moderate
Apparel: Casual
Code: Year-round, trees, birds, flowers, plants

Points of note: This walk starts at the Whakatane Trig and goes through historic country, either as far as Kohi Point (and return) or on through Otarawairere to Ohope Beach.

Access: To reach the trig, drive from Whakatane toward Ohope. After passing the cemetery, turn left at the top of Ohope Hill at Otarawairere. Take the first turn left and follow the metalled road to the trig and carpark.

The formed track begins over a stile. Immediately on the right are the remains of Toi's Pa (Kaputerangi), one of the oldest in New Zealand. The track generally follows the crest of an escarpment through regenerating forest that has been burned frequently.

Through occasional gaps you can see Whakatane town and river, Whale Island offshore and White Island, 50 kilometres out to sea. On a clear day, you can pick out Motiti Island, Mt Maunganui and the Coromandel Range. To the east the view extends to East Cape and the high country around Mt Hikurangi. Tui, pigeons, warblers and European birds can be heard.

There are both uphill and downhill stretches on this part of the walk, but only a couple of steep pinches. Past the mouth of the river the vegetation becomes more stunted and windswept.

Above Kohi Point the track turns right and continues through scrub and some bush above the coastal cliffs to Otarawairere Bay, descending the final steep drop by wooden steps. Islets offshore are occupied by seabird nests and shag rookeries. In clear weather you can see the gannet rookeries on White Island.

By following around the beach (difficult at high tide), you reach the bottom of the track leading to the Otarawairere settlement. Further on, another track leads over the spur to the west end of Ohope Beach.

From the settlement it is about a 2-kilometre walk (mostly uphill) to the trig; and from the west end of Ohope Beach, about twice that distance. Anyone not wanting to face this walk should arrange transport accordingly. An alternative is to walk as far as Kohi Point and then return to the trig.

A recent extension of the Kohi Point walk provides access to Hillcrest Road, Whakatane.

Hinehopu Track

Length: 7.5 kilometres
Time taken: 1½ hours return
Grading: Easy
Apparel: Casual; warm clothing in winter
Code: Year-round, trees, birds, flowers, historic

Points of note: A feature of this bush walk leading to the Wishing Tree on Hongi's Track and Lake Rotoehu is a thriving community of kohekohe (New Zealand mahogany).

Access: At the eastern end of Lake Rotoiti, on the main highway from Rotorua to Whakatane, turn left at the derelict Hinehopu store. Take the lake-edge road to where it ends under the steep Matawhaura Ridge. Access is signposted to the track, through the Rotoiti Scenic Reserve.

Before entering the forest it is worthwhile studying the vigorous and crowded growth of small trees and shrubs by the lake edge. Here you can see young rimu, tawa, mahoe, putaputaweta, kotukutuku, coprosma, five-finger, black and red matipo and pohue.

The track itself is easy walking all the way. In the off season the sunlight is blocked out by the ridge until late in the day. The forest contains some magnificent rimu, tawa, kahikatea, pukatea and northern rata. You will soon become aware of some large kohekohe, with their spreading branches and handsome shiny leaves comprising four or five pairs of leaflets. On the forest floor below, young seedlings and saplings of kohekohe give the effect of a garden of houseplants.

The understorey generally is sparse, consisting mainly of tree-ferns, young tawa, kotukutuku and five-finger. In some places the track passes nikau palms, which are uncommon in the Rotorua area.

The track leads out to the Wishing Tree at the edge of the busy main highway. In spite of the traffic noise, tui, bellbirds and other forest songsters are very active here, perhaps because of the food supply. The venerable rimu has a root disease and shrubs have been planted at its base on one side to try to restore its vigour.

From the highway, a glance through binoculars reveals heavy forest growth clinging to the precipitous Matawhaura Ridge. High-flying birds above the ridge are shags to-ing and fro-ing between the two lakes.

The track continues past the tree to reach Lake Rotoehu in another 15 minutes.

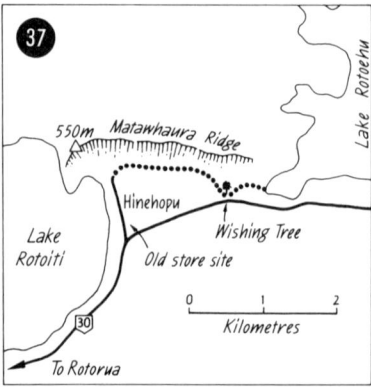

38

Lake Okataina – Eastern Walkway

Length: 8 kilometres
Time taken: 2½ hours
Grading: Average
Apparel: Good footwear and warm clothing
Code: Year-round, history, forest, views, lakes, swimming, fishing

Points of note: Lake Okataina is the only lake in the Rotorua district completely surrounded by native forest. It is also surrounded in history. The area was renowned for its carvings and canoes produced from local totara, and the carved gate of the pa at Te Koutu can be seen in the Auckland War Memorial Museum. The lake was an important link for canoes between Tarawera and Rotoiti, and the present road follows the route used to carry the canoes.

Access: The road to Lake Okataina turns off State Highway 30 at Rauto on Lake Rotoiti (29 kilometres from Rotorua) and continues about 8 kilometres to Tauranganui Bay, where there is a public shelter and the walkway begins.

The walk starts at Tauranganui Bay, passes through forest around the lake with marvellous views, and at times drops down to the shore. It continues past the southern end of the lake to Lake Tarawera. It is necessary to return the same way, unless you arrange to be picked up by boat at this bay. The lake has no outlet, so its level can rise dramatically after heavy rain.

About 15 minutes along, the track comes to a natural amphitheatre formed by volcanic cliffs. It is thought the local inhabitants used the echo produced by this cliff to relay messages along the lake. Not far past here, a side track to the right leads down to the lake at an ideal spot for picnicking and swimming. The main track continues left and bypasses Te Koutu Point, a pa site of the Ngati Tarawhai, who gifted the reserve to the Crown in 1921.

From Kaiwaka Bay, the track climbs gradually above the lake through rimu-tawa forest with totara, miro, kahikatea, rata, mangeao, hinau, mahoe, kamahi, five-finger and coprosma. Eventually it levels out and passes through dense forest of kamahi and rewarewa before rejoining the lake at Oruaroa Point. Here it passes through an impressive stand of rewarewa. Large numbers of tui and bellbirds are attracted when these trees flower during November and December. In Otangimoana Bay, pohutukawa thrive around the lakeshore. These trees are normally found on the coast, but do well here on the volcanic soils.

The track leaves the lake at the southern end of Otangimoana Bay and

71

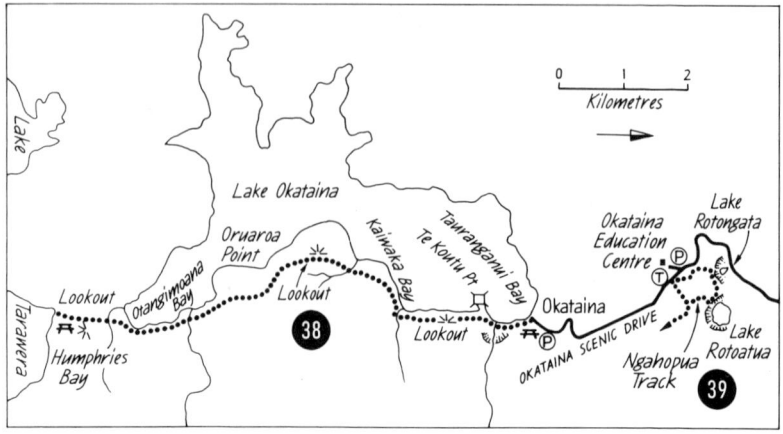

heads towards Lake Tarawera, about 20 minutes to Humphries Bay. Okataina was once part of Lake Tarawera, but the extrusion of a rhyolitic dome separated the two and raised the level of Okataina by 13 metres to 311 metres above sea level. The vegetation on this section is quite sparse compared with the rest of the walk, as a result of the porous volcanic soil from the 1886 Tarawera eruption, with heather, kanuka, manuka and various coprosma species. Bird life in the area is rich, with both forest and lake species in evidence.

Ngahopua Track

Length: 3 kilometres
Time taken: 1–1½ hours
Grading: Generally easy
Apparel: Casual; good footwear (mud patches)
Code: Year-round, trees, flowers, plants, birds, lakes

Points of note: This bush walk in the Lake Okataina Scenic Reserve offers a high-up view of Rotoatua, a crater lake. The track climbs a small ridge that can be ascended in slow stages; there are a few areas of mud, but generally the going is easy.

Access: The Lake Okataina Scenic Reserve is about 25 kilometres from Rotorua on State Highway 30. On reaching Lake Rotoiti, turn off at the bay signposted Ruato.

A sign indicates the road to Lake Okataina. Follow this road for a few kilometres to where a sign on the right announces the Okataina Education Centre. Almost opposite on the left can be found the signposted entrance to the Ngahopua Track.

A short distance from the entrance, the track takes a sharp left-hand curve. Here, on the left, lies a fallen forest giant worthy of close inspection. Its rotting flanks provide a home for a variety of plants, ferns, mosses and fungi, illustrating, in their crowded profusion, the sheer fecundity of the New Zealand rain forest. As the track winds its way up the ridge, the understorey plants become thinner, the dominant growth being tree-fern and tawa.

Here and there you can see impressive specimens of rimu, kahikatea and northern rata that have escaped the miller's saw. (Milling ceased here in 1931.) Large tangles of supplejack are evident everywhere.

The track eventually levels out along the top of a scarp, where the vegetation becomes even more interesting. Small ferns abound and the crown fern makes its appearance. Down to the left the dark waters of Rotongata come into view. The blackness of this lake lends it a sinister aspect; you almost expect to see some strange creature emerge from its depths, but the only ripples on its surface are caused by teal and other small fowl. In summer the lake resounds to a noisy chorus of frogs, competing with cuckoos and indigenous birds to fill the small valley with sound.

A few hundred metres further on, the track reaches a cleared space on the edge of a steep drop. There, far below, lies Lake Rotoatua, light greenstone in hue and encircled by thick forest growth except where a section of crater wall is exposed. There are two large wooden benches at the viewing point.

On this section of the track the forest takes on a tropical appearance. From old stumps and fallen logs the kowharawhara (*Astelia solandri*) stands out in sharp relief, as does the kiekie, which, having no length of trunk to climb, waves its tufted arms outward. Crown ferns are crowded into a garden of their own.

From a tall rimu growing hard by the track dangle the thick mature roots of a rata. The roots have been severed just above the ground, saving the host tree from eventual strangulation. On other trees can be seen an occasional root of puka, distinguishable from rata by its grey colour and fluted form.

The track descends from the scarp easily through some rather patchy bush to emerge into an old sawmill clearing, overgrown with grasses. In springtime the flowers of the makomako, or wineberry, attract bees and nectar-sipping birds. Makomako grows thickly around the clearing and on the track leading away from it, as do tawa and kotukutuku, the native fuchsia. All three constitute, with their berries and drupes, an important food supply. In summer the area is alive with birds of many varieties, tui and bellbirds being particularly active and tuneful.

The track, now following an old logging trail, comes to a grassy junction from which the Anaha Track goes off to the left. Keeping straight ahead, the walker soon emerges on to the main road at a point not far below the original entry point. A short drive down to view Lake Okataina is a satisfying way to round off the outing.

Rotorua Lakefront Walk

Length: 2 kilometres
Time taken: 30 minutes return
Grading: Easy, suitable for wheelchairs
Apparel: Casual
Code: Year-round, birds, views

Points of note: About sixty species of bird have been spotted from this lakeshore track.

Access: The walk starts by the Sea Scouts building on Memorial Drive, and ends by the boat ramp at Motutara Point, which is at the end of Queens Drive. There is a boardwalk over swampy ground.

EAST COAST

Lakes Waikareiti and Ruapani

Length: Various
Time taken: Up to 6 hours
Grading: Easy–moderate
Apparel: Good shoes
Code: Year-round, bush, trees, birds, flowers, plants

Points of note: An interesting track system offering plenty of variety, it is easy all the way except that the two longer tramps require good fitness. Apart from the risk of becoming overtired, there is a danger of becoming lost if the tramper moves away from the track, particularly on the undulating country traversed on the Ruapani Track through to Lake Waikareiti. The beech forest can make all directions look the same to the inexperienced.

Access: The track system begins near the headquarters of Te Urewera National Park at Waikaremoana on State Highway 38.

The tracks in this area are:

A 1-hour walk to Waipai Swamp, which can be continued for another hour to Lake Ruapani.

Another 1-hour walk to Lake Waikareiti, which is approximately 300 metres above Waikaremoana.

A full 5 hours (8 kilometres) to the north end of Lake Waikareiti, with a further 3-hour return trip to Kaipo Lagoon, 990 metres above sea level. (This is an overnight trip.) From the north end of Lake Waikareiti to Kaipo Lagoon is approximately 4 kilometres.

The Circuit Track takes 6 hours (10 kilometres) from Aniwaniwa to Waipai Swamp, Lake Ruapani, Lake Waikareiti and back to Aniwaniwa.

For the Lake Waikareiti Track, follow the highway for 200 metres across the bridge from the park visitor centre to the signposted start of the track. The track follows an uphill grade on a total climb (1 hour) of about 300 metres to

Lake Waikareiti, where a day shelter has been erected. The dominant bush type is beech forest, although many other species are present, especially tawa, rimu, northern rata, tawari and, in the gullies, fuchsia and tree-ferns, with many smaller varieties of trees and ferns. On one of the islands on Lake Waikareiti there is a small lake. The birdlife on the lake includes scaup, black and little shags, and paradise, grey and shoveller ducks.

The track carries on around the lake edge to a sandy beach at Tawari Bay, a walk of 20 minutes from the shelter. The main track continues on to Sandy Bay at the northern end of the lake, where an eighteen-bunk hut is situated. Although there is a stove in the hut, firewood is not available, so trampers should carry a gas or spirit stove. (It is 3 hours from the day shelter to the hut.)

From the Sandy Bay Hut you can visit the Kaipo Lagoon, often called the Tundra, an old, silted-up lakebed that is usually under water in winter. The track passes through a number of clearings with interesting vegetation. The round trip from Sandy Bay to the lagoon takes about 3 hours, through mainly beech bush, with much tawari, and two prominent ferns, the Prince of Wales feather (*Leptopteris superba*) and the similar *L. hymenophylloides*.

The Lake Ruapani Track begins a few metres past the starting point of the Waikareiti Track. After an uphill start from the road, this is a track of easy grade undulating through beech forest to the Waipai Swamp (1 hour), which gives an excellent showing of orchids and sundews in season. The track continues to the small Lake Ruapani (1 hour) and on for a further 2-hour walk to meet the track that follows the shore of Lake Waikareiti. This track can be followed back to the road (2 hours).

Ngamoko Track

Length: Various
Time taken: Up to 5 hours
Grading: Easy, becoming strenuous
Apparel: Casual to tramping gear
Code: Year-round, trees, birds, plants, flowers

Points of note: The Ngamoko Track in Te Urewera National Park is an interesting and varied bush walk, that, if the final stage to Kaitawa is taken, follows the southern rim of what appears as a huge basin some 5 kilometres long. This was

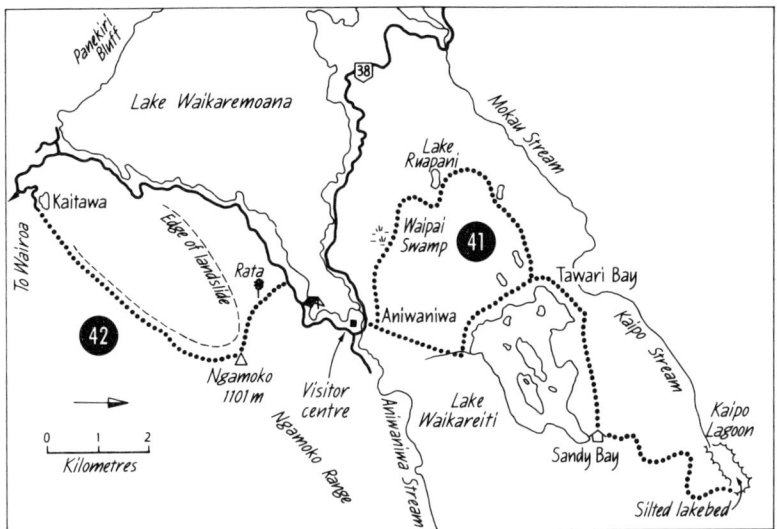

created when a huge landslide slipped away from here about 2,280 years ago and blocked the valley of the Waikare-Taheke Stream. The resulting build-up of water behind the landslide has become Lake Waikaremoana.

Access: The track begins at the main highway (State Highway 38) opposite the site of the old Lake House of the Tourist Hotel Corporation at Waikaremoana, and about 200 metres from the entrance to the Jetty Camp, which has motel units, cabins, camping facilities, a boat-launching ramp and a shop.

This track begins with a climb to the Ngamoko Trig. The first part, to an exceptionally large rata tree, is easy walking and takes about 20 minutes. Above the rata the track becomes steeper and is not as well formed, although it is well marked and easy enough to follow as it moves up the spur, finally becoming very steep on the climb to the main ridge of the Ngamoko Range. The total time up to the trig is about 2 hours. From the summit the views are superb, looking back first to Lake Waikaremoana and Panekiri Bluff. Lake Waikareiti with its seven tiny islands can also be seen. The view to the east and north-east takes in Mahia Peninsula, Poverty Bay and, on a clear day, Mt Hikurangi, the highest peak of the Raukumara Range.

The return journey can be made along the same track or you can continue down the southern side of the range to finish at the Kaitawa Power Station. This track descends through bush but then emerges into scrub country and follows an old bulldozer track. The more open parts boast many species of ground orchid during early summer.

77

The first part of the Ngamoko Track is through dense mixed podocarp forest with a thick undergrowth of smaller trees, especially tawa and tree-ferns. As the climb gets steeper, the cover changes to beech forest, with fine views down on to podocarp forest.

There are plenty of bush birds – bellbirds and tui being most noticeable with their song, and grey warblers and fantails are common. Silvereyes, tomtits, chaffinches, riflemen and pigeons are often seen or heard. Both species of cuckoos are present through the summer.

Hinerau Track

Length: 2 kilometres
Time taken: 30 minutes
Grading: Easy
Apparel: Casual
Code: Year-round, trees, birds, plants, waterfalls

Points of note: One of several scenic bush tracks that begin at Te Urewera National Park headquarters, this should be walked after an inspection of the visitor centre, which offers excellent exhibits and photographs on the history and wildlife of the park. Brochures, maps and park handbooks are also available here. The building itself is set into the bush as part of the natural setting.

Access: The track is reached from State Highway 38, 64 kilometres from Wairoa, at the park visitor centre.

The track begins alongside the visitor centre and is roughly circular, returning to the carpark at the centre. The half-hour suggested for the walk allows plenty of time for viewing the falls and other points of interest; seats are placed at vantage points.

There are three waterfalls on the Aniwaniwa Stream, seen from Hinerau Track. Where the stream divides around an island, the Momahaki Falls and the Bridal Veil Falls cascade about 15 metres over the same rock ledge. Large trout are sometimes seen in the pool at the foot of these falls. The lower falls, of about 10 metres, are named Te Tangi o Hinerau.

Further on, the track passes a short path leading to an old Maori clearing. From here you can look across the valley to a bush-clad slope with rimu and red and silver beech dominant. The dominant Panekiri Bluff rising above Lake Waikaremoana is also visible from this point.

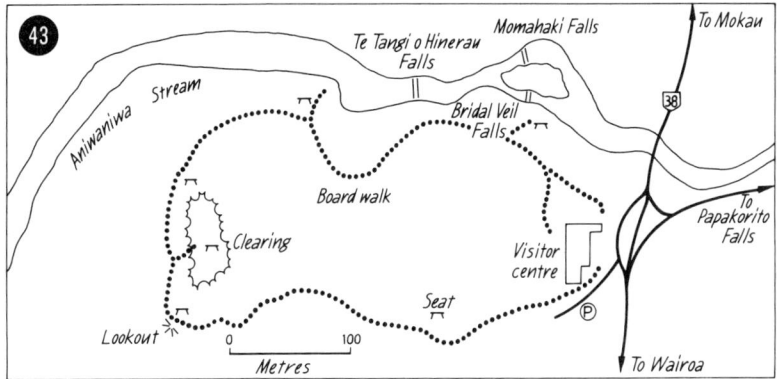

The main road bridge is often a good vantage point to look for blue ducks (whio). The principal birds on the track are tui, bellbird, rifleman, New Zealand pigeon, silvereye, grey warbler, fantail and tomtit. The North Island robin is also sometimes seen or heard, together with the kaka and whitehead, and both shining and long-tailed cuckoos in season.

The bush is typical of the southern region of the park – red and silver beech with rimu emergent. The intermediate canopy consists of mainly kamahi, tawa, northern rata (a magnificent sight when all the trees are in flower), miro and tawiri, which is common in this area and gives a fine showing of starry white flowers early in summer.

Smaller species are numerous and include putaputaweta, kohuhu, mahoe and tree-ferns, especially wheki. Ferns are numerous, with *Leptopteris hymenophylloides* and the hen and chicken giving a fine showing.

The other falls on the Aniwaniwa Stream are the well-known Papakorito Falls. To reach these, take the old Gisborne Road, opposite the visitor centre, for 2 kilometres. It is then a walk of only 100 metres to the falls.

Waihirere Domain

Length: 1 kilometre
Time taken: 20 minutes
Grading: Easy
Apparel: Casual
Code: Year-round, trees, flowers, birds, plants

Points of note: An area of approximately 47 hectares, this reserve gains its character from an attractive stream running through a gorge-like bush-clad valley.

Access: The reserve lies off Back Ormond Road, 13 kilometres north-west of Gisborne.

This walk passes through a piece of typical tawa forest with a generous sprinkling of kohekohe, pukatea, pigeonwood, pate and many subcanopy types. The streambed, with moss-covered boulders and ferny banks, is a delight, and the track terminates at a small attractive waterfall. Bird life abounds, with moreporks, shining and long-tailed cuckoos, pigeons, tui and fantails being the predominant species.

The domain includes a recreation area with swings, slides and swimming pool.

Grays Bush

Length: 600 metres
Time taken: 20–30 minutes
Grading: Easy
Apparel: Casual
Code: Year-round, trees, birds, flowers, plants

Points of note: Grays Bush comprises 12 hectares of a very vital remnant of the kahikatea forest that once covered a substantial part of the Gisborne plain.

Access: The reserve lies approximately 10 kilometres from Gisborne on Back Ormond Road.

A network of easy flat tracks makes Grays Bush a very pleasant place in which to botanise, perhaps as part of an outing that embraces the whole locality.

The reserve contains a mixture of very fine trees – kahikatea, rimu, matai, puriri, kohekohe, tawa, titoki, pukatea, with an abundance of nikau palms and smaller trees and shrubs of the subcanopy type.

Bird life includes tui, pigeons, warblers, fantails and weka. Up Grays Hill nearby, on the Waimata Valley Road, is a lookout giving one of the best panoramic views of the Poverty Bay flats.

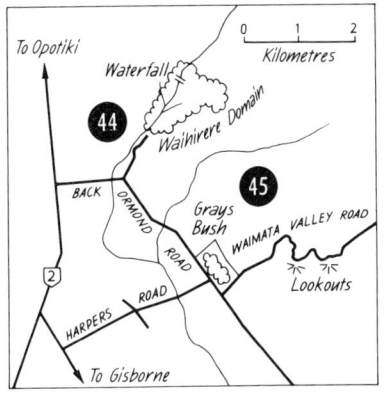

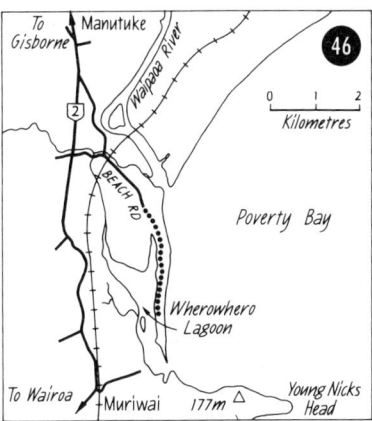

Wherowhero Lagoon

Length: Various
Time taken: Up to 3 hours
Grading: Easy
Apparel: Casual
Code: Year-round, birds, swimming

Points of note: This lagoon is the only substantial feeding ground for migratory and wading birds between Napier and East Cape.

Access: Wherowhero Lagoon is approximately 24 kilometres south-west of Gisborne. Access is off State Highway 2. If travelling south, turn hard left immediately over the bridge at the south end of the long straight beyond Manutuke. If north-bound, turn right 5 kilometres north of Muriwai School.

Beach Road leads over the railway line and terminates at the property owned by the Wall Estate and farmed as a trust for the Foundation for the Blind. Continue through the gate to the left opposite the estate. At the sand dunes a right turn pursues a somewhat rough track to a clump of silver poplars.

The long lagoon to the right extends for about 2 kilometres. In season many migratory birds are to be found during a most rewarding walk along the lagoon. The interesting return along the beachfront gives a close-up view of historic Young Nicks Head and Poverty Bay. There is good safe swimming here.

The many types of bird you may see at Wherowhero Lagoon include

81

white-faced herons, black swans, red-billed and black-backed gulls, wrybills, paradise shelducks, little terns (rare), three species of shags, pied stilts, Asiatic whimbrels, godwits, turnstones, black-fronted and white-fronted terns, harriers, golden plovers, banded dotterels, Caspian terns, oyster-catchers, knots, mallards, red-necked stints, curlews and welcome swallows.

Morere Springs

Length: Various
Time taken: Up to 2½ hours
Grading: Moderate
Apparel: Good footwear
Code: Year-round, trees, birds, plants, swimming

Points of note: The tracks are in the Morere Hot Springs Reserve, administered by the Department of Conservation and with a resident conservation officer. This bush is the only good-sized protected piece of northern Hawke's Bay coastal forest. Although the reserve is better known for its hot springs, the tracks offer the impression of being deep in bush throughout, although open farmland surrounds the reserve. Facilities include hot pools and an outdoor swimming pool, toilets, picnic tables, coin-operated barbecues, an open grassed area and a nearby shop and hotel.

Access: The reserve is on State Highway 2, 40 kilometres north of Wairoa and 65 kilometres south of Gisborne.

Mangakawa Track offers an interesting variety of flora through its length. It takes 2½ hours of steady walking and can be wet in places (and slippery when following the stream), with some steep downhill stretches. The track, which passes through extensive nikau groves, starts a short way inside the bush, following an asphalt path past the main pools. The start of the track is signposted to the right of the path. There is a steady but fairly easy rise to the halfway point, the lower part being through nikau palms, which dominate with kohekohe and tawa, and an understorey of kawakawa, supplejack and silver fern. As the track rises, nikau becomes less frequent and kohuhu more plentiful, with a very large specimen just to the left of the track. An opening where the track is almost on the edge of a sharp ridge gives a magnificent view across farmland to Mt Moumakai, the dominant landform in the district.

As the track rises, the bush becomes more open with the brake fern

(*Pteris tremula*) and wheki. The downhill section is short and sharp, down a steep ridge, passing through a number of medium-sized black beech. Smaller trees now become numerous, mainly rewarewa and kohuhu, but also lancewood, coprosmas, mingimingi and a few broadleaf. The track descends into the Mangakawa Stream, which is followed, with a couple of crossings, until the nikau pools are reached. The stream section is very picturesque, with mosses, ferns and many small plants on the banks and nikau, kohekohe and tawa overhead. At one point the track gives beautiful views down the stream.

Two other tracks lead off the asphalt path to the left, both starting at the same point. The Nikau Track is short (20 minutes) and circles to join the main track again. This track passes through the best of the nikau groves; many of the palms are very tall with trunks up to 8 metres.

The Ridge Track, taking 2 hours, covers the left of the reserve, working up the hill to the ridge and circling down to join the main path again above the top pools.

Two uncommon plants in the reserve are *Helichrysum glomeratum*, a shrub up to 3 metres high found in the drier area of beech, and *Jovellana sinclairii*, a small erect herb that bears panicles of little white flowers from December to February and is restricted to the Hawke's Bay-East Cape region.

Tui and bellbirds are the most notable of the bird life, which includes fantails, grey warblers, and native pigeons throughout, kingfishers near the picnic area, and shining cuckoos, blackbirds and chaffinches.

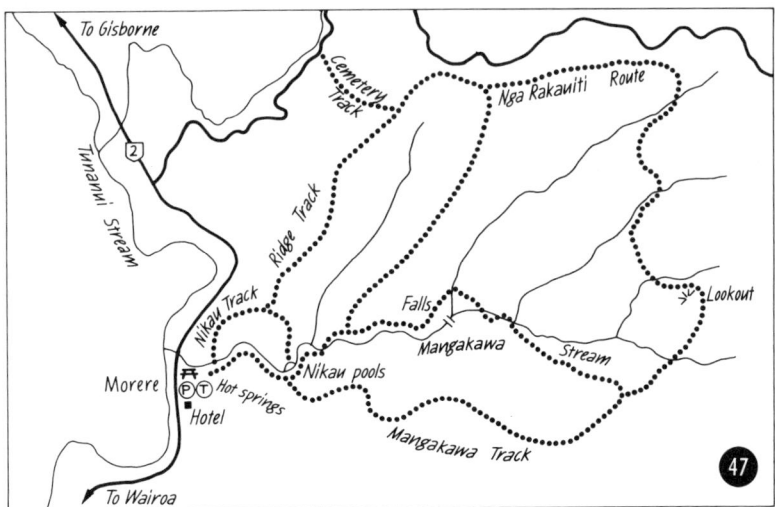

48

Mahia Peninsula Scenic Reserve

Length: 3.5 kilometres
Time taken: 1½-2 hours
Grading: Easy to moderate, steep in places
Apparel: Good footwear
Code: Year-round (can be slippery after rain), trees, birds, views

Points of note: This reserve is one of the last tracts of lowland coastal forest remaining between East Cape and Cape Palliser.

Access: 48 kilometres east of Wairoa on State Highway 2, and 7 kilometres south of the Mahia Beach settlement, on the narrow, winding Kinikini Road. There is parking at the entrance.

The best direction to walk the track is from the carpark south-west to the lookout. The track heads briefly out to the road again before heading down to follow the stream. About halfway along, a clearing by a fork in the stream provides an ideal spot for picnicking. The track then heads north-west back to the carpark. The forest is a mixture of tawa, podocarps (rimu, matai and kahikatea) and hardwoods (particularly rewarewa). Tarata, karaka, mahoe, ngaio, cabbage tree and lancewood make up the subcanopy.

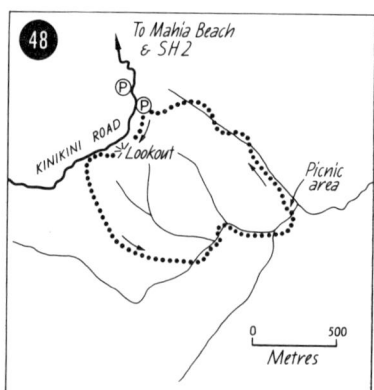

HAWKE'S BAY

Hawke Bay Coastal Walkway

Length: 16 kilometres
Time taken: Up to 9 hours return
Grading: Average
Apparel: Good footwear and windproof clothing
Code: Summer, trees, birds, views

Points of note: Originally part of the early settlers' route from Napier to Wairoa, this walkway can be used only in fine weather, and a portion can be passed only 2 hours either side of low tide.

Access: From the south, the walk starts from Aropaoanui Road, 48 kilometres north of Napier. From the north, the walk starts at the end of Waikari Road, which turns off State Highway 2 at Putorino, 59 kilometres north of Napier.

Starting from the south, the walk follows a massive earthquake slip ledge under high cliffs overlooking the sea. Native plants grow well here, and water-loving plants cling to the seepage on the towering cliffs. The first place of interest is where the Waipapa Stream tumbles over a waterfall into a pool by the sea. This makes a good hour-long return walk from the carpark. Between this point and Moeangiangi River the tide has to be watched.

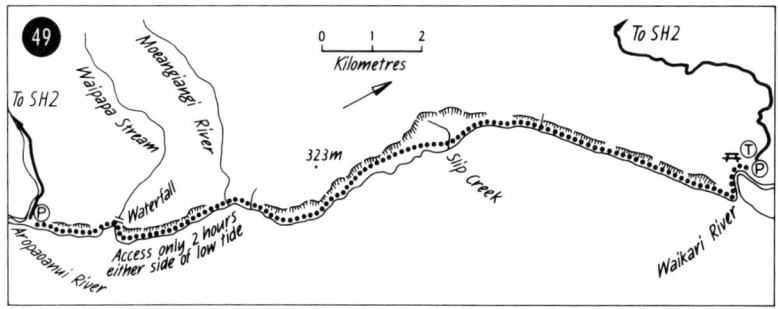

The next 12 kilometres ranges from wide, impressive beaches to massive slips bounded by 400-metre-high cliffs. The walk is lightly marked, but an added interest is to assess the best route around large boulders.

Note that this walk is along predominantly beach topography, which is subject to constant change. Slips occur every winter but are usually passable.

Lake Tutira

Length: Various
Time taken: Up to 4½ hours
Grading: Steep in places; otherwise average
Apparel: Good footwear
Code: From October to July (muddy at times), water birds, open country, views

Points of note: Tutira Station, through which the two walks pass, was part of the run operated by W. H. Guthrie-Smith in the early days of Hawke's Bay. A keen naturalist and observer, Guthrie-Smith left behind a vast amount of information on the breaking-in and development of this area. These two walkways are closed during August and September each year for lambing.

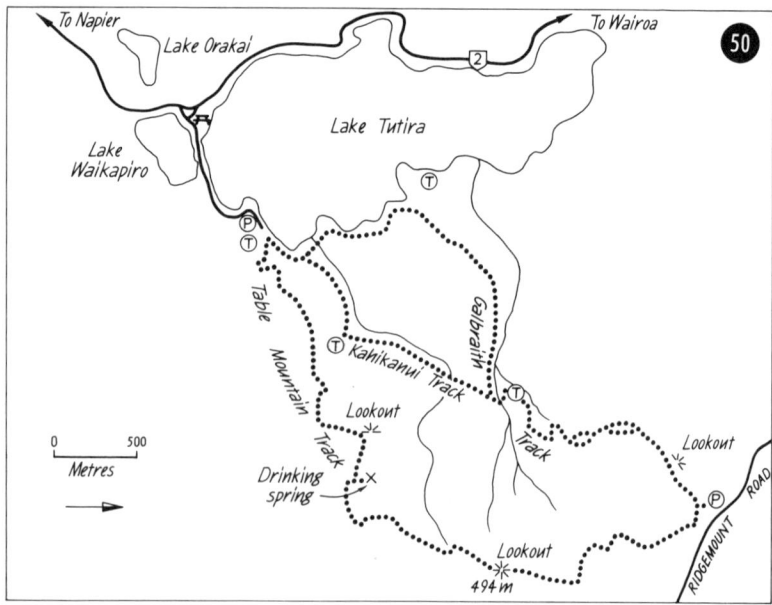

Access: A parking area is located at Lake Tutira Recreation Reserve, 45 kilometres north of Napier on State Highway 2.

The walkway begins by skirting the eastern shoreline of Lake Tutira, where wide protective bands of native trees and shrubs are being planted. Galbraith Track then swings away from the lake and climbs to the top of Table Mountain, leaving the shorter Kahikanui Track below.

From the crest of the Table Mountain Track there are magnificent views of coastal Hawke's Bay, from Cape Kidnappers to Mahia Peninsula and the inland ranges. The walkway continues south, following the crest of the range to a lookout before dropping down an easy ridge to the edge of the lake and a short walk back to the carpark.

51

Cape Kidnappers Gannet Reserve

Length: 8 kilometres
Time taken: 4 hours return
Grading: Easy (at low tide)
Apparel: Protection against sun and dehydration
Code: Summer, seabirds, geology

Points of note: The gannets start to arrive at the reserve around late July, and eggs are usually laid in October, hatching 43–44 days later. The best time to visit the reserve is from early November to late February. From late February/March, the birds start to disperse and the chicks begin their epic migration to Australia, not returning to the colony for about three or four years. By April most of the birds have left.

Access: The beach walk starts at the coastal settlement of Clifton, which is 18 kilometres east of Hastings and 21 kilometres south-east of Napier. There is a campground at Clifton and another at Te Awanga, from where concessionaire-operated tractor and trailer transport to the reserve departs. The walk can only be made during low tide. It is best to leave Clifton about 3 hours after the high tide and leave the Cape no later than 1½ hours after low tide. Wind and sea conditions may affect this walk. There are two private transport operators who visit the gannet colony via the beach (with tractor and trailor) and over farmland respectively. For less energetic walkers, it is possible to walk one way and ride the other.

Towering cliffs above the beach are unstable, so visitors should avoid stopping for picnics below them. The cliffs have been cut by streams to form

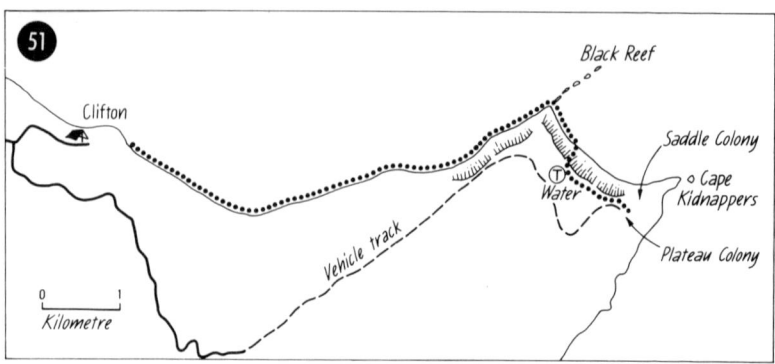

impressive canyons and are dramatically layered by bands of different-coloured strata. In places, fossils can be seen jutting out of the rock. A small publication on the geology of the area and another on the gannets can be purchased at the Department of Conservation visitor centre at Napier.

There are a multitude of seabirds in the area. There are two colonies of black-backed gulls, and white-fronted terns nest in the cliffs near the Black Reef gannet colony. Less than 1 kilometre along from the reef, a track leads up to the rest area. Here there are display panels, shelter, water and toilets. A track then leads up past a residence to the Plateau Colony and a view of the Saddle Colony, access to which is prohibited. About 2,200 pairs of birds return annually to the same nest sites.

Te Mata Trust Park

Length: Various
Time taken: Up to 2 hours
Grading: Easy to average (Peak Trail has one steep section)
Apparel: Casual
Code: Year-round, trees, birds, geology, rock formations, views

Points of note: Te Mata Peak was given to the people of Hawke's Bay in trust by the Chambers family in 1927 and dominates the Hastings-Havelock North skyline. It has the reputation of being the driest hill in the area and any plantings are made with extreme difficulty.

Access: Access is by way of Te Mata Peak Road from Havelock North.

The Nature Trail (2 hours) starts just inside the main gates by the carpark and winds around Tui Bluff, where there are many varieties of eucalyptus and views out over the Heretaunga Plains. Dropping down through a native bush area, the track passes through a plantation of young redwoods before crossing Chambers Walk to a gentle climb up a track cut out of the limestone bedrock. At the crest of the ridge is another fine lookout and a plane table pointing out places of interest. The trail now enters and descends through exotic forest to the Redwood Grove, a stand of semi-mature trees with a cathedral-like atmosphere. From the head of this stand the Peak Trail (45 minutes) circles the base of the southern ridge and climbs up to Te Mata Peak by way of fossil beds and viewpoints. Te Mata Peak offers a full 360° view of Hawke's Bay and is the end of Te Mata Peak Road. The Peak Trail continues down, winding between the road and the cliff line to rejoin the Nature Trail just above Peak House, a restaurant.

Te Mata Walk (30 minutes) also starts from the head of the Redwood Grove, passing through a wetlands area to climb steadily up the valley and on to Farnsworth Ridge. The track then passes above Webbs Bush through open pasture to rejoin the Nature Trail above Peak House.

The Nature Trail leaves the head of the Redwood Grove to climb through

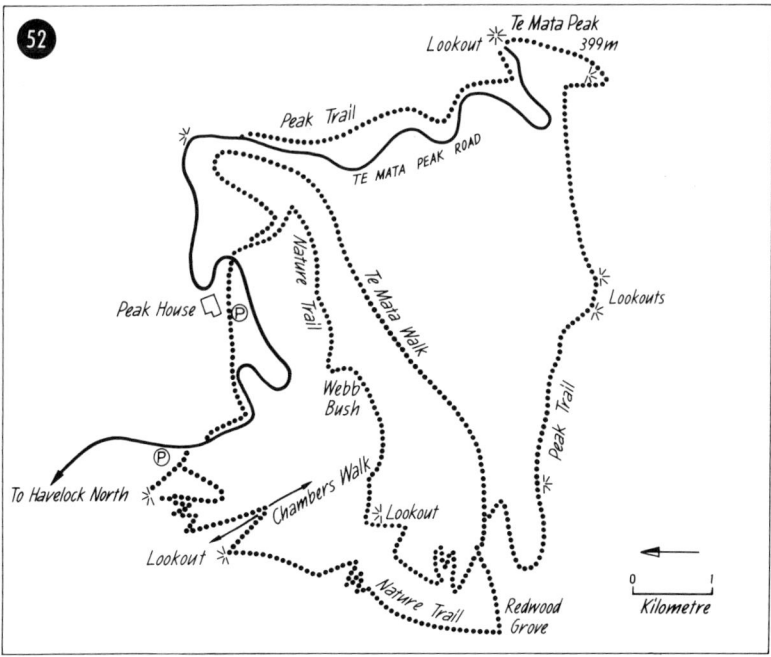

89

exotic forest to the Plains Lookout and on over Farnsworth Ridge to drop down into Webbs Bush, an area of native trees planted in the main valley. At the top of Webbs Bush the trail enters open pasture and climbs to pass Peak House and enter a regenerating native plant area. From here the trail circles one last lookout before dropping down to the carpark.

There are marked exits from the Nature Trail along its full length to enable walkers to leave as it suits them.

Mohi Bush Scenic Reserve

Length: 5 kilometres
Time taken: 1½ hours
Grading: Easy
Apparel: Good footwear
Code: Year-round, trees, birds, geology, views

Points of note: This reserve is situated on the Maraetotara Plateau, a prominent landform to the south-east of Hastings rising to a height of 450 metres above sea level. Capped with a layer of fairly hard limestone overlaying thick mudstone, the plateau has steep eroded edges and areas of coastal-type forest contained in a series of scenic reserves. Where sections of limestone have been badly undercut by weathering on the seaward side, great blocks of rock up to 500 metres wide and 3 kilometres long have sheared off and rafted down the slippery mudstone to tip on edge to form coastal ranges.

Access: The Maraetotara Plateau may be reached by road from Hastings by way of the Waimarama, Maraetotara and Waipoapoa Roads, and is 18 kilometres from Havelock North.

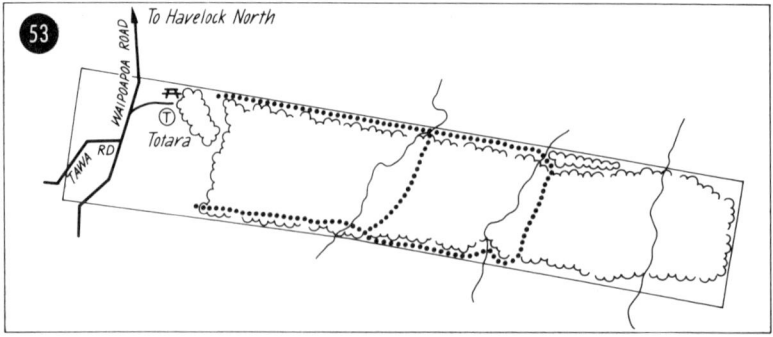

Mohi Bush Scenic Reserve is clearly marked and has shelters and toilets. A track starts from the south-eastern side of the picnic area. Across the fenceline, an old logging track wanders down into dense forest, predominantly tawa, overshadowed in places by mature matai, rimu and kahikatea. The track passes through tawa glades of great beauty before emerging to skirt farmland. It then re-enters bush and crosses to the northern boundary of the reserve, where it follows the fenceline back to the carpark.

William Hartree Reserve

Length: Various
Time taken: Up to 2 hours
Grading: Moderate
Apparel: Short walks, casual; longer, tramping gear
Code: Year-round (except midwinter and after heavy rain), regenerating trees, birds, flowers, plants

Points of note: On the hills of Te Waka Range, the William Hartree Reserve is in regenerating bush with clearings often high in bracken fern. Tracks have been made through the more interesting areas. Although there are few big trees left, the reserve is rich in ferns and ground and epiphytic orchids. There are two small waterfalls.

Access: The reserve is reached from the Napier–Puketitiri Road, 51 kilometres north-west of Napier, 8 kilometres beyond Patoka. A car track leads up to the lodge parking area and the start of the track system.

This reserve was the centre of co-operation between William Hartree and Reg Williams, who from 1953 encouraged Junior Wildlife Wardens to study the regenerating bush. When Hartree died in 1961, his widow donated the bush as a scenic reserve. A house was built as a research station and this was opened in 1967. When Williams died in 1976, the house became the William Hartree Memorial Lodge and was donated to the Forest and Bird Society. It is managed by the society's Napier branch.

Kanuka Track: This half-hour walk follows the main ridge up through regenerating forest, festooned with lycopodiums. At its highest point the track turns right and crosses a bracken dividing strip to drop down into a grove of mature trees with ground orchids and ferns.

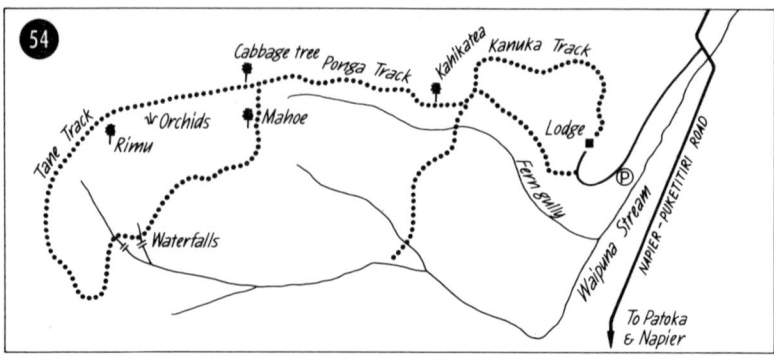

Ponga Track: (1 hour return from lodge) starts from the top of the Kanuka Track, where it turns off to the left, dropping down through young kahikatea to a ferny creek that is followed upstream until the walls close in. Here the track climbs through bush to a bracken clearing dominated by large cabbage trees decked with epiphytic orchids and ferns. You retrace your steps to the lodge.

Tane Track: (2 hours return from lodge) follows the whole of the Ponga Track route to the cabbage trees, before following the leading ridge through forest out on to a wide ledge where there are many birds. The track then drops down to the tops of two waterfalls tumbling into ferny gorges, an excellent viewpoint surrounded by tree fuchsias. Crossing a small stream, the track winds its way through ferny groves and trees to rejoin the Ponga Track.

Blowhard Bush

Length: Various
Time taken: Up to 2½ hours
Grading: Easy
Apparel: Casual, but be prepared for cold weather
Code: Year-round, trees, birds, geology, views

Points of note: Blowhard Bush is an island of extremely varied podocarp forest, with walks ranging from very sedate paths through massive blocks of Waitotara Limestone, festooned with vines and plants, to windswept viewpoints and tall mature forest. The bush is owned and serviced by the Hastings-Havelock North branch of the Forest and Bird Society, who have built Lowry Lodge as a shelter for day visitors.

Access: Blowhard Bush lies at the junction of the Napier–Taihape and Lawrence Roads, 64 kilometres west of Hastings.

Rimu Track: (1 hour loop) winds its way through a podocarp-broadleaf forest that is unusual for an altitude of 800 metres, a height normally producing mountain or red beech in this area. The track passes through moss-covered stone passages, festooned with ferns, where trees scramble for rooting space, out into the forest proper where giant rimu, matai, black beech, turepo, red beech, totara and many other uncommon trees grow.

Hoheria and Tui Tracks: From a short distance along the Rimu Track, the Hoheria Track branches off to the left to climb in easy, sweeping grades around massive, water-worn limestone blocks, through groves of tree fuchsias, with their papery bark and purple flowers. As the track meanders higher, the forest changes to kanuka before giving way to regenerating bush and, in turn, to tutu and tussock. Here alpine flowers add a splash of colour to the varied foliage and viewpoints add to the interest. The scrub gives way to a bare pumice landscape, the result of rabbit burrows eroding away under heavy rainfall, but even this inhospitable area is healing slowly as tutu and tussock make use of every patch of cover.

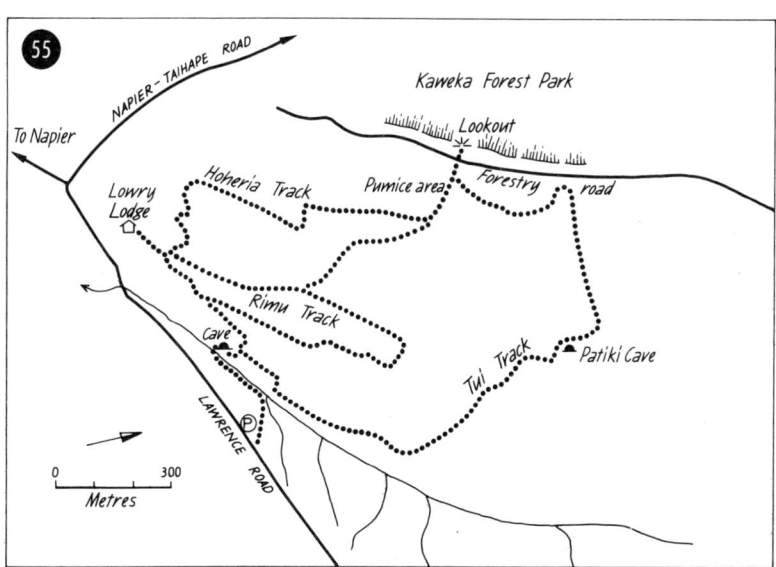

93

The track here reaches the top of the reserve and crosses to a fine lookout on the other side of the forestry road. From here may be viewed, from south to north, Mts Miroroa, Kohinga, Kuripapanga and the Kaweka Ranges, with the Blowhard in the foreground. From this point it is possible to drop down to the Rimu Track or continue on the Tui Track through tussock back into kanuka forest and Patiki Cave, once the home of an outcast Waimarama Maori family. Back in mature forest, the track passes through limestone passages until the Rimu Track is once more reached.

From Lowry Lodge to the summit takes 40 minutes, the Hoheria Track and return via the Rimu Track takes 1½ hours and the full loop of the Hoheria and Tui Tracks takes 2½ hours.

Within the bush are several other walks, such as a cave by the stream (30 minutes) or to the almost underground stream, lined with glow-worms by night.

Makairo Track

Length: Various
Time taken: Various
Grading: Easy to moderate
Apparel: Short walks, casual; longer, tramping gear
Code: Year-round, trees, birds, flowers

Points of note: The Makairo Track provides walks through montane bush of the Waewaepa Scenic Reserve, on a route where an abandoned road crosses the Waewaepa Range from Coonoor to Makairo. This road was officially closed about 1975, and lack of maintenance has now reduced the route to a walking track only.

The forest is on easy to steep country, reaching an altitude of a little over 700 metres. The summit ridges are mostly broad and allow moderately easy travelling through bush and scrub. The area is suitable for picnicking, easy walking and tramping.

Access: The Makairo Track may be reached by road from either Pahiatua or Dannevirke. From Pahiatua, you can travel either to the western end of the track (at the roadend at Makairo) or to its eastern end at Coonoor. From Dannevirke, Coonoor is reached by a 30-minute car trip. Motorists should head west from Coonoor and leave their vehicles at the quarry site at the foot of the track.

The most popular trip is a family walk from the Coonoor end up the road formation to the saddle at the summit of the range (2 hours return). On a winding, easy grade, the track affords views of podocarp trees and a few large northern rata in the valley below. Most of the bush is possum-damaged montane vegetation with a good representation of the hardwood species characteristic of the Wellington province. Pleasing features are some fine specimens of *Cordyline indivisa,* while the shady south-facing banks of the side cuttings of the road are a striking sight in the spring when the gnaphaliums are in bloom.

You can cross the saddle at the road summit and continue to the road end at Makairo (1½ hours). This west side of the road descends through bush on a route high above the spectacular gorge of the Makairo Stream.

A longer and steeper walk is available from the road saddle to the range summit, Waewaepa, on the north side of the saddle. Ascent time from the saddle is 30 minutes.

An interesting tramping route from the road saddle is to climb south along the range toward the Ohinereiata Trig to an open grassed ridge top surrounded by subalpine scrub. Reaching this area involves following ridges along a poorly defined old track through montane bush and scrub along the spine of the Waewaepa Range. In one locality on the eastern side of the summit ridge grows a small colony of the shrub *Senecio elaeagnifolius.* This is its only known occurrence in this area, east of the Ruahine–Tararua main divide. Time from road saddle and return is about 5 hours.

Bird life in the area includes tui, bellbirds, fantails, tomtits, silvereyes, wood pigeons, moreporks, grey warblers, harrier hawks, falcons, whiteheads and riflemen.

Klein Track

Length: 3 kilometres
Time taken: 2 hours return
Grading: Average
Apparel: Casual
Code: Year-round, trees, birds, flowers

Points of note: The Klein Track is situated on a steep hillside on the south side of the Manawatu River, close to State Highway 2 just before it enters the eastern end of the Manawatu Gorge. It traverses a bush reserve known as the Woodville Domain, most of which is visible to highway travellers.

Access: The track enters the reserve from a small parking area on the left of the main highway immediately over the Manawatu Bridge at the entrance to the gorge.

Indicated by round white markers, the Klein Track is suitable for a family walk, although it is rather steep in places. It climbs through mixed forest, with a predominance of tawa, especially in the lower areas. There is a good variety of ferns, tree-ferns and filmy ferns. Several big trees – matai, totara and rimu – stand beside the track. These are surrounded by mixed forest, with mahoe, rewarewa, pigeonwood, titoki, kamahi, miro, manatu, pate, mapou, rangiora, maire, kawakawa, hoheria and several nikau palms. Climbing plants include parsonsia, kohia, supplejack and clematis. Interesting fungi and lichens abound. The New Zealand gloxinia, taurepo, is also to be seen.

Birds you may see or hear along the track include fantails, silvereyes, warblers, pigeons, tui, bellbirds, shining cuckoos, kingfishers and riflemen.

The track rises sharply to a point above the bush, a resting place from which there is an extensive view over the Manawatu River, which here is the boundary between the Wellington and Hawke's Bay provinces. Wharite Peak is seen to the north and the Waewaepa and Puketoi Ranges away to the east.

The track then descends, very steeply in places, with one slightly difficult section where there is a sharp descent to a small stream crossing.

It finishes at a pleasant picnic area in a grove of tawa trees, with swings, a paddling pool, fireplaces and tables, on the road to Ballance. An easy walk of about 1 kilometre across the Ballance Bridge and along the main highway takes walkers back to the carpark. The walk can be done in reverse.

This track is named after a Woodville resident, Stan Klein, who was a keen naturalist and a foundation member of the Southern Hawke's Bay branch of the Forest and Bird Society. He cut and formed the track in the early 1960s with the help of a few friends.

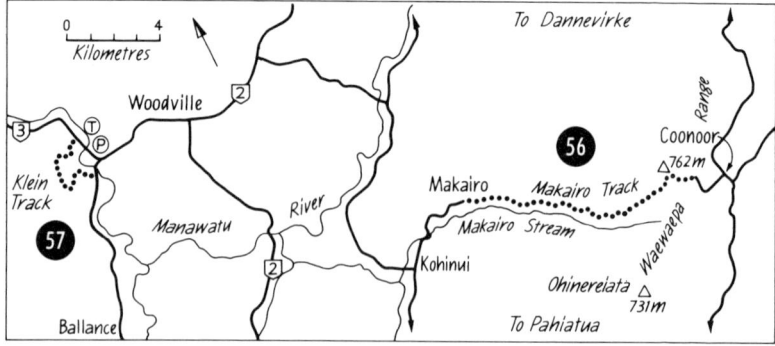

Cape Maria van Diemen from Cape Reinga

Hinerau Falls, Te Urewera National Park

Red Rocks, Wellington
Fossilised sea urchin, Hawke Bay Coastal Walk

Northern rata, Upper Hutt

Cape Kidnappers gannet colony

Wilkies Pools, Egmont National Park

Pukatea and kiekie, Marlborough Sounds

Kahikatea, Pelorus Bridge Scenic Reserve

Truman Track, West Coast

View from Otepatotu Reserve, Banks Peninsula

Boardwalk, Lake Wilkie

TONGARIRO-TAUPO

58

Opepe Bush Scenic and Historic Reserve

Length: Two walks, 1.5 kilometres and 3 kilometres
Time taken: 45 minutes and 1½ hours return
Grading: Easy, suitable for families
Apparel: Casual
Code: Year-round, plants, history

Points of note: There are two loop walks in the reserve, which start on opposite sides of the road. These pass through superb forest with a number of historic sights.

Access: The reserve is about 17 kilometres south-east of Taupo on the Napier–Taupo Highway. A parking area on the left is adjacent to the highway.

Opepe Reserve: This 3-kilometre walk starts across the highway from the carpark. The Opepe Reserve comprises regenerating podocarp forest in an area that saw significant milling of large totara during the last century. Most of the trees taken from here were used to provide telegraph poles for the Napier–Taupo line. Evidence of past milling can be seen along the track. There is an old saw pit where a totara log has been re-established, enabling the visitor to see how timber was cut in the old days. During the time of settlement, stock and horses were driven 1 kilometre each day to a water trough, which is still visible on the track.

Opepe Engagement site: This walk starts from the carpark, passes through native bush and leads to the historical Opepe graves. From here a loop track brings you back to the carpark.

At the Opepe Engagement site provides an atmosphere of peace and beauty far removed from the attack that took place in 1869 when a detachment of Armed Constabulary were ambushed and killed by Te Kooti's men. The Opepe graves site remains a monument to this event.

At Opepe are the last remaining stands of mature podocarps of any

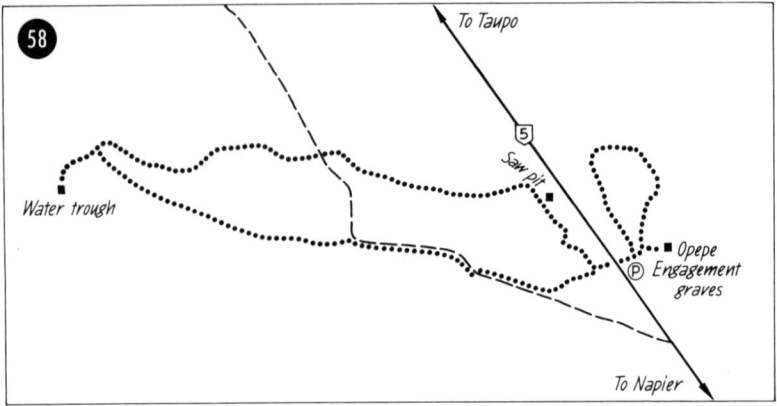

consequence close to Taupo, with trees that survived the early volcanic eruptions. A wide range of indigenous plants including kamahi, mahoe, manuka, kanuka, native fuchsia and orchids make this an interesting place for botanising. Opepe is also a popular habitat for native birds and a species of native frog.

Pureora Forest Park

Length: Various
Time taken: Various
Grading: Easy to strenuous
Apparel: Short walks, casual; longer, tramping gear
Code: Most tracks are year-round (except in bad weather), trees, plants, birds

Points of note: Pureora Forest Park contains the gigantic trees and the dense forests of the Hauhungaroa Range, famous throughout the world as the most splendid example of New Zealand's temperate rain forests. The forest park was set aside in 1979 to preserve this high forest, following public outcry at the logging that had greatly reduced the forests of the central North Island to this last remnant. Here you can hear kokako, kaka, robins and the full range of the birds of the temperate rain forests still in their native habitat.

All the walks are to the south of the Forest Park Headquarters at Pureora. There are facilities for picnicking and overnight camping, places for fishing, swimming and basic facilities such as toilets, barbecues, picnic tables and a good water supply. Camping is prohibited in the areas planted in exotic pines.

The walks have a range to suit family groups and also the experienced tramper. There are also many old logging tracks to be explored.

Access: The main road access is from State Highway 30 (Te Kuiti–Mangakino) at Pureora, where there is an information centre. There are several access roads off State Highway 32 on the eastern side from Arataki (walking), Kakaho Road (vehicle), Waihora Access (vehicle), Waihaha River (walking) and Waitaia Access (walking). There is access from east and west via the Link Road (vehicle), which joins Pureora to Kakaho Road and State Highway 32.

Totara Track: A 30-minute walk through some exceptional virgin bush that begins opposite the headquarters carpark and picnic area, where there is a barbecue and firewood supplied.

As soon as you enter the forest you are surrounded by huge matai and totara, with straight trunks reaching high above the other trees. This easy track is a good introduction to the type of forest you will meet on the other tracks. Remember to pick up a brochure on podocarps from the visitor centre.

Rimu Track: This 30-minute walk into high forest from beside the Kakaho Road picnic area, among virgin podocarp trees, is good after picnicking. It is easy going, but wear strong shoes, as it is rather up and down. The floor of the forest is worth examining for the hundreds of small plants, such as orchids and mosses, that have their habitat in the dim interior light of the high forests. Note the secretive bird life of the native forest.

Arataki Track: The track to the summit of Titiraupenga (1,042 metres) begins from the head of Arataki Road, which can be reached by driving via Link, Waimonoa and Titiraupenga Roads. This is a 3-hour return trip, which climbs the ridge to just below Titiraupenga.

This imposing pointed rock summit gives unrivalled views over the whole region, and the track is the most suitable route for those who want to climb to the top of the mountain as part of a day's outing. Wear strong boots and warm clothing against the winds that tend to swirl around the ridge and mountain.

Link Track: The whole route from below Titiraupenga to the summit of Pureora takes 4 hours. You can divide the track into two by starting from the carpark on Link Road, which bisects the track. Walk from the carpark to Mt Titiraupenga, crossing many small valleys and ridges and passing through a selectively logged area. Return by same route; the round trip takes 6 hours.

Alternatively, walk from the carpark to the summit of Pureora (1,160 metres). Of interest here is the change in plant life as you climb up the slopes of the mountain. On the top, the mountain trees are contorted by the winds and snows of winter. Here the New Zealand falcon and the harrier fly high. On a clear day it is a delight to lie on the summit and gaze at the skies above, realising that you are isolated on the roof of the West Taupo highlands. The return trip takes 2 hours.

Toi Toi Track: This is an alternative route (2 hours return) to the summit of Pureora. Turn right off Link Road about 3 kilometres from the Headquarters on to Cabbage Tree Road. Then turn right on to Toi Toi Road. The track passes through a grove of Douglas fir planted in 1962 and then enters native bush for the rest of the route to the top. Note how the vegetation changes to subalpine plants as you approach the summit. Wear strong boots and warm windproof clothes on this and the following tracks.

Bog Inn Track: This track (40 minutes one way) has an easy grade and travels from the end of Bog Inn Road to Bog Inn.

Starting just beyond the Kakaho Road picnic area, turn left on to Tihoi Road then right into Mill Road before veering left into Bog Inn Road;

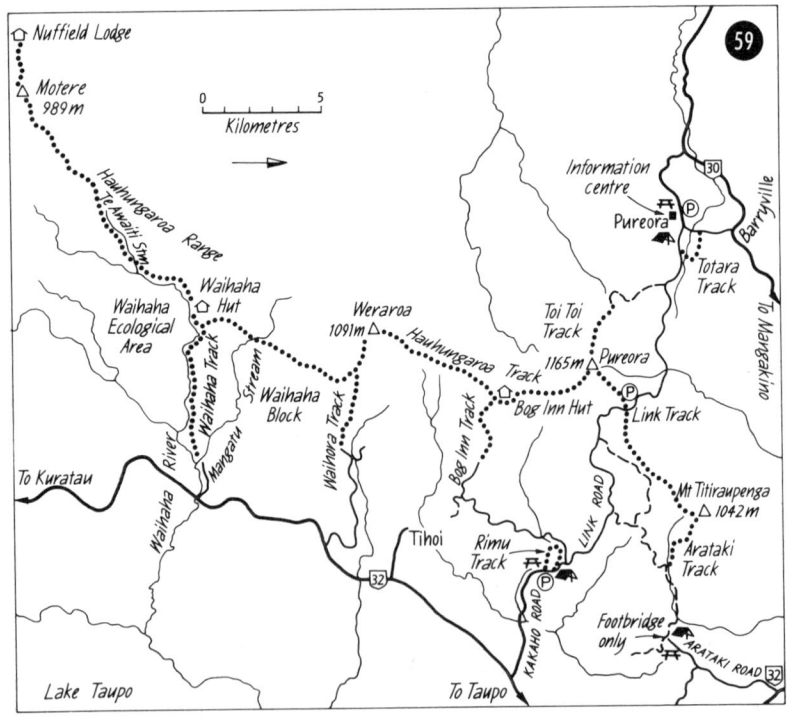

vehicles may be parked at the end. The track takes you up to the crest of the range to join the Hauhungaroa Track and a short walk north brings you to the Bog Inn Hut.

Waihora Track: This is a slightly longer walk to the ridge (45 minutes one way). From the end of Waihora Access Road (an old logging road) the track crosses the stream and climbs to the plateau on the crest of the range where it joins the Hauhungaroa Track. Two kilometres to the north is Weraroa Trig (1,091 metres). Looking south, you can see the extent of the Waihaha Block, largely unmodified native forest that was of great concern to conservationists in the late 1970s and early 1980s when it was threatened by logging proposals. Now part of the forest park, it has earned a reprieve.

Waihaha Track: Starting from the Waihaha River Bridge on State Highway 32, a benched track (2½ hours) follows up the river and soon enters the glorious Waihaha Forest. To the south of the route is the Waihaha Ecological Area. The route generally winds up along the river course in virgin forest and arrives at the Waihaha Hut (six bunks) on the Hauhungaroa Track. This is one of the best walks in the area for forest appreciation; there are many birds.

Lake Rotopounamu

Length: 4 kilometres
Time taken: 1½ hours return
Grading: Easy
Apparel: Casual
Code: Year-round (except in snow), trees, plants, flowers

Points of note: Situated near Tokaanu, Lake Rotopounamu (Greenstone Lake) is remarkable for the beauty of its changing colours. It can be jade green, as suggested by its name, but is just as often pure blue, grey blue or dark steel grey.

Access: The lake is reached from Te Ponanga Saddle Road, off State Highway 47.

An excellent track leads up through tall podocarp forest, with many rimu and kahikatea. From the open space at the top, the lake track takes about 1½ hours' easy walking.

Travelling clockwise around the lake, the visitor soon reaches two open beaches of coarse white pumice sand. The first of these has a fine grove of pokaka trees, and entangled juveniles of these can be seen in many places along the track.

Beech forest soon predominates, with a mixed understorey of shrubs and young trees and wide areas of filmy and kidney ferns. The huge moss *Dawsonia superba*, like a young pine, is also common. Both the epiphytic *Earina* orchids are found here, along with the *Dendrobium* and various ground orchids, especially *Corybas* and *Pterostylis*. The area is also good for fungi and liverworts. The larger of the two beaches is backed by subalpine scrub and stunted bush, with snowberry, dwarf muehlenbeckia and *Olearia nummularifolia*.

After this stretch of beach, the track rises for a time with many *Asplenium colenso* and *A. hookerianum* enjoying the drier conditions. Some huge and ancient red beeches grow here, and there is striking regeneration of other trees, especially white and black maire, matai and rimu.

Bird life is profuse in the bush. Robins, riflemen, kaka, pigeons and especially whiteheads are heard and seen, as well as the commoner bush birds. Both the shining and long-tailed cuckoo are heard in the summer. There are shags and grey duck on and around the lake, and dabchicks can usually be seen feeding and diving.

Tongariro National Park

Length: Various
Time taken: Up to full day
Grading: Easy to moderate
Apparel: Short walks, boots preferable, parka essential; longer, tramping gear
Code: Summer months best for nature walks and recommended for longer walks; trees, plants, birds, rock formations, springs, waterfalls, views

Points of note: The walks are chosen to be representative of the varied flora and other features of the national park. They are mainly in the Whakapapa area, where the vegetation is beech forest and shrubland, the area opposite the visitor centre being well forested and watered by streams.

Access: The road to Park Headquarters turns off from the National Park–Taupo Road (State Highway 47) 9 kilometres from National Park at an altitude of 870 metres. Park Headquarters is 6.5 kilometres from the turn-off, a little above the Chateau Tongariro hotel, at 1,125 metres.

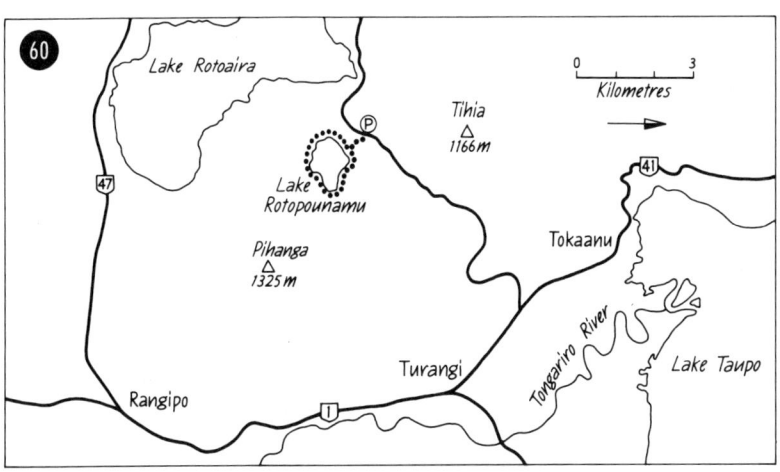

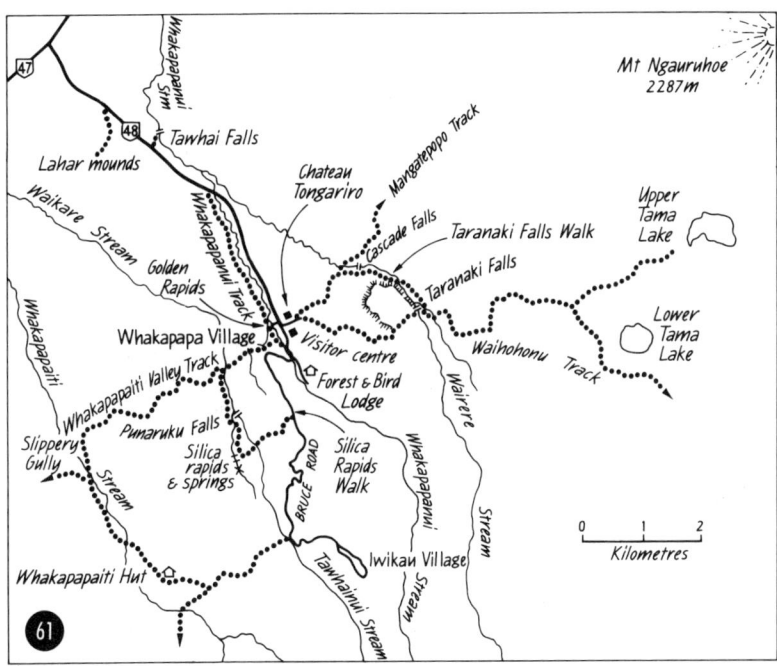

Lahar Mounds: These are 1.5 kilometres from the highway turn-off and take 20 minutes return. The short, easy track across open shrubland was made as a school project to give access to an area of lahar deposits left by a Ruapehu debris avalanche.

Tawhai Falls: This half-hour return walk is 2.5 kilometres above the turn-off. The track follows the tussock edge beside the left bank of the Whakapapanui Stream before turning to descend toward the base of the attractive 13-metre falls. In summer an occasional sun orchid may be found along the track.

Taranaki Falls Walk: A 2½-hour round trip, starting from the road a short distance above Park Headquarters. The lower track descends to cross a stream and then proceeds through tussock country to beech forest and the Wairere Stream (where the Mangatepopo Track heads off to the left). Follow the pleasantly bushed track up the stream to see the falls plunging over the lip of a great lava flow. The track climbs above the falls and then turns back right (the Waihohonu Track heads off left) across the stream toward Park Headquarters, mainly through tussock. The walk can be done in either direction.

Whakapapanui Walk: Starts from the footbridge reached by turning right 250 metres above Park Headquarters on to the short road above the campsite. This takes 1½ hours one way, for a 6-kilometre round trip. It follows the stream down through mountain beech – a good introduction to the beech forest of the Whakapapaiti Valley. Eight minutes from the footbridge is the turn-off (left) to Silica Springs and the Whakapapaiti Valley. The bush growth is notable here, particularly umbrella fern (waewaekotuku – the feet of the white heron). The track crosses over the Golden Rapids (on a side stream) and overlooks the main stream at intervals. About halfway along the track there is a bush-framed view of Ngauruhoe. A boardwalk crosses an open, poorly drained area of wire-rush and tussock before the track crosses the stream to finish at the road.

Silica Rapids Walk: Same access as for Whakapapanui Walk. This is perhaps the most enjoyable half-day walk in the park (8 kilometres, 3 hours return). Sunlight is needed to appreciate fully the beauty of the rapids and the stream.

Turn left a few minutes from the footbridge to leave the Whakapapanui Track and ascend steadily. Notice that, as elsewhere, some of the mature beech is dying. Golden rocks in the stream give a foretaste of the rapids area. An open boggy area crossed on a boardwalk gives a good view of Ruapehu behind the beech trees, and a view back to Ngauruhoe.

Re-enter the forest and soon cross the Waikare Stream to reach another track junction (40 minutes). Turn left (the Whakapapaiti Valley Track bears right) to follow the Waikare Stream up to the rapids. Half an hour from the junction is the Punaruku Waterfall, formed from old lava and lahar deposits. Higher up, the forest tapers off, reducing to mountain toatoa and bog pine and then largely tussock with some shrub snow totara and semi-alpines as the stream is recrossed. The Silica Rapids area is 1 hour from the junction. The creamy silica deposit on the rocks is in places overlaid with rust-coloured iron compounds.

Above the rapids a streambed leads up to a plateau with tussock and more alpines. The return track heads back from this stream area. It descends steeply to the Tawhainui Stream, before rising again to sidle down a steep hummock. Watch for small plants in the tussock – snow totara, pigmy pine, snowberry, inaka and celmisia – as you approach Bruce Road. There is a 2-kilometre walk back to Park Headquarters.

Whakapapaiti Valley: This track (5½ hours) goes beyond the short nature walks with their fully formed paths into regions of poled tracks and fewer notices.

Start on the Silica Rapids Walk, but at the Waikare Stream junction bear right and soon descend to about 1,130 metres. Ascend steadily to the top of a long, low spur and continue through forest with more kaikawaka and less beech than before, but with the canopy broken by dead or dying trees. The understorey is, however, healthy and regenerating. Continue on an undulating track, descending for stream crossings. At the Slippery Gully crossing (1¾ hours) there is an outlook to the plains below, the twin fans of the gully separated by a ribbon of forest.

The track can be muddy here. Descend sharply to reach the stream and bridge. Across the stream on the right is the track to the Hauhungatahi Wilderness Area (2½ hours). The Whakapapaiti Track shortly passes an old bivouac, where it can be muddy and slippery, in fairly open bush. Two stream crossings should not pose any problems. Leave the beech forest and ascend to the Whakapapaiti Hut in subalpine tussock. At 1,350 metres (3½ hours) a track branches right to Lake Surprise, Mangaturuturu Hut and Blyth Hut.

Bear left to leave the tussock at the climb up the zigzag, which rises to the scoria gravel field. A close look will reveal much variety in ground plants springing up in moss and clinging to tenuous footholds in the gravel and rock. Whipcord hebe, small and low-growing senecio and celmesias are among the plants to be discovered.

The track drops across the Scoria Flat and over a few streams to return to the Bruce Road (4½ hours) with an hour's downhill walk back to Park Headquarters.

Tama Lakes: The 6-hour return trip to the Tama Lakes starts on the upper track to the Taranaki Falls and continues ahead on the Waihohonu Track. At Tama Saddle (2 hours) turn left to reach the elevation overlooking the Lower Tama Lake after a few minutes. The upper lake (nestling below the slopes of Ngauruhoe) is reached by an exposed scoria ridge. There are good views back to Ruapehu over the Lower Tama Lake.

Mangawhero Forest

Length: Various
Time taken: Up to 1½ hours
Grading: Easy; Rimu Walk suitable for wheelchairs and pushchairs
Apparel: Jerseys and parka always advisable
Code: Year-round

Points of note: Podocarp forest (giant rimu, kahikatea) with a kahami understorey.

Access: Off Ohakune Mountain Road opposite the Ohakune ranger station, 2 kilometres from Ohakune township. Good carpark.

The well-graded and surfaced track crosses the Mangawhero River, and passes old volcanic craters before climbing a short hill. A limestone cliff where fossilised shells are exposed is found before the Mangawhero picnic area is reached. After crossing the river and road, the bush is re-entered. Old railway sleepers, relics of timber milling in the 1940s and 1950s, lie close to the track. A large variety of ferns line the return to the ranger station.

The Rimu Walk is a short loop, with identification labels, near the beginning of the longer track.

Lake Rotokura

Length: 3.5 kilometres
Time taken: 1½–2 hours
Grading: Easy
Apparel: Jersey and parka, especially in winter

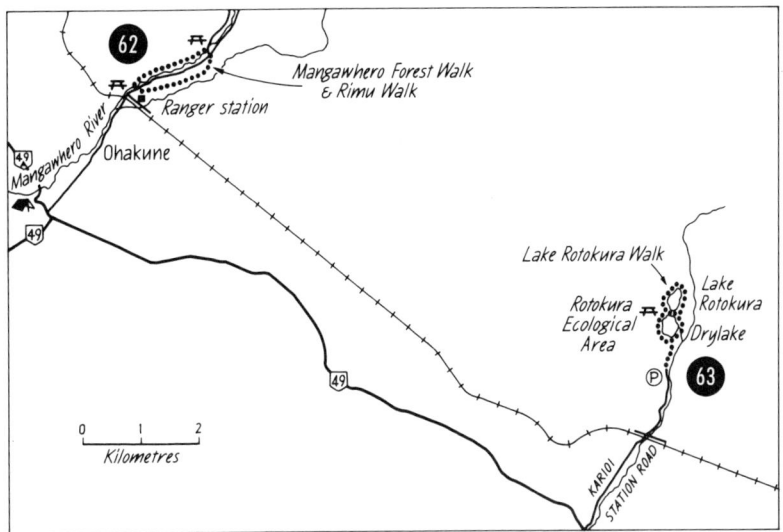

Code: Year-round, swimming, fishing

Points of note: A man-made and a natural lake. Giant red beech trees plus equally large podocarps and a rich understorey cover. Waterfowl, especially on Drylake. Abundant bird life.

Access: Off State Highway 49, 11 kilometres east of Ohakune, 17 kilometres west of Waiouru. Turn north on Karioi Station Road, cross the railway line and continue to a good carpark.

After a short climb Drylake and the picnic spot is reached. Quietness here will be rewarded with good sightings of waterfowl. The track to the west of the lake is uneven and should be walked first or ignored. The track to the east has a good surface and leads to Rotokura, which can be walked around in either direction. Good views of Girdlestone on Ruapehu when the weather is right. Bird sightings could include kaka, parakeets, kingfishers, dabchicks and Australian coots.

WANGANUI

Rerekapa Falls

Length: 6 kilometres
Time taken: 2–3 hours
Grading: Average
Apparel: Good footwear, parka
Code: Year-round, trees, plants, birds, waterfall

Points of note: The walk through bush, mainly along an old bridle path, leads to falls in a beautiful setting near a former farm homestead. Although previously logged, the bush is a magnificent stand of regenerating podocarp forest, with rimu, kahikatea and other species.

Access: It is a 2-hour drive from New Plymouth to the start of the track. Take State Highway 3 east past Mt Messenger to Ahititi then turn right to State Highway 40 through Okau and continue on 5 kilometres to the Kiwi Road turn-off to the right. Just over a small bridge turn left and park inside the gateway.

The track rises gently from left to right on the other side of a small swampy area. Until Rerekapa Hut – about 2 hours' walk – the track is in forest all the

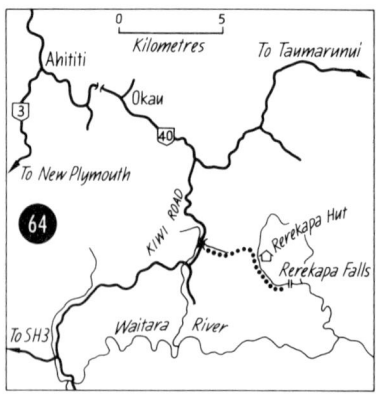

way and easy going. Here are honey fern, hinau, kamahi, kowhai, tree-ferns, rewarewa and kaikawaka.

The kokako has been seen in this area recently, moreporks abound in the forest behind Rerekapa Hut, the long-tailed cuckoo can be heard frequently and there are fantails and warblers.

A walk of 45 minutes from the hut leads to the Rerekapa Falls, the track following the Waitara River in more open country. The falls are not very high but are in a beautiful setting, falling into a deep circular pool. On the steep, bush-clad hillside opposite is a very large rimu.

Pukearuhe

Length: Various
Time taken: Up to 5 hours
Grading: Average
Apparel: Good footwear with non-slip soles
Code: Year-round (closed July–September), trees, birds, beaches, views

Points of note: The track is part of the National Walkway – the Whitecliffs section – and for a considerable distance follows the route of the Kapuni pipeline, which opened a way through dramatic forest and coastal scenery. Using the beach as a return route (safe only at low water), the track may be taken at different lengths. Exposed slopes along the route carry mainly tawa-rewarewa forest, with hard beech further inland and nikau palms, karaka and puriri in more sheltered areas.
Note: The walkway is closed because of lambing from July to September, inclusive.

Access: Turn off State Highway 3 down Pukearuhe Road (36 kilometres north of central New Plymouth and just past Urenui township) and drive 11 kilometres to the end of the road and the Pukearuhe Historic Reserve. Park near the bridge.

The track begins on the other side of the bridge, a signpost pointing the way through a gate and a stile. Follow it across farmland (privately owned) on a well-formed road, with stiles over fences, gradually rising through a cutting and along a ridge before descending steeply to the Waipingau Stream (1½ hours). The track continues but you can follow the stream down to the beach to return that way (tide permitting) to the starting point.

Beyond the stream (turn right and cross a footbridge) the track zigzags up another ridge (keep left where the track seemingly divides) for good coastal and rural views, before descending to the Waikorora Stream. Walkers

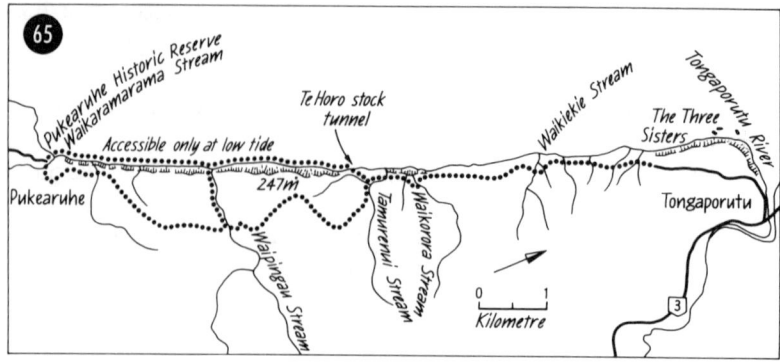

can return from here along the beach (tide permitting), by cutting back via a track rising to the Te Horo stock tunnel giving access to the beach. This is 2 hours' walk from the Waipingau Stream, and the walk back along the beach to Pukearuhe, which should be completed within 2 hours of low water, takes 1½ hours. The coastal walk continues, for those who wish to carry on, over farmland to a recreation reserve on the Tongaporutu River.

Onaero River

Length: 1 kilometre
Time taken: 45 minutes
Grading: Easy
Apparel: Casual; good footwear
Code: Year-round, trees, birds, swimming, views, history

Points of note: The Onaero River Reserve was one of the first set aside when legislation authorised the establishment of scenic reserves in 1903. Like the adjoining Onaero Domain and Pukemiro and Kaipikari Scenic Reserves, it is a steep, bush-clad area, with historic pa sites, and fronts on to a sandy beach. It is a popular picnic and camping area.

Access: The area is reached on State Highway 3, 29 kilometres from New Plymouth on the route to Te Kuiti and 3 kilometres short of Urenui. There is a parking space in the domain to the left.

Proceed toward the beach from the domain. Two stiles lead across a fence on the left into dense bush, with a track to the summit of the hill, and the sites of

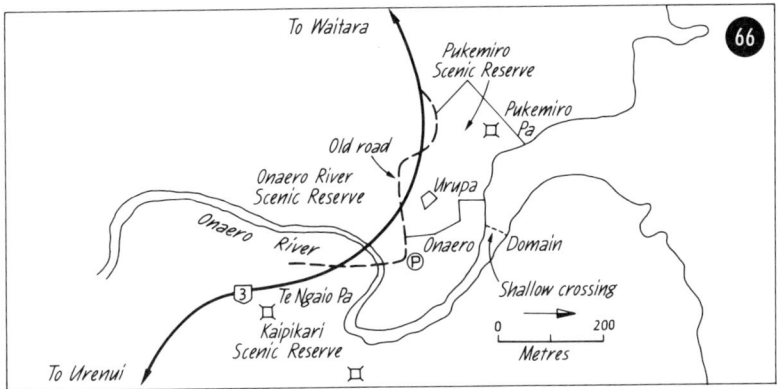

two pa and an old burial ground, all of which remain in Maori ownership. The larger pa, Pukemiro, was built and occupied by Ngati Matunga, a subtribe of the great Atiawa. The trenches and ramparts are still well preserved. Forward trenches facing the sea are remarkable for their depth and width.

On the western side of the river a steep bank is covered with bush, mainly kowhai and puriri, species also surround the pa sites, along with karaka (some of them very large on the summit), matipo, hangehange, kawakawa, kohekohe and rewarewa. A tree of interest is the whau, which is like cork when dry and was used by the Maori for their fishing floats.

Other parts of the domain and reserve can be reached from the sweeps of the old road. Some of these areas are being replanted. Tui, bellbirds, pigeons and fantails can be seen and heard in the bush. There is safe swimming for small children in the river (which also produces whitebait), and a sandy beach offers ocean swimming.

Te Henui

Length: Various
Time taken: Up to 3 hours
Grading: Easy
Apparel: Casual
Code: Year-round, trees, plants, birds

Points of note: This New Plymouth city walk up a bush-lined stream is part of the

National Walkway and is in three parts:

1. From the mouth of Te Henui Stream, East End Reserve, to Cumberland Street (75 minutes);

2. From Cumberland Street to either Welbourn Terrace or Durham Street (25 minutes);

3. From Oriental Street returning on the opposite side of the river to the starting point (80 minutes).

Access: East End Reserve, where the start of the walk is signposted and which offers ample parking space, can be reached from Devon Street either via Hobson Street and Buller Street, or via Nobs Line, with a turn left at the beach.

The walk crosses the river over a footbridge between bowling and croquet lawns and passes under Devon Street, except in times of flood, into Ebrington Place. The walkway user may like to wander a short distance up Lower Courtenay Street to visit the old stone vicarage – now the home and sales centre of the local potters' society. It continues through Waiwaka Reserve, with plantings of natives and exotics, including an extensive collection of magnolias and camellias, that flower in elegant succession from winter through to early spring.

Directly over the next footbridge, the walkway comes to Pukewarangi Reserve, named for the pa on the hilltop. Along this next stretch, which is grazed by sheep, there are popular swimming spots where karaka, titoki and kohekohe hang out over the river, and kiekie scrambles up the banks. As you approach Cumberland Street, through a fine stand of tawa, there are many native ferns and plants of interest, such as epiphytic lycopodiums, a large specimen of which hangs from kamahi on the streambank, and the keen botanist will find several varieties of orchid – *Dendrobium cunninghamii, Earina autumnalis, Gastrodia cunninghamii, Pterostylis banksii* and *Corybas*

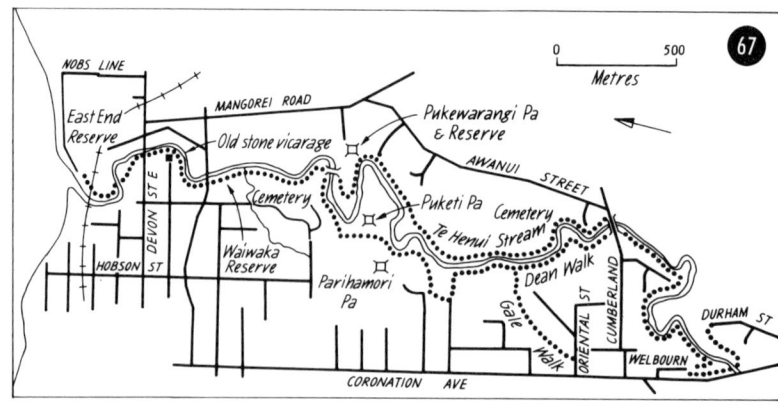

species. There are vines such as bush lawyer, clematis, parsonsia and supple-jack, and a large kahikatea by the Cumberland Street bridge.

One can return on the other side of the river down the Dean Walk or proceed further upstream also on the western bank, which is signposted. Opposite a swimming pool a short distance upstream is a fine hinau, and on one side of the walk is a bank planted with South African proteas. The track turns right into bush, with kohekohe, lancewood and tawa dominant; then into a steep incline, to the right to Welbourn Terrace. The walk to Durham Street is longer and leads up the river to a fine stand of mamaku, several notable puriri (complete with moth holes), tawa, kohekohe and titoki.

The return walk proper starts from a sign in Oriental Street, the Gale Walk leading down the valley to the Te Henui Stream, passing through Avery Reserve between the sites of two pa: Puketi and Parihamori. The latter was once besieged by a distinguished chief, Potaka, for the prize of Urukinaki, a beautiful girl whom he won for his wife.

The bush-lined banks of the Te Henui provide a home for many native birds – fantails, silvereyes, grey warblers, pigeons, tui, bellbirds, kingfishers, black and pied shags, and a few black fantails and an occasional kaka, probably a visitor from Egmont National Park. The number of native pigeons seems to be increasing with the extensive tree planting by the city's park division and residents whose properties fringe the valley.

Huatoki Stream

Length: 5 kilometres
Time taken: 1½ hours
Grading: Easy
Apparel: Casual
Code: Year-round, trees, birds

Points of note: This walkway follows the Huatoki Stream from Sir Victor Davies Park to the outskirts of New Plymouth city. The Huatoki Domain offers further short walks.

Access: The walk starts at the entrance to the park, in Powderham Street, near the 2ZP building.

Follow the stream to the Vivian Street overbridge. Cross the road and pass under the bridge to follow the stream again. A new alignment of the walkway

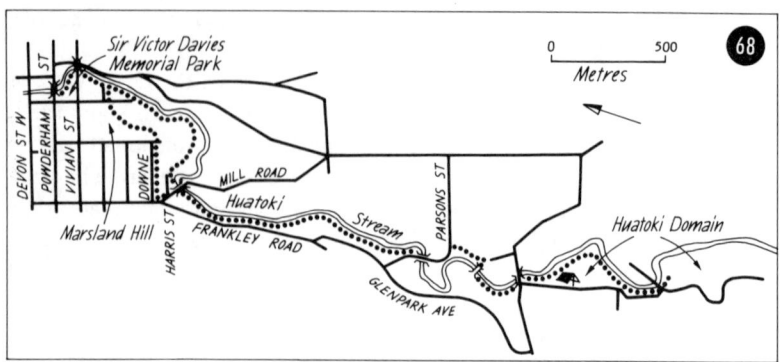

commences at the Red Coat Lane Bridge (signposted). Turn left where the track emerges on a road and follow the road to a sign indicating a continuation of the track alongside the stream to Harris Street and into Mill Road.

As an alternative in wet weather, when the new track can be slippery, take a short uphill walk to the top of Marsland Hill, which was the site of the army barracks set up to protect New Plymouth from Maori attack last century.

From the top of Marsland Hill, with the observatory to the left, descend to and turn left into Downe Street, which turns right at the entrance to the prison. Take the left-hand turn into Mill Road and proceed to the bridge, which could be an alternative starting point.

Walk upstream on the true left bank. The track passes under the Parsons Street Bridge and then turns sharply right up onto the road. Cross the bridge and follow the road to a large macrocarpa tree, where the track recommences.

Take the downhill route to the bank of the stream and along to a footbridge. Cross this and follow the track on the other side of the stream. On emerging at the next road, cross diagonally to the left but do not cross the bridge.

Enter the Huatoki Domain and camping ground. After crossing a fence and the main entrance road, enter the playing area and proceed a short distance uphill to the right and find the track again on the left. The track emerges at the entrance in Huatoki Street to the upper part of the domain. The Bendell and Therkelson Walks here are well signposted and both can be walked in 30 minutes.

69

Barrett Domain

Length: 2 kilometres
Time taken: 1 hour
Grading: Average
Apparel: Good footwear
Code: Year-round, lake, swampland, birds, trees

Points of note: Barrett Domain and Lagoon, part of which is a wildlife refuge, are named after Dicky Barrett, an early settler and whaler, whose Maori wife, Rawinia, lived beside the lagoon after his death. The major forest remnant is modified semi-coastal forest, with the canopy dominated by kohekohe, tawa and pukatea, with some rewarewa, karaka, puriri and manuka, and an understorey containing kohekohe, hangehange, silver fern, kawakawa, pukatea and wheki.

Access: Follow Tukapa Street, New Plymouth, to just past Francis Douglas College, turn right into Wallath Road and the main access, Roto Street, where there is room to park.

On the walk in to the lagoon, a number of kauri can be seen on the right, a legacy of F. J. Cowling, who planted the 2-hectare block. These, together with another group, the Mary Reilly Grove, make up one of the largest plantations

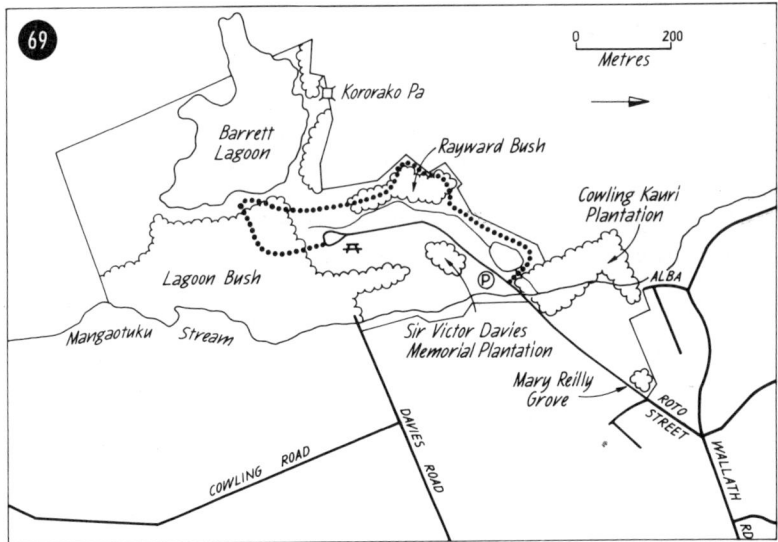

outside the species' natural distribution range.

On crossing the Mangaotuku Stream, next to a picnic table is a map describing three walks. Straight ahead, kowhai and other native trees have been planted on a hillside to the left as a memorial to Sir Victor Davies. On crossing a stile, it is only a short distance to the lagoon, where there are many waterfowl, including a large population of Canada geese. Tainui trees are planted by the lagoon (legend has it that the tree was originally brought to New Zealand by the *Tainui* canoe).

On your return, if you take the track to the right over a stile next to a gate and walk through the signposted Rayward Bush area, passing through hinau, kamahi, puriri, tawa, karaka and titoki, this track leads to the pond near the picnic table mentioned earlier. From here, a walk can be taken through the kauri plantation and past the Riding for the Disabled area back to the entrance.

Pukeiti Rhododendron Trust

Length: Various
Time taken: Up to 1½ hours
Grading: Easy
Apparel: Good footwear
Code: Year-round, trees, flowers, views

Points of note: The Pukeiti Rhododendron Trust was formed in 1951 to promote interest in this species, using them to beautify the whole area, and to preserve and add to the native flora. Two long walks and several short walks, all well signposted, lead through the reserve. A gatehouse at the main entrance provides information and maps, souvenir and plant sales, and refreshment at the restaurant.

Access: Proceed 20 kilometres up Carrington Road, west from New Plymouth.

The Loop Walk, plus a diversion to Pukeiti Hill, provides a great variety of vegetation from low montane to alpine. The path is flanked at first with borders of New Zealand native plants, but once Post 17 is passed, the species change to rhododendrons and azaleas, seen at their best in early October.

Once the grassed walk ends, the route descends to the junction with the Richardson Walk. Two native plants can be seen on this section above the path on the right – *Cordyline banksii*, the forest cabbage tree, and the barrier pine, *Dacrydium kirkii*.

At Post 19 the Richardson Walk swings away and the Loop Walk continues straight ahead. Crown fern is abundant along the margins. The track then crosses the boundary of the Egmont National Park, with tall rewarewa on the skyline, rata and tawa and, further on, hinau trees clothed in epiphytes.

From the park boundary the route descends rapidly to the bridge at Puketewhiti Stream, which is typical of the Egmont system of mountain streams. The banks are clothed with mosses, ferns and liverworts, and other shade- and moisture-loving plants. Along Loop Track a 45-minute diversion to the summit of Pukeiti gives extensive views of the coastline.

The Richardson Walk (1½ hours) proceeds along the native border, through the major plantings of evergreen azaleas and then into native bush, across three bridges and through the native aboretum, where many natives not endemic to the area have been planted. The track then offers a brief detour along the Maxwell Walk to the Kauri Entrance and return, and then leads to the Carrington Road entrance, with a stroll back along the road to the gatehouse.

Kiwi still roam at night in Pukeiti, and there are pigeons, fantails, tomtits, moreporks and grey warblers.

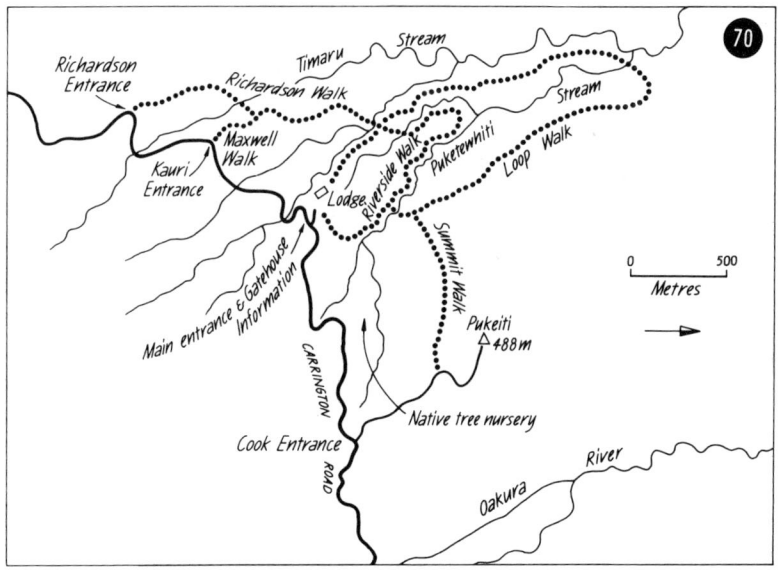

Wilkies Pools

Length: Various
Time taken: Up to 2 hours
Grading: Moderate
Apparel: Casual
Code: Year-round, trees, plants, flowers, views

Points of note: The Wilkies Pools walk in the Dawson Falls area of Egmont National Park is interesting botanically and geologically, and suited to the casual visitor or the not-so-fit.

Access: The Dawson Falls area on the southern slopes of Mt Egmont is reached by a 30-minute drive via the Upper Manaia Road from State Highway 45. From the park entrance a drive of 5 kilometres on a sealed road through the canopy forest and an avenue of roadside shrubs brings you to the parking area and public facilities.

Several walks radiate from the Dawson Falls display centre. Each is colour-coded and well signposted along its route. At the entrance to most walks large map boards give details of the code and time taken. For maximum appreciation of each walk, browse first through the display centre's information panels and exhibits of the geology, vegetation and history of Egmont.

The Wilkies Pools walk starts through young forest in which the vegetation is small, including manuka shown by annular ring dating to be about ninety years old. Soon, however, the track enters older forest with dominant kamahi, Hall's totara and mountain fuchsia festooned with lichens and mosses, and an understorey of coprosma, five-finger, leatherwood,

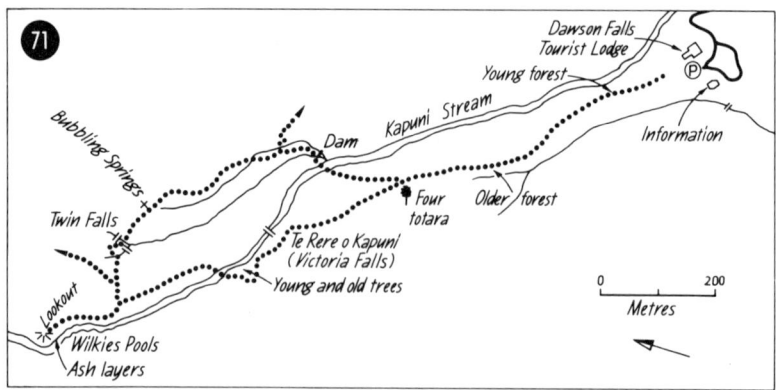

118

horopito and mahoe. Astelias and mosses are thick on the sides of the track. In summer, ourisias, pratia and New Zealand eyebright flourish, with ground orchids in November and December.

At the Kapuni Stream and lookout there is a good view of the regeneration on the older courses of the stream, with daisies, raoulia, willowherb and mountain tutu. Mosses and lichens are seedbeds for other larger plants, which in turn become a nursery and coloniser for larger trees.

Another few minutes' walk brings you to the junction to Wilkies Pools, named after farming brothers who were climbers and explorers in the region. Deeply cut channels through the lava flows show the cutting and abrasive effect of water-borne rocks and shingle. The lava rock – the older flows date to about 21,000 years ago – supports harebell, daisies and cottonwoods. Ash layer profiles on the cliff faces represent various eruptions of Egmont and, latterly, of Fanthams Peak.

A few minutes' walk on is the junction of the Round-the-Mountain Track to the Stratford Plateau. Past a thick bankside growth of ourisia and tutu, bubbling springs flow out of volcanic rock. The track leads on past the dam that feeds the power generator for the Dawson Falls Tourist Lodge and, at four totara, joins the main track back to the display centre.

There are many other walks on Mt Egmont. Brochures and details are available at information centres.

Maraekowhai

Length: 1 kilometre
Time taken: 15 minutes
Grading: Easy
Apparel: Casual; good footwear
Code: Year-round, plants, historical sites, birds, waterfalls

Points of note: A track winds through native forest to a swingbridge over the Ohura River near its confluence with the Whanganui River. Features include waterfalls and ancient niu poles. Ideal for a short visit, Maraekowhai is a good place to immerse yourself in the area's unique history and beauty. Camping is permitted.

Access: To reach Maraekowhai by car, turn off the main Taumarunui–Ohura Road 35 kilometres south of Taumarunui onto Tokirima Road and follow this 18 kilometres to its end, where the short walk begins. Maraekowhai can also be reached by travellers on the Whanganui River.

The track leads into native forest and then crosses to Maraekowhai via a swingbridge. This makes a good vantage point to view the three individual waterfalls, all within a few hundred metres as the Ohura River drops towards the Whanganui River. These were important fishing places for the Maori, who travelled great distances to catch the small eels that may still be seen making their way up the falls during summer.

The historic nature of the whole reserve area can be sensed from the two ceremonial niu poles. The oldest, the War Pole or Rongo Niu, which was erected in 1864 when Maraekowhai was a stronghold for rebellious Hauhau warriors, has two cross arms pointing to the four points of the compass. It is said that a spirit in the pole radiated out through the arms to warriors everywhere calling upon them to fight the Europeans. The Hauhau, followers of the Pai Marire religion, a combination of Old Testament and ancient Maori beliefs, used to dress the pole with flags and parade around it chanting prayers and incantations.

The second pole, known as the Peace Pole or Rere Kore, was built when the Hauhau fighting ceased on the Whanganui River, 'to counter the influence of the War Pole'. The Pai Marire religion continued peacefully on the upper Whanganui for some years after the wars ended in the 1860s.

A flour mill, constructed with the help of missionaries, once stood on this site, and was one of many built on the Whanganui River in the 1860s to process the wheat then grown by local Maori. Perhaps because of the land mass, this mill was never used. (Some say it was wrecked by the Hauhau.) By 1872, missionary Richard Taylor recorded that the mill was in ruins. Its wheel was to have been supplied with water from the second fall and carried along a flume and channel cut in the papa rock face to the mill, which was sited below the Peace Pole and below the first fall on the river bank. Nothing remains of the mill today.

From 1904 to 1927, Hatrick and Co. ran a popular three-day Whanganui River paddle-steamer trip, which became as famous as the Milford Track. The houseboat *Makere*, moored at Maraekowhai, allowed for boat changes to shallower-draught canoes to explore higher up the river. Overnight stopping with excellent food made *Makere* a mecca and, because of the number of tourists making the round trip to include Tongariro and Rotorua, a swingbridge was built to allow road access to it.

The bush is typical of the upper Whanganui reaches – ferns and mosses abound, and the bird life on a summer's day is very lively. Many different varieties of native orchids and flowers can be seen over the spring and summer.

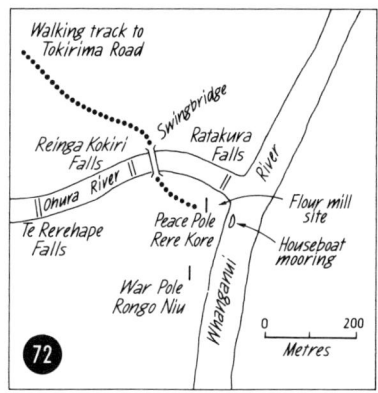

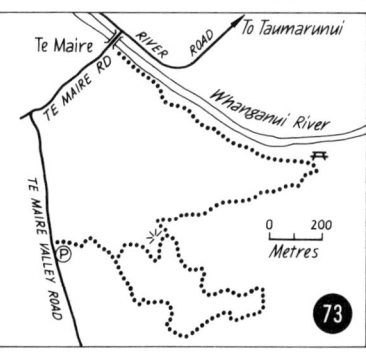

73

Te Maire

Length: Various
Time taken: Up to 2 hours
Grading: Easy to moderate
Apparel: Casual; good footwear
Code: Year-round, trees, birds, view, swimming

Points of note: Te Maire is part of the Whanganui National Park and a fine remnant of the forest that once covered much of the King Country.

Access: Te Maire is 15 kilometres south-west of Taumarunui on the Whanganui River Road. A bridge crosses to the south bank of the river opposite Te Maire Bluff. An entrance here gives foot access to the river flats, where there are picnic and barbecue facilities and good swimming. The main entrance is 3 kilometres up Te Maire Valley Road, which turns off here.

A loop track begins at the main entrance and leads through mixed broadleaf-podocarp forest to a lookout at the top. Hinau and tawa are the most common broadleaf species, with large totara, rimu, kahikatea and matai the predominant podocarps. The forest is extremely dense, with masses of epiphytes growing on the trees. The northern slopes tend to be drier, with kowhai and titoki.

Between October and March, many varieties of native orchids can be seen flowering. White rata flower over January, along with fine examples of native gloxinia, supplejack and clematis. Many different varieties of ferns (some not found anywhere else) are also a most attractive feature of this walk.

Look too for the distinctive blistered leaves of ramarama. It is found in other areas, but Te Maire has some fine examples.

Tui, bellbirds and pigeons are found in large numbers, particularly when the kowhai are in flower. The North Island robin is also present.

From the lookout, a track heads steeply down (15 minutes) to a picnic area by the river. It is another 15 minutes along the river from here to the bridge. The loop track starting and ending at the main entrance takes about 2 hours.

74

Sutherlands Reserve

Length: Various
Time taken: Up to 4 hours
Grading: Easy
Apparel: Casual; good footwear in winter
Code: Year-round, trees, birds

Points of note: Bequeathed by Archie Sutherland in 1967, this reserve contains a total of 71 hectares of podocarp forest in two separate stands. The larger portion lies between the Turakina Valley Road and the Turakina River.

Access: From State Highway 3 at Turakina, the reserve lies 26 kilometres up the Turakina Valley Road at its junction with Mangahoe Road. The smaller reserve, on Mangahoe Road, lies 5 kilometres past the larger stand. Access is also available from Hunterville via Ongo Road to Mangahoe Road, a distance of 13 kilometres.

There are three walks in this Forest and Bird Society reserve. Two of them are in the main area of bush, where the original track (now called the Reynolds Track) starts about 1 kilometre from the entrance. Roughly circular and marked with yellow discs, it takes about 1½ hours to walk. Of the two others in the main area, the one with blue markers takes 2½–3 hours, and the one marked with orange up to 4 hours. This is predominantly used for eradication of old man's beard and passes through long fescue grass above the river. There is a sign inside the reserve at the junction of the yellow and blue tracks showing the layout of the walks.

The larger trees are mainly kahikatea, totara, rimu and tawa, with some big rewarewa. A row of Maori sleeping pits, of pre-European origin, lies just short of the start of the yellow track. From the same track a small area of regenerating tawa is visible.

Access to the smaller bush from Mangahoe Road is across a bridge at a signposted point. The track in this reserve is also marked with circular yellow discs and is roughly circular.

A somewhat unusual feature of both reserves is the large number of sulphur-crested cockatoos that inhabit the area. Native bird life is not prolific.

Marton 1990 Walkway

Length: 2 kilometres
Time taken: 30 minutes
Grading: Easy, suitable for wheelchairs
Apparel: Casual
Code: Year-round, trees, stream

Points of note: The walk and native plantings were developed as part of the 1990 celebrations. At either end of the walk, impressive carved Maori gateways, called Tomokanga, mark the entrance ways.

Access: The track starts by a carpark in Cobber Kain Avenue, which turns off Wellington Road in Marton, and ends on Hereford Street.

From Cobber Kain Avenue, the track passes through a 1-hectare area of native plantings before winding along the bank of the Tutaenui Stream and through exotic trees toward Hereford Street. There is another area of well-established native trees by the northern entrance.

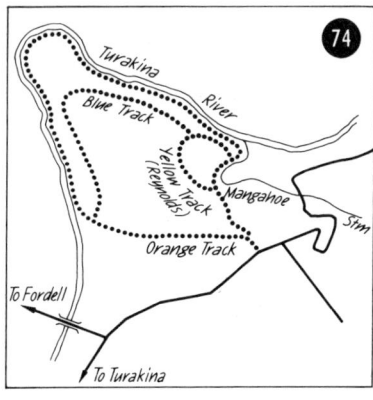

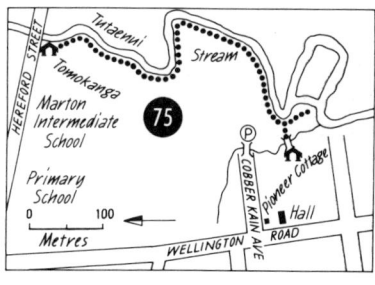

Mt Lees Reserve

Length: 1.5 kilometres
Time taken: 1 hour
Grading: Easy
Apparel: Casual
Code: Closed whenever conditions are unfavourable, trees, birds, plants

Points of note: The area traversed by this nature walk is one of the last remnants of native bush in the Sanson district. While much of it is now regenerated growth, many of the original trees still stand, and these are enhanced by selective plantings of exotics and shrubs. Spring and autumn are the most colourful times to visit.

Access: Turn right from State Highway 3 up Halcombe Road, just short of Sanson, coming from Palmerston North. The turn-off is clearly marked by the Mt Stewart memorial. Follow the signposts thereafter.

After passing through a field where daffodils bloom in August, commence the walk at the gate of the homestead, with its one old yew tree. An even pathway leads through labelled matai and totara trees among banks of exotics interspersed with *Pittosporum tenuifolium*, red matipo and large-leafed rangiora. The New Zealand rock lily (rengarenga), which flowers in early summer, grows along the banks. Opposite, the unique growth of a puka tree should be noticed. Behind an open glade with three lancewood trees showing different formations of leaf growth is a lofty kahikatea said to be 600–1,000 years old.

Among the many varieties of trees easily seen without strenuous climbing are a *Ginkgo biloba*, fronted by a native tree daisy (*Senecio greyii*), a dawn redwood (*Metasequoia glyptostroboides*), varieties of magnolias (spring-flowering) and colourful maples (autumn foliage). A rubber tree grows in the midst of a fern glade shaded by large native trees. The banks on the return path carry korokia cultivars, olearias and golden tainui. Of special note is a pukatea tree that could be 200 years old. Its trunk is hollow but it has huge buttress roots and gnarled heavy branches. Agapanthus borders a path to a lookout point.

There are native pigeons, tui, bellbirds and grey warblers in this 33-hectare reserve, which was created as a result of a gift to the Crown by Ormond Wilson and is controlled by the Manawatu District Council. For arrangements for group visits, phone 733 Sanson.

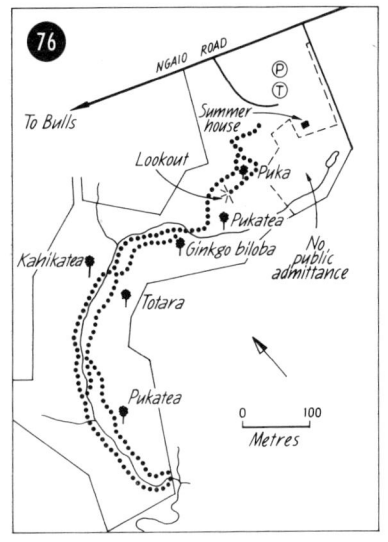

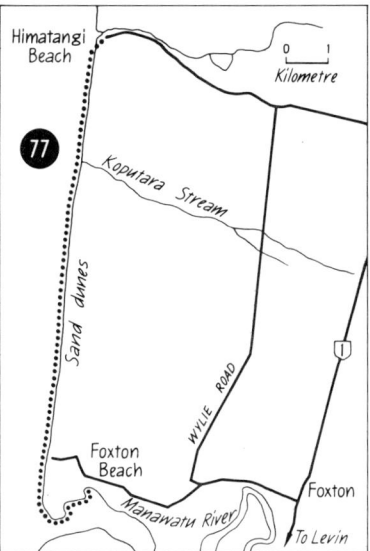

Foxton and Himatangi Beaches

Length: 8 kilometres
Time taken: 3 hours
Grading: Easy to moderate
Apparel: Casual
Code: Year-round, plants, birds, crustacea

Points of note: This is a beach walk from a large estuary at the mouth of the Manawatu River at Foxton Beach settlement. The town of Foxton, 1.6 kilometres from the beach, is the oldest in the Manawatu. From its beginning as a small port at the mouth of the river, it became the hub of the district as the main outlet for large quantities of timber and flax. Later the railway bypassed the town and the river proved too shallow for larger vessels.

Access: Travel 30 kilometres down Highway 1 from Palmerston North to Foxton and turn right to the beach. Proceed to the camping area beside the estuary, where the walk starts in front of the yacht club building.

The estuary is the habitat of many wading and seabirds including royal spoonbills, oyster-catchers, Far Eastern curlews, sandpipers, wrybills, banded dotterels, godwits and knots, white-faced herons, pied stilts, black shags, terns and gulls. It also houses a variety of molluscs and crustacea, thousands of mud snails, pipi, cockles and mussels. The salt flats have glasswort and spartina grass where subject to immersion.

The walk north to Himatangi Beach normally takes 3 hours but can easily, because of its interest, be extended. It is safe and easy except when there is a gale or rough seas, and is most pleasant on the firm sand from half to low tide. Back from the beach and its small marine inhabitants, the seaward sand dunes yield a variety of plants that have adapted to the harsh environment. Pingao, which trails over the sand dunes in horizontal runners, was used by the Maori for weaving the yellow sections of the tukutuku panels decorating the interior of meeting houses.

WELLINGTON

Mangaone Track

Length: 5 kilometres
Time taken: 1½ hours
Grading: Moderate
Apparel: Footwear suitable for river crossings, parka and jersey
Code: Year-round (river crossings may be difficult if water level high), trees, ferns, birds

Points of note: This bush walk, which is part of the national walkways system, is best walked from the southern end to the halfway point on the track and return. This saves arranging for transport at the other end and misses out less interesting open country.

Access: Turn east off State Highway 1 at the traffic lights in the middle of Waikanae. Cross the railway line and follow the road to Upper Hutt for 3 kilometres as far as Reikorangi, where you turn left along Ngatiawa Road for approximately 1 kilometre. Then turn left, 2 kilometres up Mangaone South Road to the carpark.

From the carpark, the site of an old sawmill that worked from 1900 to 1930, the track leads across a stile into a large area of fine native bush crossed by the Kapakapanui and Waterfall Streams. The route leads down to and up beyond a shallow river-crossing into a profusion of kiokio ferns hanging from the right bank of the river, and then left at the walkway sign into a beautiful track, which almost tunnels through a dense forest of wheki tree-ferns, leading into the Kaitawa Scenic Reserve. Here are many other ferns – climbing, perching and ground-based – including large numbers of filmy ferns on the wheki stems.

Over another stile is a crossing (below knee-deep in normal conditions) of the Waikanae River – the unstable, algae-covered boulder dam invites a ducking or a sprained ankle. The track now generally follows the route of the old bush tramway, with a few sleepers still visible.

Soon after the crossing, you reach an open area with tree-ferns all

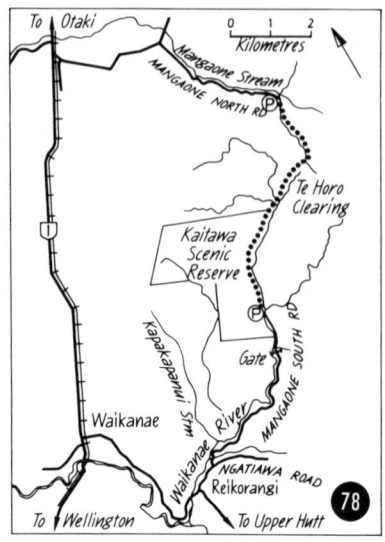

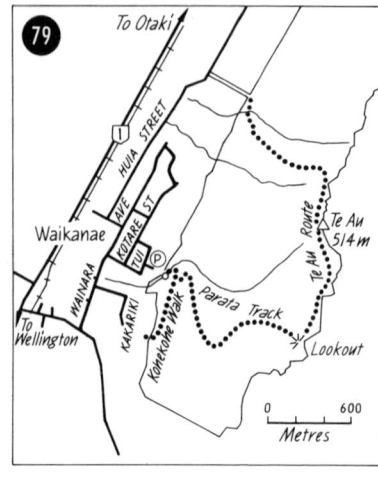

around. A kahikatea in the centre has a lancewood inside it, festooned with *Rubus australis* (a species of bushlawyer). Towards the west you can see heavy regenerating bush with some towering northern rata and rimu. Further on, where the track runs high above the river because the tramway track has broken away, a small clearing gives good views of a similar eastern skyline.

From here on the nature of the bush changes to include many horopito and miro, a few young matai and many wheki-ponga tree-ferns, a close relative of the wheki with very thick red-brown trunks.

A locked gate ahead marks the end of the bush area and of the Kaitawa Scenic Reserve. This is the halfway point, at which bush-lovers may choose to turn back. Beyond the stile you are on private farmland and soon meet a road leading over the Mangaone Saddle to the other track entrance, on the Mangaone North Road.

Hemi Matenga Scenic Reserve

Length: 1.5 kilometres
Time taken: 1 hour return
Grading: Average

Apparel: Casual but warm; good footwear when wet

Code: Year-round, trees, plants, flowers, birds, views

Points of note: The reserve is an area of mixed bush providing a rewarding walk, which should not be undertaken in very strong winds, when pieces of the old forest tend to fall.

Access: Hemi Matenga is 1.5 kilometres from the Waikanae Railway Station. Cross the railway at the traffic lights and take the third left turn along Elizabeth Street into Wainara Avenue. Then turn into Kereru Street (second right) and, at the top end, turn left into Tui Crescent. Watch for an open pipegate on the right with the sign 'Bushwalk'. The site of a big water-tank is the start of the Kohekohe Walk. There is good parking on grass at the top of the access road. Alternate access can be gained from Kakariki Street.

From the start of the walk you see tall rimu emerging from the bush canopy with its variety of shades of green, the brightest indicating the puka, the epiphytic broadleaf. Some tawa trees are the worse for lack of protection from high winds.

Entering the bush, with its semi-darkness under a high canopy, and the sound of running water, the track follows a stream for a short while. Here is one of the highlights of this nature walk – very tall pukatea trees with conspicuous plank-buttresses, standing in the creekbed. Some show the vertically grooved roots of the puka, with its bright green leathery leaves high in the crown of the host tree. Here also are many tall tawa, with smooth black trunks, and a great many kohekohe, typical of coastal forest.

The view from the bridge shows a good sample of subtropical, high-rainfall coastal forest. The track climbs, at first alongside the creek through supplejack and ferns, and then away from it. A clearing at the highest point offers a good view. Below is an enormous northern rata, and the clear space below the clearing is covered with the delightful native iris, mikoikoi, which displays abundant white flowers in late November and early December. A short distance further on a magnificent rimu stands about 10 metres above the track, and a fine miro, tall and straight like a ship's mast, the same distance below.

Ahead, the only real climbing of the walk, a line of easy steps, zigzags up to a grove of young lancewood 2–3 metres high. The track levels out in an opening with a view and a small grove of wharangi trees, with very light green foliage; every leaf is in three parts. From here a descent leads to a magnificent view over Waikanae and out to Kapiti Island.

It is best to return to the carpark the same way, but for visitors with more time there is the Parata Track (1–2 hours return) and the longer Te Au Route (3–4 hours).

80

Maungakotukutuku

Length: 3 kilometres to summit
Time taken: 4 hours return
Grading: Average
Apparel: Warm clothing (end of track crosses open tops)
Code: Year-round, trees, birds, flowers

Points of note: This hill track climbs to the top of Mt Maunganui through mixed podocarp-hardwood forest with a belt of kamahi on the middle to upper slopes.

Access: From the Paraparaumu traffic lights proceed over the railway lines. Turn right into Hinemoa Street, then left up Ruapehu Street and continue on into Valley Road, passing the golf course to the right. After about 1.5 kilometres, take the first turn left, an unsealed road up into the hills. Proceed through the farm gates across the road and on for another 1.5 kilometres to a picnic area on the right.

The marked track begins over the creek from the picnic area. As you climb, the predominant tree types change. First you encounter kahikatea, emergent rimu, tawa, pukatea, rewarewa, lancewood (canopy), mahoe and ferns; then rimu, rewarewa, kamahi, rata, putaputaweta, pigeonwood, mahoe, rata and ferns; followed by miro, rimu, toro, *Griselinia lucida*, mapou, *Coprosma spathulata*; and finally Hall's totara, coprosma, kamahi, dracophyllum, five-finger, olearia, ferns and mosses.

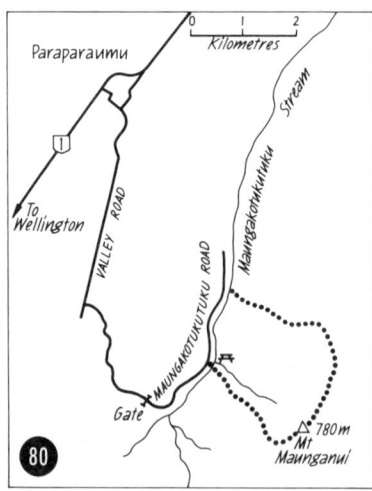

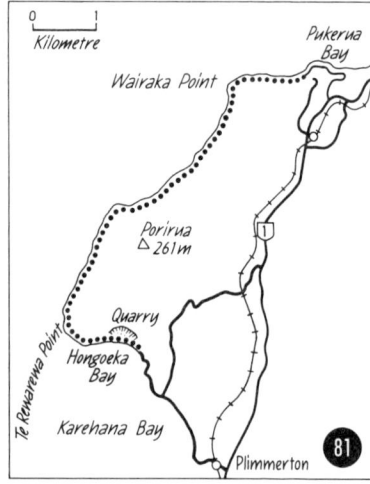

A wide variety of birds inhabits the bush – tui, bellbirds, grey warblers, fantails, silvereyes, North Island tits, whiteheads, riflemen, native pigeons, eastern rosellas, long-tailed cuckoos and native falcons. From the summit the track continues roughly north, then descends to the road about 1 kilometre north of the start.

Pukerua Bay and Plimmerton

Length: 8 kilometres
Time taken: 3–4 hours
Grading: Easy but uneven
Apparel: Warm, windproof clothing
Code: Year-round, birds, coast

Points of note: An exhilarating, rocky and windswept walk along the coast, this excursion is memorable, especially in fine weather, for the wild beauty of the shore and the magnificent views across Cook Strait. There is a great feeling of space and solitude. Although graded easy, the walk is not very suitable for older people, being very rocky, with an uneven track and some scrambling to be done. Although the walk can be made in either direction, it is preferable to travel from north to south, as this will ensure views towards the South Island.

Access: Catch the train to Pukerua Bay. Leave the station and walk for a short distance along a tree-lined road to the main highway. Turn right up the highway, cross at the pedestrian overbridge and go down Beach Road, which leads very steeply down to the beach and a small parking area. A zigzag short cut, on the left about 100 metres along the road, leads down the cliff to the beach.

Turn left along the sealed road between houses and the beach, with a view of Kapiti Island and many rock pools. There is another larger carpark at the end of the sealed road.

Go through a barrier on to a rough track that leads along the foot of a steep, flax-covered hillside beside a wild and rocky beach, with piles of driftwood. Small groves of stunted karaka cling to the hillside, and rough tussock grass and small-leaved pohuehue line the track.

High, rugged rocks (some of which can be climbed) are common along the shore. There are gulls, terns and herons; seals are sometimes seen, swimming and playing. Hawks hunt across the steep faces, and sheep feed precariously and have their lambs on the abrupt slopes. The very rare

Whitaker's skink may be seen between Wairaka Point and Pukerua Bay.

The views include Kapiti and Mana Islands, with the Kaikoura Ranges and snowcapped Mt Tapuaenuku clear across Cook Strait on a fine day.

The latter part of the walk is less attractive because of quarry workings, but the views – toward Paremata, Titahi Bay and the South Island – are still very fine, and a high-pointed rock just offshore, with nesting and diving terns, is well worth stopping for.

At Hongoeka Bay the walk meets the road from Karehana Bay to Plimmerton.

Pauatahanui Wildlife Reserve

Length: Various
Time taken: Various
Grading: Easy, with wheelchair access
Code: Year-round, plants, birds

Points of note: The Pauatahanui Inlet supports the largest concentration of birds to be found in the south of the North Island. The most commonly seen birds are Caspian tern, pied stilt, New Zealand shoveler, paradise shelduck, little and black shags, spur-winged plover, banded dotterel, godwit, pukeko, white-faced heron, kingfisher, welcome swallow, fantail and harrier hawk. Take binoculars for bird-watching.

Access: From Wellington, take State Highway 1 to Paremata and turn right to Pauatahanui. From Upper Hutt, turn off State Highway 2 at Haywards. The entrance to the reserve is behind the Pauatahanui Community Hall, where there is a carpark and information board.

At the entrance to the reserve there are picnic tables, a pond and a plant nursery. Tracks have been boardwalked, giving access to wheelchairs, and there are four hides to facilitate bird-watching. The vegetation of the reserve contains a succession from tidal mudflats to exotic grassland. Wetland species include swamp flax, raupo, reeds, rushes, glasswort, sea primrose, half-star, New Zealand spinach and wild celery. Areas of coastal scrub include marsh ribbonwood, coastal tree daisy, taupata, ngaio, kanuka and manuka. The wetland area has been reduced in the last hundred years by a number of factors: deforestation has caused the inlet to silt up, an earthquake in 1855 raised the level of the land, and the Pauatahanui Stream has been diverted.

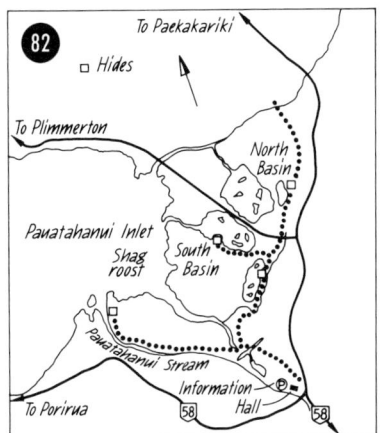

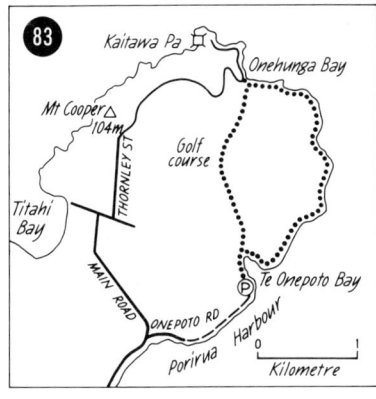

The Forest and Bird Society is working to restore the wetland and has undertaken an extensive replanting programme.

Whitireia Park

Length: 4 kilometres
Time taken: 2–3 hours return
Grading: Easy
Apparel: Casual
Code: Year-round, birds, swimming, picnic areas

Points of note: Offering a quiet recreational walk, with many birds present, Whitireia Park is mostly open grassland, but there is a forest remnant above Onehunga Bay and salt-marsh associations at the head of the bay.

Access: The park is on Te Onepoto Peninsula, north-east of Titahi Bay. There are two points of entrance. From the main entrance at Thornley Street there is vehicle access to Onehunga Bay, which is the focal point for visitors. The walk described here, however, is approached from Te Onepoto, the second access point, on the shore of Porirua Harbour.

From Titahi Bay Road turn right at the rugby club buildings into Onepoto Road and follow the vehicle track (subject to tides) past the boatsheds and along the edge of the Porirua Harbour. This will lead to the estuary at Te

Onepoto Bay, where there is often an interesting variety of birds feeding. White-faced herons are always present, with occasionally both pied and variable oystercatchers, and kingfishers and most of the introduced small species can be seen.

A track from the head of the estuary leads to the interior of the park, reaching, after 15–20 minutes of gradual climbing, the top of a gully overlooking Onehunga Bay. Continue in a northerly direction. A small area of native bush on a hillside to the right is a remnant of the coastal forest that probably covered the peninsula in pre-European times.

Further on, past the radio masts, on the hillside beyond the road, can be seen the Maori kumara terraces of earlier times. On the point below is the site of Kaitawa Pa. It is easy to descend across the pasture to this point and then to the beach below.

The return in the southerly direction leads soon to Onehunga Bay, which is a good place to stop for refreshments or a swim at the excellent beach.

Follow on past several small bays, where a number of coastal birds can be identified, including three species of shags – large black, little black and little shag – often seen drying out after fishing. Gulls are common, both black-backed and red-billed; you may also see white-fronted and Caspian terns, oystercatchers, pied stilts, waterfowl including paradise ducks, herons, and at times a gannet diving for food in the sheltered waters.

On arrival at Te Onepoto estuary, follow the track round the edge of the inlet to the starting point.

Tararua Forest Park

Length: 13 kilometres
Time taken: Full day
Grading: Strenuous
Apparel: Full tramping gear
Code: Fair weather, trees, birds, plants, huts

Points of note: The walk along the Puffer Track to Dobsons Hut, the Tauherenikau River and the return up Smith Creek introduces parts of the route followed by Captain W. M. Smith in 1859 to reach the Wairarapa. The area was also considered as a route for the Wellington–Wairarapa railway line, but was found to be too difficult. This, fortunately, has left us with a very attractive area for a more than usually adventurous tramp, in a forest park close to an urban area.

The walk is classed as strenuous but is not difficult for anyone who regularly undertakes steep hill walking. Boots are essential and wet-weather gear must be carried, as the weather in the Tararua Ranges is capricious. The walk provides a variety of terrain (from high country, up to 650 metres, to grassy river flats) and of flora (a mix of forest types such as beech, podocarp and manuka).

Access: Proceeding north from Upper Hutt, turn left at the Kaitoke Youth Hostel on State Highway 2, immediately after crossing the Pakuratahi River bridge. Three kilometres up the sealed side road is the entrance to the Tararua Forest Park, and the walk commences at the upper carpark.

You should allow a day for this walk, although the total walking time is less than 4 hours, without stops. It is suggested that you start from the Kaitoke carpark at 9–10 a.m. and walk to Dobsons Hut (1½ hours) for morning tea, descending to the confluence of the Tauherenikau River and Smith Creek for lunch (50 minutes). A gentle walk up the Smith Creek catchment back to the carpark (1½ hours) completes the trip.

The track climbs gently, and an occasional look back gives extensive views over the Upper Hutt Valley and the Kaitoke Basin. On a clear day the Inland Kaikouras can be seen with Mt Tapuaenuku, at a distance of 170 kilometres, showing its snow-capped peak for most of the year. After 20 minutes take the branch to the left.

At the firebreak the track narrows and levels off through manuka before ascending gently again through montane forest to Dobsons Hut. This stage of the walk follows the ridge of the watershed between the western (Hutt) and eastern (Wairarapa) catchments flanking the Tararua Range. Ahead, on Marchant Ridge, can be seen tree skeletons from an extensive fire in 1938. Regeneration at this exposed altitude is slow.

From Dobsons the track leaves from the side opposite the hut door and descends for a short distance before rising over a small knob to fall steeply away on the other side. Ten minutes after leaving the hut, the track divides. Take the right branch, signposted to Smith Creek.

Here the understorey is open, with the track descending through predominantly beech forest with an increasing mixture of trees as the Tauherenikau River flat is reached. In some parts down this spur the track is not well defined, but orange discs blaze the trail to the bottom, where tracks cross. Keep straight ahead for 50 metres to a grassy area on the right of the track at the junction of Smith Creek and the Tauherenikau River.

Birds, although well concealed, are plentiful, and can be more easily observed in the open areas near the rivers. Tui, native pigeons, fantails and grey warblers are common, and bellbirds, parakeets, pied tits and white-backed magpies are often seen. Black and white-throated shags and black-backed gulls frequent the river areas, along with grey duck. Traces of pig and deer can occasionally be found, but numbers are decreasing.

The Smith Creek Shelter can be found by retracing the path to the crossed tracks and turning north-east for 80 metres. The return journey is along a well-formed track from the crossed tracks junction in a south-westerly direction. This follows Smith Creek for some distance before veering away to avoid a river crossing.

Pockets of rimu can be seen breaking through the forest canopy in many places, and fern, miro, rewarewa, kahikatea and totara are conspicuous. After 50 minutes, Halfway Creek provides a useful resting place. Cross the stream (there is a litter bin to the left) and the track zigzags up a spur before levelling off to continue to the ridge firebreak above Kaitoke. Continue straight ahead and descend the track to the carpark.

Karapoti

Length: 2 kilometres
Time taken: 1 hour return
Grading: Easy
Apparel: Casual
Code: Year-round, trees, plants, swimming, picnic area

Points of note: Karapoti is part of a large area owned and managed by the Wellington Regional Council. Although nearly all the bush and forest areas have been logged and only small pockets of original bush remain in some valleys, regeneration is taking place. The Karapoti area is suitable for picnics, camping and swimming. Regional Council service roads lead to the hilltops with some fine views of the Akatarawa Ranges and Hutt Valley.

Access: Karapoti can be reached by road from the west side of Akatarawa Road. Turn left off State Highway 2 at Brown Owl and travel for approximately 5 kilometres down Akatarawa Road. Turn left into Karapoti Road (metalled surface), where vehicles can be parked, and cross the Akatarawa River by swingbridge; or, if in a four-wheel-drive vehicle, ford the river and follow the road up a gradual incline to the picnic area.

This is a popular area for picnickers and campers in the summer season, and the walks are within the capabilities of school-age children. In the early 1900s Karapoti was heavily milled for its native timbers, chiefly rimu, matai and a

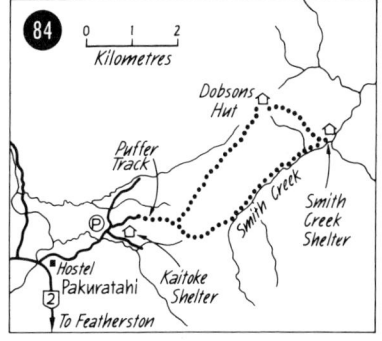

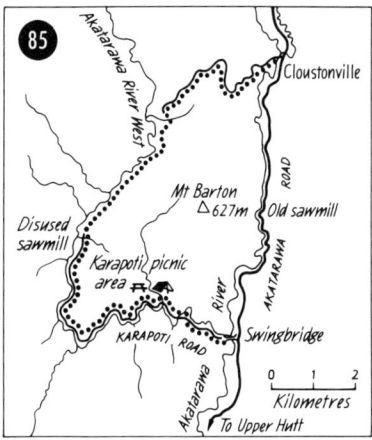

little totara. The community had its own twenty-pupil school. The mill and school closed in the early 1920s and all that remain are some rusty old machinery and concrete foundations.

As you walk through to the picnic area you can still see the odd rimu, but predominant among many other species are kamahi, mingimingi, rangiora, lemonwood, matipo, bracken, tutu, hinau, ponga and coprosma. Bird life is not abundant, but wood pigeons, tui, bellbirds, warblers, fantails and an occasional parakeet may be seen or heard.

A more strenuous, 3–4 hour tramp continues up the Karapoti Gorge. The walk starts by following the road through the gorge, which becomes very narrow. There is some fine bush here, with ferns, regenerating beech, rewarewa and an occasional pukatea. After about an hour's walk the valley opens up to areas of pine forest and of toetoe. About 30 minutes through here is a lovely grassy area (a former mill site), which makes an ideal spot to have lunch by the river. There are some good swimming holes, but the water seldom warms up very much.

A fairly steep climb passes through mixed forest to the top of the ridge, where there are good views of the main Tararua Range. From this point a road drops steeply through cut-over bush and pine forest to the Cloustonville area, where there used to be a mill settlement, and on to the Akatarawa Road. It is about 8 kilometres back down the road to the start of the walk, and it is a good idea to have a car at either end of the walk.

137

86

Rimutaka Incline

Length: 16 kilometres
Time taken: 4½–5 hours; Cross Creek to summit and back 3 hours
Grading: Strenuous
Apparel: Full tramping gear; torch for tunnels
Code: Year-round, history

Points of note: This historic walk follows the route of one of the world's few rack railways, which was the lifeline of the early Wairarapa. Regenerating bush, large rata and bush birds can be seen.

Access: From the Kaitoke (west) end, on State Highway 2, look for the AA sign: 'Gliding Club; Upper Valley', 'Motocross Park' and 'Go-kart Raceway'. The metalled road that turns off at this point is the start of the walk. From the Featherston (east) end, access is by way of a short road signposted 'State Forest Park', leading up Cross Creek towards the hills from Western Lake Road, about 9 kilometres south of Featherston.

The track runs at an easy grade (1 in 14) past the sites of old railway stations and through tunnels, including Siberia Tunnel in a wild, windswept area, and Summit Tunnel, the longest, extending for 576 metres. There is little bush on the Wairarapa side of the track but much secondary growth on the Kaitoke side, where several very large rata trees make a great showing when they flower in December. All the small bush birds abound, including fantails,

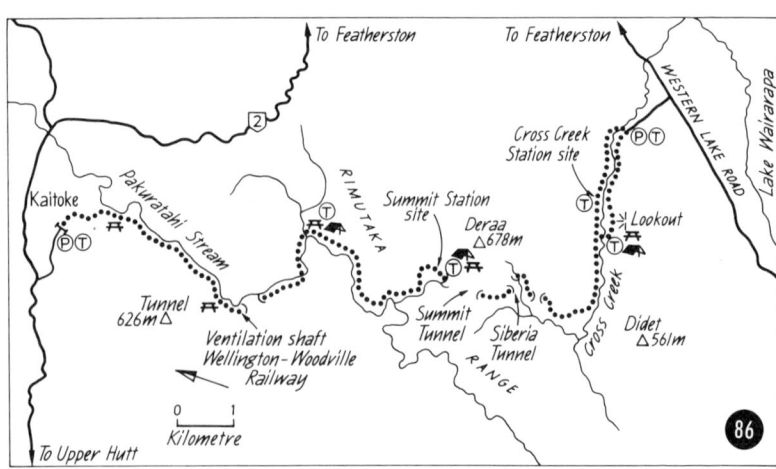

which collect the harvest of insects disturbed by walkers along the track.

Open fires are prohibited except in fireplaces provided at picnic and camping areas. From the eastern side, the first 1.5 kilometres are through farmlands. Dogs are prohibited. Follow the white posts and leave gates the way you find them.

Keith George Memorial Park

Length: 5 kilometres
Time taken: 2 hours
Grading: Moderate
Apparel: Good footwear
Code: Year-round, trees, birds, plants, views, swimming

Points of note: At one stage this area was threatened by the encroaching motorway, but strong protests from local people delayed decisions and the building of the motorway has receded into the distant future. This park was gifted by his family as a memorial to Keith George, who died in the First World War. There are no picnic spots as such, just a beautiful, quiet hillside, which is a joy in itself, but there are swimming holes in the Hutt River beside the Silverstream Bridge.

Access: The park is at the lower end of the Upper Hutt Valley, near the western end of the Silverstream Bridge.

At the entrance to the park a fine old ribbonwood, one of the few deciduous natives, stands guard. Totara and kahikatea also grow well there, but the main forest at the start is tawa, with a lovely groundcover of ferns. The track leads steeply up the hill and the ground is almost always damp. In the winter an abundance of fungi can be found in many different varieties and colours; one to look for is the pale-pink dead men's fingers.

About halfway up the hill there is an area where all the beech trees were blown down in the Wahine storm of 1968. This allows some good views, giving a different perspective of the Silverstream Bridge and motorways, and the Silverstream Hospital across the valley.

The track leads over the ridge and through some attractive beech forest. It soon tails off into gorse, but it is easy to get out on to the power pylon access road. Turn left and follow the road down toward the Haywards substation, keeping to the old road right down the hill and emerging on to State Highway 2 almost opposite Manor Park railway station. From there it is about 15

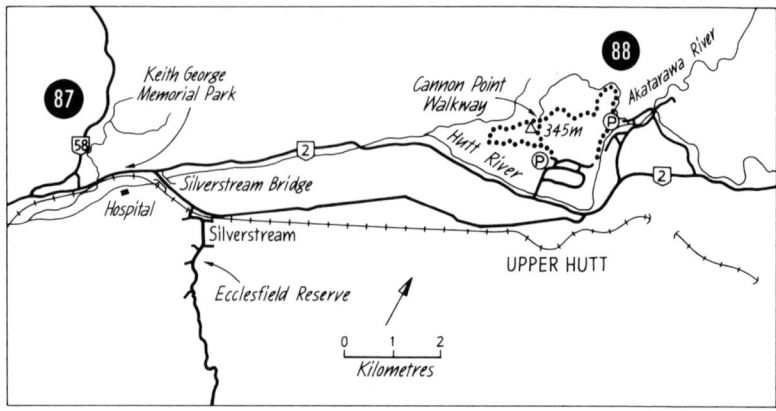

minutes' walk back along the road to the parking area at the entrance to the park.

Small bush birds are common on the walk, including grey warblers, whiteheads, fantails, tui, pigeons, silvereyes and moreporks.

Cannon Point Walkway

Length: Two walks: 6 and 10 kilometres
Time taken: 2 and 4 hours
Grading: Moderate
Apparel: Casual
Code: Year-round, trees, birds, flowers

Points of note: This walkway gains its name from the hill on top of which grew a tree resembling a cannon when viewed from Upper Hutt.

Access: Turn left off the main road through Upper Hutt, about 1 kilometre north of Upper Hutt railway station. The walkway is well signposted to the carpark.

The Cannon Point Walkway provides a 2-hour walk for people of average fitness, with a gradual slope up a road through the bush and a magnificent view from the trig point at the top of the hill, from Wellington Harbour right up the Hutt Valley to the Tararuas. The bush is mainly beech and kamahi, but one or two magnificent hinau trees can be seen flowering in November.

The walkway also borders on a pine plantation, and a longer walk is

140

possible along the ridge to the north, coming down at Akatarawa Bridge Road and returning along the foot of the hills to the carpark.

Some of the birds to be seen are rosellas, tui, wood pigeons, shining cuckoos, grey warblers, pipits and fantails.

Butterfly Creek

Length: Various
Time taken: Up to 3 hours
Grading: Easy
Apparel: Casual; good footwear
Code: Year-round, trees, birds

Points of note: The walks are through part of the Eastbourne Reserve, which extends to the Wainuiomata Valley. Parts of the reserve have been farmed in the past, but regeneration has been rapid and the reserve has a large variety of trees, shrubs and ferns. The picnic area has a swimming hole and there are ideal camping spots.

Access: The walk starts at Muritai Park, 1 kilometre south of Eastbourne Post Office, and ends at Kowhai Street, 1 kilometre further south. The shorter trip enters and returns via Kowhai Street.

The track from Muritai Park zigzags up the face of the hill through mixed regenerating bush, including hinau, titoki, rewarewa, manuka, mingimingi, kamahi, karaka, hangehange, kawakawa, rangiora, wharangi and heketara. In places there are areas of hard and black beech. On the ground you can see hood orchids, blueberry, lycopodium, New Zealand iris and the common maidenhair.

There are splendid views of Wellington, the harbour, the heads and the Kaikoura Ranges from points along the track. At the ridge a signpost shows a return to Eastbourne via the very steep McKenzie Track, and the track to Butterfly Creek. Beyond the ridge the beech forest is mature; northern and southern rata are prominent, miro and maire common, and podocarps are seen as you approach the valley floor.

The valley through which Butterfly Creek runs has some good specimens of kahikatea, rimu, pukatea, nikau palms, tawa, karaka, rewarewa and a variety of ferns: filmy, fragrant, shield, umbrella and ladder, maidenhairs, spleenworts, blechnums and tree-ferns. The track down the sheltered valley

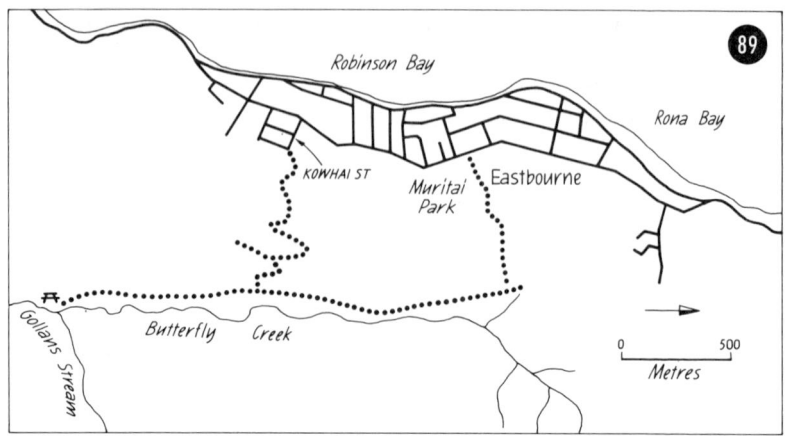

crosses the creek on good wooden bridges and, apart from some soggy areas in winter, is an easy walk. Lower down, the valley widens and podocarps become dominant, with kahikatea regeneration in all stages of growth.

The next junction provides the return track to Eastbourne, via Kowhai Street, but it is worthwhile carrying on to the picnic area, at the confluence of Butterfly Creek and Gollans Stream. A track proceeds up Gollans Stream, but this should be approached with caution, as it is indistinct in parts.

Days Bay Ridge

Length: 4 kilometres
Time taken: 2½–3 hours
Grading: Easy
Apparel: Casual
Code: Year-round, bush, birds, scenery

Points of note: The top of this hill walk follows the ridge dividing the Wainuiomata Valley from Wellington Harbour.

Access: The walk begins at the lookout carpark on the summit of the Wainuiomata Hill Road.

The summit lookout provides fine views of Wellington Harbour and the eastern bays. The track follows the length of the ridge before dropping steeply down into Days Bay.

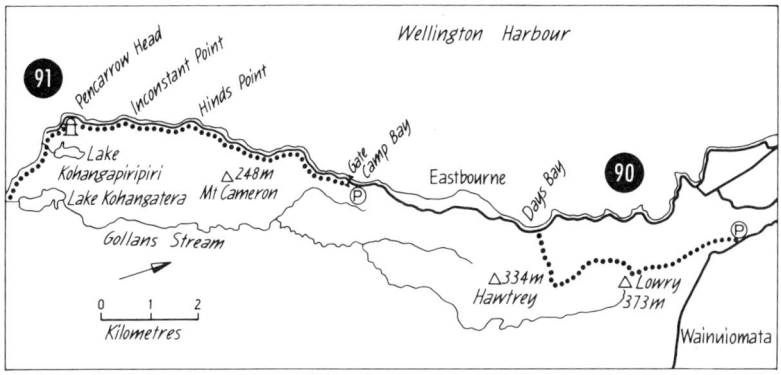

This is an all-year-round walk, and for the most part dry. There is no water supply of any description along the entire walk, nor are there camping areas or huts. Do not attempt to light an open fire anywhere on this ridge walk, as the beech forest is dry and vulnerable at all times of the year. Although the track is used frequently, you can drift well off the ridge in foggy conditions if you are not alert.

Tui, bellbirds, fantails, pigeons, tomtits, grey warblers and shining and long-tailed cuckoos can be heard or seen.

Pencarrow Lighthouse

Length: 14 kilometres
Time taken: 3½ hours
Grading: Easy
Apparel: Weatherproof
Code: Year-round, birds, history, wildlife reserve

Points of note: This varied coastal walk ends at the Pencarrow Lighthouse, which was erected in 1859. The first lighthouse in New Zealand, it functioned until 1935, when the Baring Head light was commissioned. Staff were retained at Pencarrow to operate the fog signal until 1960, when an automatic lighthouse and foghorn were installed at beach level. In 1959 the shell of the old lighthouse was declared a historic place by the Historic Places Trust.

Access: The walk starts at the carpark south of Eastbourne, where locked gates bar the entrance to vehicular traffic.

A well-maintained metalled road leads along the coast, providing good walking conditions. There are good views of Wellington's eastern suburbs, Barrett Reef and the South Island. Bird life is fairly plentiful and, according to season, may include black, little black and pied shags, black and pied oystercatchers, reef herons, white-fronted terns, black-backed and red-billed gulls, gannets and blue penguins. Inland, New Zealand pipits and the more common introduced birds can be seen.

About 400 metres from the start of the walk, there are signs of a track leading up to a saddle that provided one of the first routes to the Wairarapa. Travellers were rowed across the harbour from Wellington and from here made their way up the cliff. Stock for the stations in the Wairarapa was driven around the coast.

Inconstant Point is named after a barque that went ashore in 1849, was refloated and towed into Wellington Harbour and then used as a jetty and warehouse by a prominent early settler, John Plimmer.

On the foreshore at the foot of Pencarrow Lighthouse, a remnant of the steamer *Devon* is often exposed after southerly storms. On the hillside near the track leading up to the lighthouse, an enclosure marks the grave of a young child, the daughter of one of the keepers.

Continue from the lighthouse to Lakes Kohangapiripiri and Kohangatera. Extensive wetlands around these lakes are part of a wildlife reserve.

Makara Track

Length: Various
Time taken: Up to 3–4 hours
Grading: Moderate
Apparel: Casual but warm; non-slip footwear
Code: Year-round (except farm portion during lambing time, August and September), birds, plants, views, swimming

Points of note: The complete nature walk from Makara Beach to Opau Stream and return is recommended, covering shoreline, clifftops, a farm road and rock scrambling. Shorter walks include along the shoreline both ways; up to the fence and notice board (defining limit of access during the lambing season) and return downhill to the beach; or (a popular walk) to the summit to see the remains of old gun emplacements and views of the northern ranges of the South Island and the waters of Cook Strait.

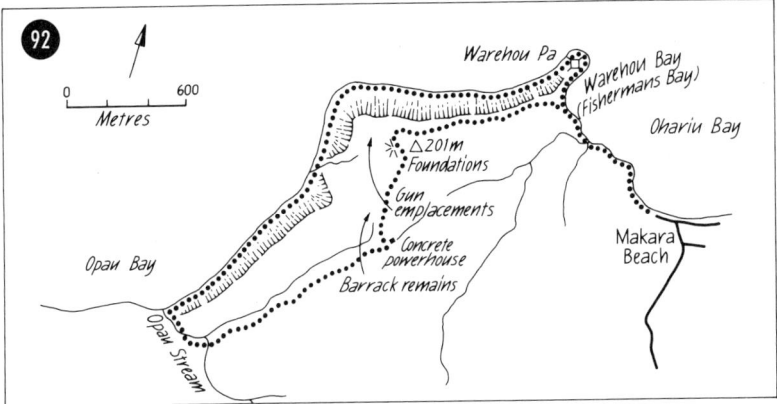

Access: Makara Beach, the starting point, is 16 kilometres west of Wellington, via Karori.

From the coast of the settlement at Makara Beach the walk passes changing sheds and toilets to a well-formed track above high-water mark at the base of extremely steep slopes. After less than 500 metres the first headland is passed, with a variety of interesting rock pools.

Next is Warehou (Fishermans) Bay, popular for skindiving, family picnicking and swimming. At the end of the beach cross a small stream and climb a gully to the site of an old Maori pa, revealed by terracing. The track ahead is well marked up the fenceline, but the long grass can be slippery. Over a stile are the concrete remains of gun emplacements, now being clothed with the creeping fern *Pyrrosia serpens*. The view from here is breathtaking, over Cook Strait to the South Island, and north up the Makara coast.

As the track angles inland, you can see below the tattered remnant of the totara and broadleaf-podocarp forest that originally covered these hills. After crossing a level area, which once carried a barracks and parade ground, the track becomes a gravel road, steeply descending past a pine plantation to another stile. The valley to the south and the gully now being traversed proclaim the existence of the Pukerua Fault.

You now cross Opau Stream and soon reach Opau Bay. On the walk back along the log-strewn stony beach, many native ground-covering plants and some unusual garden escapers can be seen growing on the shoreline and cliffs.

Makara Track is administered by the Department of Conservation and crosses land farmed by Landcorp. Dogs and firearms are not permitted, nor any radio equipment that would interfere with telecommunications from the nearby tower. Please respect the property and livestock.

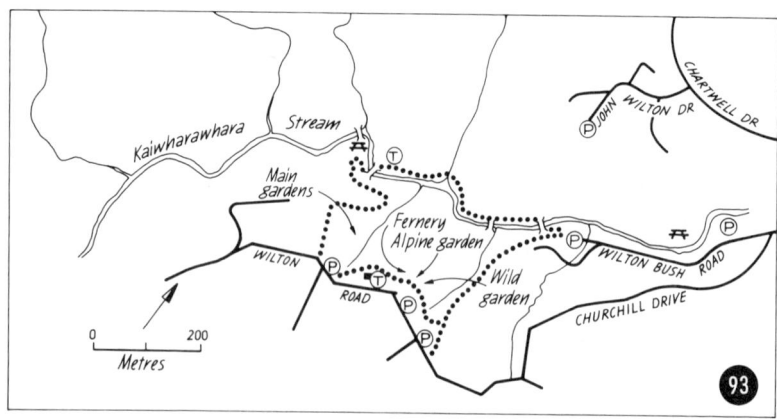

93

Otari Native Plant Museum

Length: Various
Time taken: Up to 1 hour
Grading: Easy to moderate
Apparel: Casual
Code: Year-round, trees, shrubs, grasses, ferns, orchids, birds

Points of note: The Otari Plant Museum covers 80 hectares of native forest, including 2 hectares of gardens where a comprehensive collection of plants are cultivated for horticultural and botanic interest. There are approximately 1,200 species, hybrids and cultivars, and about 500 labelled with common and botanic names.

The bush tracks lead away from the Kaiwharawhara Stream up into 150–200-year-old forest, with a section more or less virgin, including rimu, kahikatea and northern rata. There is an interpretive centre, with a sizable lecture theatre, near the carpark off Wilton Road.

Access: Take a No. 14 Wilton bus from the centre of Wellington city to the main gate at Wilton Road, opposite Gloucester Street. You can also enter from the south end of Wilton Bush Road near the junction of Churchill Drive and Blackbridge Road, and from above Chartwell.

The circular route, beginning at the main entrance and joined at other entrances in Wilton or Wilton Bush Roads, is a popular all-weather walk with a very gentle grade. This 30-minute stroll encompasses a collection of cultivars, a picnic green, and the west bank of the Kaiwharawhara Stream,

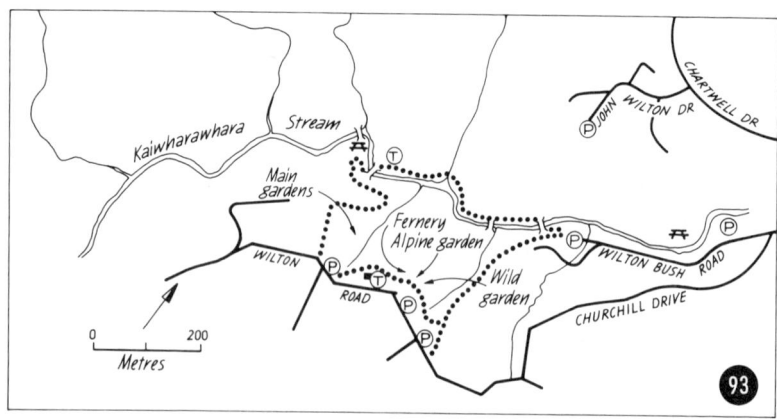

with indigenous forest on both sides. Near Wilton Road, rare flora from offshore islands is grown, while an area near the main entrance is devoted to plants of New Zealand's montane and alpine regions. The more challenging tracks through the forest are well marked with a primary colour.

Native birds seen, especially in the spring, are native pigeons, tui, grey warblers and fantails. There is also a wide range of introduced species. The picnic ground on the east bank of the stream is well sheltered, with fine grassy areas.

The idea of the Otari Native Plant Museum (originally known as Wilton Bush) was formulated in 1926 by Dr L. Cockayne, then honorary botanist to the Wellington City Council, together with J. G. MacKenzie, who was Director of Parks and Reserves. Dr Cockayne later became president of Forest and Bird. The 'museum' is a living wilderness environment, where New Zealand plants are grown and protected from extinction, so that the country's botanical heritage is not lost.

Northern Walk

Length: Various
Time taken: Up to full day
Grading: Moderate to strenuous
Apparel: Windbreaker
Code: Year-round, trees, birds, flowers, plants, panoramas

Points of note: Passing through areas of farmland and exotic and native bush, linked by short stretches of suburban streets, this walk offers changing panoramas of the city and can be made in shorter segments.

Access: Access to the start of the walk can be gained from the Botanic Garden lookout, at the top of the cable-car terminus in Upland Road, Kelburn. The other end of the track is reached from the Raroa Station, Johnsonville, by walking to the entrance of Johnsonville Park on Truscott Avenue.

Botanic Garden (25 minutes): From the lookout, walk down the path past the Meteorological Service Building and the DSIR to the Garden of Remembrance and around the rose garden to the exit.

Tinakori Hills (1 hour): Cross Glenmore Street, climb St Mary Street and follow directional markers to the entrance of the Town Belt. The track leads through native and exotic forest to the open upper ridge. A side track leads to a tunnel on the right of the main track, above the Scout hall. It is not certain why this 40-metre-long tunnel was constructed. Fantails, tui and silvereyes are common in this area, along with kingfishers, grey warblers, finches and thrushes.

Trelissick Park (20 minutes): From the Tinakori Hills, the walk follows Weld Street and passes through Wadestown to Trelissick Park. The track winds down through the park to Kaiwharawhara Stream and up the Ngaio Gorge to Trelissick Crescent. Tawa and rewarewa are common trees in this area, which has been regenerating for about a hundred years. Follow Kenya Street, turn left into Crofton and right into Ottawa to Cummings Park, which has a children's play area. Then continue to Khandallah Road and Simla Crescent to Khandallah Park.

Khandallah Park (50 minutes): The walk passes through hundred-year-old regenerating native forest and climbs to Mt Kaukau, with some exotic trees near the top, before moving onto farmland. There are extensive views from the lookout, from which the walk heads northward to a T junction. To the right, a track heads down to the northern boundary of Khandallah Park. The left-hand track enters Johnsonville Park.

Johnsonville Park (35 minutes): The walk passes a disused water reservoir and a tunnel, hewn out of solid rock, for the outlet pipe. The track continues to the exit of the park and follows streets to the station.

Eastern Walk

Length: Various
Time taken: Up to 2 hours
Grading: Moderate
Apparel: Warm clothing, good footwear
Code: Year-round (weather permitting), trees, shrubs, flowers, views, birds, swimming

Points of note: This exposed walk around the hilltops between Seatoun and Taraki Bay offers great views, changing along the way. Although the walk is steep in places, steps have been built on these sections and seats are placed along the way.

Access: The walk starts at the Pass of Branda, Seatoun, on the Miramar Peninsula,

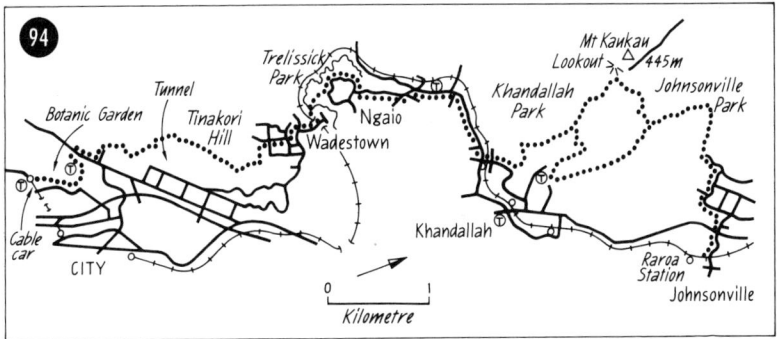

and ends at Taraki Bay, with other points of access at Beacon Hill Road, Sidlaw Street and Bowes Crescent. It is about a 30-minute walk back along the coast from Taraki Bay to the Pass of Branda.

The track starts toward the south above the Pass of Branda and zigzags up a steep hill through a plantation of macrocarpa and pine to the first viewpoint. From here, an open pathway continues up to Beacon Hill. Around and below the signal station a groundcover of native vegetation competes with gorse and broom. An exit to Beacon Hill Road is signposted just before the lookout.

The track continues in a southerly direction, with pine trees giving some protection from the wind. Further along is a second exit, to Sidlaw Street, and there is another constructed lookout. At Palmer Head lookout picnic

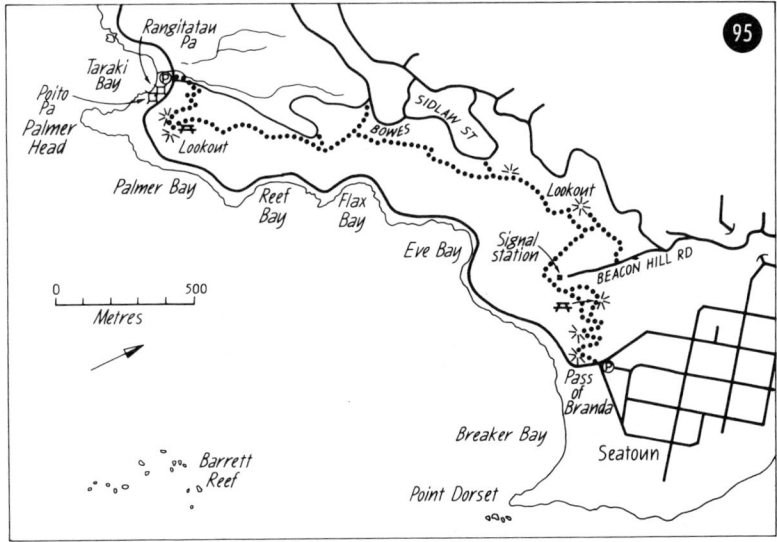

tables are placed to enjoy the view of Wellington Heads and Taraki Bay below. On a clear day, the Kaikoura Range may be seen across Cook Strait. Steps lead steeply down to the end of the walk at Taraki Bay. A walk back to the start along the coast makes a pleasant contrast to the hills.

On the southerly windswept slopes of the walk, mountain flax predominates, with cabbage trees in a damp, sheltered valley. There are large specimens of poroporo, and taupata gives shelter to stands of mahoe, whiteywood and kawakawa. Near the shore are many ice plants; the evergreen *Coprosma propinqua* clothes shingle margins, and the orange lichen *Xanthoria parietina* colours the rocks.

Southern Walk

Length: Various
Time taken: Up to 3 hours
Grading: Easy to moderate
Apparel: Casual; strong footwear
Code: Year-round, trees, panoramas

Points of note: This walk between Oriental and Island Bays traverses the Wellington Town Belt. Most of this area was cleared of native bush last century and grassed; work horses grazed here in off-duty hours and dairy cows were milked on some of the slopes. It has been planted with more than a million exotic conifers.

Access: Take a bus from Courtenay Place to the start of the track at Oriental Parade. The walk can be joined at the junction of Crawford and Wellington Roads near Hataitai Park or along the eastern boundary of the Zoological Gardens.

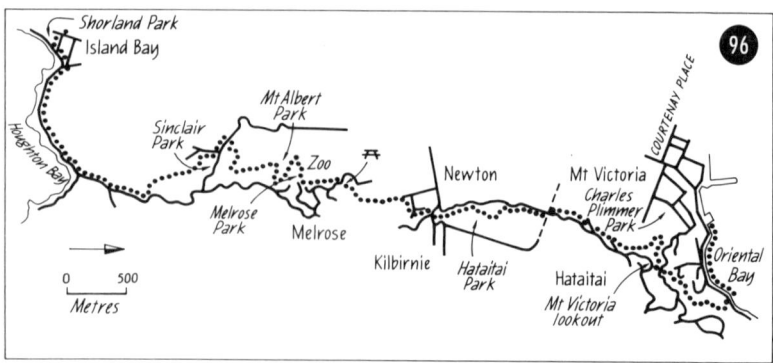

The walk is well marked with small brown posts painted with directional arrows. From the Oriental Parade (northern) end, the track zigzags up the hill, beneath many spreading pohutukawa, and soon passes into regenerating forest, with mahoe predominant. Across Palliser Road the track continues to the left up the hill, through exotic plantation. Good picnic spots are found in the Charles Plimmer Park to the right. A short way to the left, back along Alexander Road, brings you to the Byrd Memorial and Mt Victoria lookout (196 metres), which offers sweeping views of the Wellington area.

From Alexander Road the walk leads down through Hataitai Park to Crawford Road, Newtown, then above Kilbirnie to Melrose, passing the zoo. From Melrose Park there is a steep climb to the summit of Mt Albert (178 metres), but the view is extremely rewarding. On a fine day the Kaikoura Range may be seen in the distance.

The track descends through Sinclair Park and Houghton Valley reserve and play areas to Houghton Bay. From here the walk follows the coastline (exposed to the south) to Island Bay, where, at Shorland Park, a bus can be caught back to the city.

Red Rocks

Length: 4 kilometres
Time taken: 2–3 hours return
Grading: Easy if wind moderate
Apparel: Good footwear and windproof clothing
Code: Year-round, scientific reserve, seals, geology

Points of note: A family walk, this excursion offers wild and magnificent scenery and a close view of a seal colony. Red Rocks and the surrounding scientific reserve are of national significance. There are six archaeological sites in the area, including the site of the Ngati Mamoe Pa at Sinclair Head. There is a karaka grove, thought to be the site of an old Maori village, and also in the area are middens, storage pits and terraces.

Access: You can reach Owhiro Bay, where the walk starts, by car, travelling either through Brooklyn and down Happy Valley; or from Island Bay, following the coast. Sunday is the best day to go, when the gate at the road end is locked, thus barring trail bikes and motor vehicles.

The Red Rocks Track has always been popular with family groups. Small

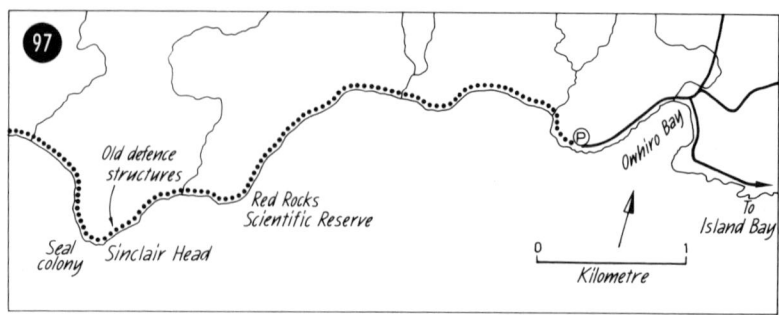

children can be taken in pushchairs, but the track is stony. The shadow of the hill comes across the track just after noon, so it is an advantage to do the walk in the morning. The track starts at a carpark at a quarry and leads around the coast to the scientific reserve.

The rocks were formed about two million years ago by submarine volcanic activity. The purple rocks are pillow lava that erupted onto the seafloor and were rapidly cooled. The red colour is caused by iron oxide (hematite), and the green by illite, a clay mineral. The red and white banded rocks contain silica. The rocks have been compressed, tilted, uplifted and finally eroded to be exposed on the shoreline between greywacke and argillite.

After passing the reserve on the seaward side of the track, you will see Sinclair Head, with the track rising and passing through a narrow corridor of rock. Immediately before and beyond this pass are stones stained and polished from the contact of the seals that bask there.

Beware of a strong fishy smell – it means that you are nearer to the seals than you suspect. If the seals are not immediately visible, stop and look hard; it is surprising how well they blend into the rocks. And the flippers of those swimming immediately offshore are often mistaken for giant kelp.

On clear days the scenery includes Mt Tapuaenuku on the Inland Kaikoura Range across Cook Strait. On other days, with a wild southerly, the sea is boiling and the coast exposed and exhilarating.

The birds of the coast include black-backed and red-billed gulls, white-fronted terns and shags, with petrels, shearwaters and albatrosses out in the strait.

The vegetation of the area consists of tough plants such as flax, the native linen flax and speargrass. Taupata is trimmed by the wind on the cliffs, and on the beaches *Coprosma propinqua* forms low cushions. Other plants include shore groundsel, bachelors button, glasswort, *Pimelea prostrata* and *Muehlenbeckia* – a springy, mattress-like shrub.

NELSON-MARLBOROUGH

Whites Bay

Length: Various
Time taken: Up to full day
Grading: Easy to moderate
Apparel: Good footwear for short walks; boots and parkas for longer
Code: Year-round, bush, views

Points of note: These coastal walks through bush, mainly regenerating, offer fine views.

Access: Whites Reserve is 20 kilometres north-east of Blenheim.

Rarangi–Whites Bay (45 minutes one way): This easy family walk starts at Rarangi, opposite the children's play area, and climbs through bush to the road. Walk along the road for about 10 minutes to the marked turn-off, where the track descends to Whites Bay.

Pukatea Track (15 minutes): The track leads from near the cable station in Whites Bay to the road. An easy walk, mostly on the flat through bush, it follows the stream.

Black Jack Track (45 minutes): This begins across the stream from the picnic area opposite the cable station. The track leads through regenerating bush, including koromiko, whiteywood, rangiora and manuka. The climb to the top and the lookout is best done in the direction of the arrows.

Mautaku Track (30 minutes): An easy walk back from the top of Black Jack Track through heath and manuka, this track has good views of Whites Bay.

Loop Track (3 hours): Access to the track is from four-wheel-drive roads on the left-hand side of the Port Underwood Road. (It is approximately an hour's walk by road between the starting points.) Of a moderate grade, the Loop Track is most easily walked from the northern end. The walk begins through

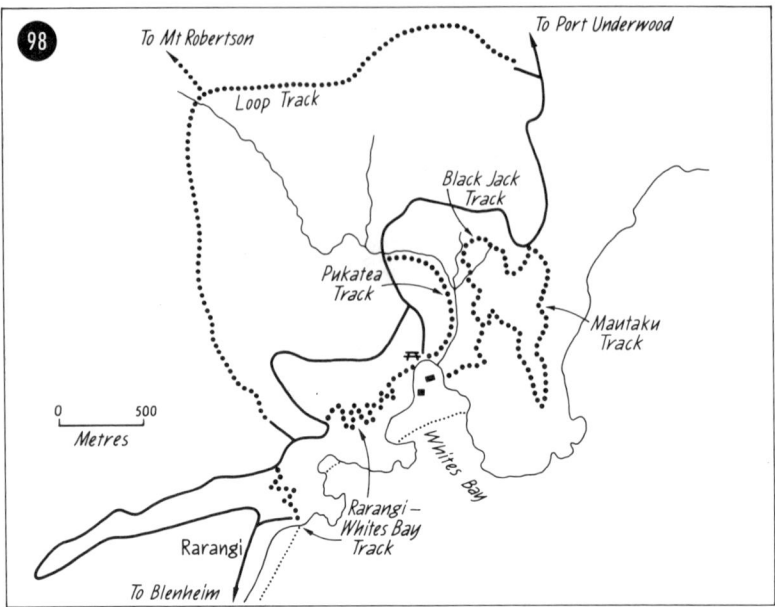

To Mt Robertson
To Port Underwood
Loop Track
Black Jack Track
Pukatea Track
Mautaku Track
0   500
Metres
Whites Bay
Rarangi – Whites Bay Track
Rarangi
To Blenheim

regenerating heath and manuka and then enters beech forest, with some rata at the top and thick clumps of ferns off the track. The track is well marked; watch for the turn-off to Mt Robertson.

There are excellent views of Port Underwood, Pukaka Valley, the Wairau Plain, the Kaikoura Ranges, Cape Campbell and across Cook Strait. It is often cool on exposed ridges, and parka and boots are recommended.

Mt Robertson (6–8 hours return): This track begins halfway along the Loop Track and climbs a ridge to the summit of Mt Robertson (1,036 metres).

Anakiwa and Davies Bay

Length: 5 kilometres
Time taken: 1½–2 hours return
Grading: Easy
Apparel: According to weather; good footwear
Code: Year-round, trees, birds, swimming, boating

Points of note: The track passes through the 719-hectare Iwatuaroa Scenic Reserve, which extends from the water's edge to the top of the ridge dividing the Grove Arm of Queen Charlotte Sound from Mahau Sound, a reach of Pelorus Sound.

Access: Access is from the end of Anakiwa Road near Cobham Outward Bound School, 25 kilometres from Picton and 19 kilometres from Havelock. There is off-road parking in front of the Outward Bound School.

The track first passes through a good representative example of Inner Sounds mixed broadleaf forest. Some fine examples of mamaku fill the damper gullies, contrasting with towering black beech as the track leads on to the well-drained ridges. An occasional nikau palm can be found, but this is not its best habitat. In the watercourses, pukatea and tawa provide support for kiekie. Hen and chicken ferns are abundant.

All the common bush birds are in the area – silvereyes, grey warblers, bellbirds, tui, pigeons and the occasional cheeky weka lying in ambush.

Thirty-five minutes from Anakiwa, the track runs close to the beach at Davies Bay. At low tide this is a fine feeding ground for waders and kingfishers. Resuming the walk, a further 10 minutes through mainly

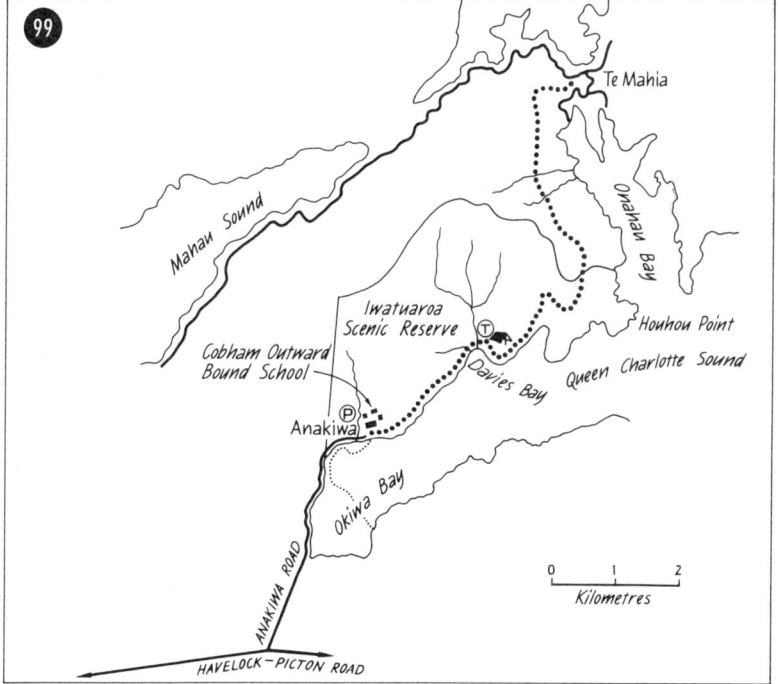

regenerating bush – ponga, mahoe, five-finger and wineberry – leads to a fine campsite. A large grassed clearing has a backdrop of dense tawa and pukatea. A good all-year stream runs on one side, and there are toilets and a fireplace.

A further track leads from near the beach at Davies Bay to the head of Onahau Bay and Te Mahia. This involves a further 2-hour walk for the moderately fit.

Pelorus Bridge

Length: Various
Time taken: Up to 3 hours
Grading: Moderate
Apparel: According to weather; good footwear
Code: Year-round, trees, flowers, birds, swimming, fishing

Points of note: The walks are through the Pelorus Bridge Scenic Reserve, which comprises 1,008 hectares of native bush, including one of the southernmost stands of tawa in the country.

Access: Pelorus Bridge is on Highway 6, approximately halfway between Blenheim and Nelson.

There are three short walks in the reserve: Tawa, Totara and Circle; the first two being suitable for the disabled. The reserve is well posted with information boards. The longer Trig K Track is described below. In addition to the walks, there is excellent swimming below the bridge.

The track starts at the northern end of the campsite, which is reached by taking the road through the bush beside the tearooms.

The track plunges immediately into vegetation of great diversity. High podocarps reach overhead, with an undercanopy of tawa, tarata, pate, putaputaweta and kamahi crowded beneath. Below these again are crown ferns, hen and chicken ferns, rice grass, tree-ferns and many seedlings.

For a while the trail follows the same track walked by early gold miners and, before them, Maori war parties using the Maungatapu Trail. Ten minutes' walking brings the visitor to the junction of the tracks for the round trip. The Falls Track, to the right, keeps to a river terrace with glimpses of the Pelorus River. The first waterfall, soon reached, does not always run after dry weather.

The drier sites further on are covered by black and hard beech, with

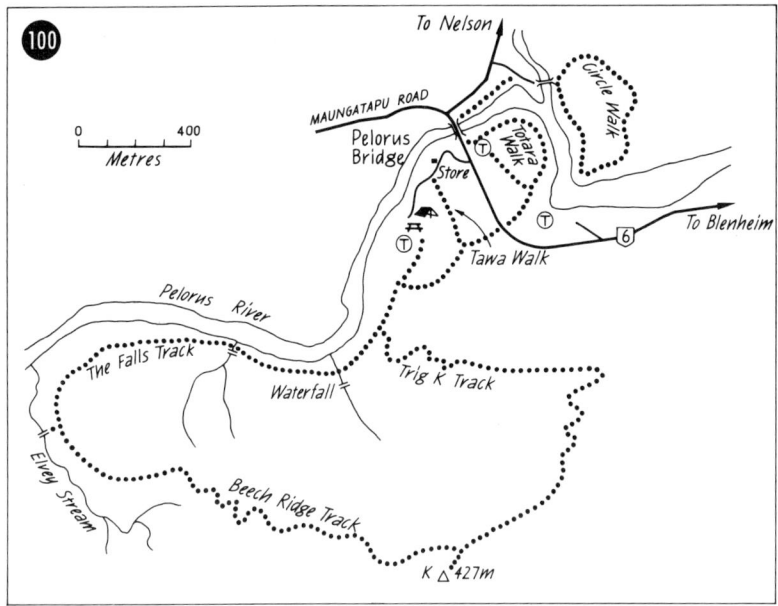

kanuka the dominant tree nearer the river. *Helichrysum glomeratum* grows here too, as does an occasional silver beech, the seed for which has perhaps been washed down from higher altitudes.

About 40 minutes from the start of the walk, you reach the Elvey Stream, and a few steps off the track take you to a strong-flowing waterfall, several metres high, surrounded by lush vegetation. The track climbs on past hard beech, with buttressed trunks, and great carpets of crown ferns, then through a dense stand of tawa on the sheltered side of the hill and soon to the ridge with a first view of the farming area of the Rai Valley.

A steady climb up this ridge, passing an area of wind-thrown beech, leads to Trig K, set in a regenerating clearing at a height of 427 metres. On a clear day there is a splendid view from Pelorus Sound in the north-east to the back of Mt Richmond Range in the far south-west.

The track leads down through a thicket of kamahi, putaputaweta, wineberry and black and hard beech into high-canopy forest again. Ten minutes after leaving the top, you can see a very large rimu on the lower side of the track, and another 10 minutes down there is a magnificent totara. The trail then rejoins the main track leading back to the campsite.

101

Hira State Forest

Length: Various
Time taken: Up to 3 hours
Grading: Average
Apparel: Casual; good footwear
Code: Year-round (except at time of fire danger), trees, birds

Points of note: The public has access to the forest except in times of fire risk. Well-formed tracks can be reached by car, using forest roads.

Access: Drive from Nelson up the Maitai Valley and turn left after 5 kilometres, opposite the Waahi Taakaro Golf Course, up the Sharlands Creek Road. At the next junction keep left for the three Sharlands Creek bush walks. The right-hand fork leads to the Pukatea and Totara Trails and the Zigzag Track.

Sharlands Creek: A track sign on the left about 7 kilometres up the left-hand road leads into an interesting remnant of indigenous bush where there are three trails. Supplejack can be walked as a circuit in 2–3 hours; Matai and Rimu Trails are return routes. From the top of the trails a track leads up to Kaka Point, where an excellent view can be had over Nelson City and Tasman Bay.

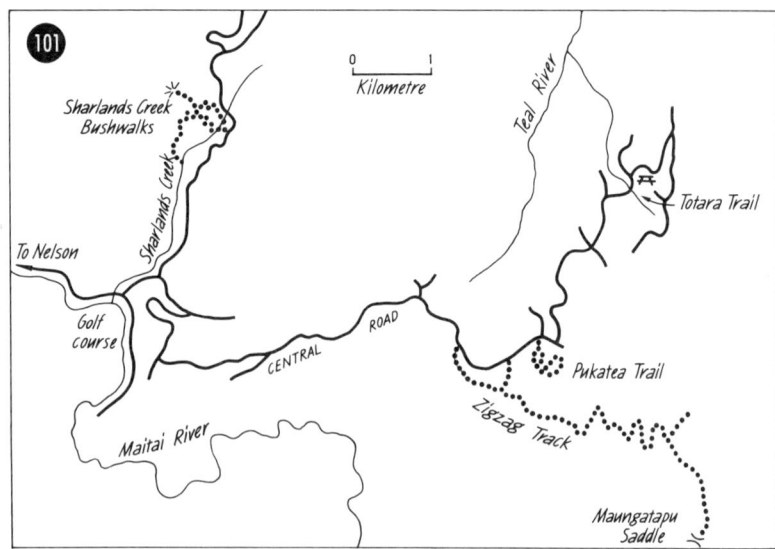

The tracks run through a good variety of trees and ferns. Rimu and matai stands in the more sheltered parts give way to beech higher up the hill. Near the stream are some unusual filmy ferns. In other places there are patches of tree-ferns, climbing ferns and epiphytes, the variety and changing associations making each of these trails different and interesting.

Pukatea Trail: The start of this trail is reached by keeping to the right at the road junction instead of carrying on to Sharlands Creek, climbing up to the Teal Saddle and continuing along Central Road until, 12 kilometres from the golf course, there is a remnant of bush on the right. Pukatea Trail has been cut through this bush in the form of a figure 8, which gives a choice of length of walk and exit points. The whole walk can be covered in 1½–2 hours.

The interesting patch of bush climbs steeply up the valley and merges at the top into beech protection forest, which covers the slopes of the ridge known as the Doubles. Some big rimu, matai, rata and kahikatea remain. Other trees represented are pukatea and tawa, which are at their southern limit. There is a good specimen of raukawa, which is unusual in the district. The ferns are very beautiful.

Totara Trail: Reached 4 kilometres further along Central Road, the Totara Trail winds through a patch of tall native forest distinguished by the large number of big trees remaining, the area not having been touched by early logging. A one-way track, this can be walked both ways in an hour.

Zigzag Track: Between the Teal Saddle and Pukatea Trail is Zigzag Track, which leads up into the beech forest to the top of the Doubles. Keep to the right and the track leads down into the Maungatapu Saddle, scene of famous murders during the gold rush of the last century. A four-wheel-drive route crosses the Maungatapu Saddle from Pelorus to the Matai Valley.

Pupu Springs

Length: Various
Time taken: Up to 1 hour
Grading: Easy
Apparel: Casual
Code: Year-round, forest, birds, springs

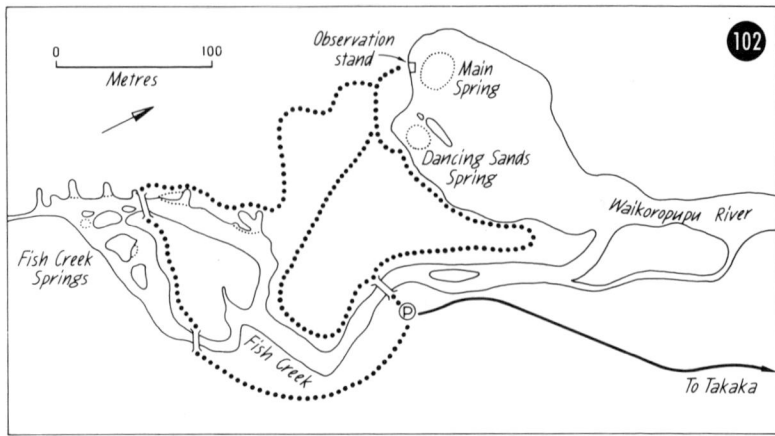

Points of note: Pupu Springs are New Zealand's largest freshwater springs. Cool, crystal-clear waters bubble up from subterranean systems in the Takaka Valley, at about 14 cubic metres per second and at times up to 21 cubic metres per second.

Access: The springs are a 10-minute drive from Takaka. The road to the springs turns off State Highway 60 north of Takaka, across the Waitapu Bridge on the western side of the Takaka River.

Two tracks lead off from the carpark. The shorter track crosses Fish Creek immediately and splits to make a loop, which rejoins by the Dancing Sands Spring and continues to the main spring. A longer round trip is possible via the Fish Creek Springs.

The vegetation of the reserve is predominantly regenerating shrubland, with one pocket of original bush remaining upstream of the bridge. This is dense podocarp-beech forest, dominated by kahikatea, with rimu, matai, totara and black beech. The rest of the forest was burnt off, with a history of gold sluicing and farming in the area.

Lake Rotoiti Peninsula

Length: 3 kilometres
Time taken: 1–2 hours
Grading: Easy
Code: Year-round, lakeshore, views, forest, interpretation markers

Points of note: The peninsula is formed by rock and debris known as moraine, deposited by a glacier during the last ice age. The ice carved out the depression that now forms Lake Rotoiti and extended either side of the peninsula to form West and Kerr Bays.

Access: The Nelson Lakes National Park Visitor Centre is at St Arnaud, about 100 kilometres south-west of Blenheim on State Highway 63, and 120 kilometres south of Nelson.

From the visitor centre, continue down to the lake shore towards the bush-edge at the western end of Kerr Bay. The track leads around the outer edge of the peninsula through beech and kanuka-manuka forest in varying stages of regeneration as a result of past fire damage. Three species of beech are present – black, red and silver. Marker posts aid interpretation of the walk and correspond to a booklet available at the visitor centre. The nature walk ends on the opposite side of the peninsula. From here one track continues around the lake shore to West Bay, and another leads back to the visitor centre on View Road (about 10 minutes), or to Rotoiti Lodge on a side track to the left.

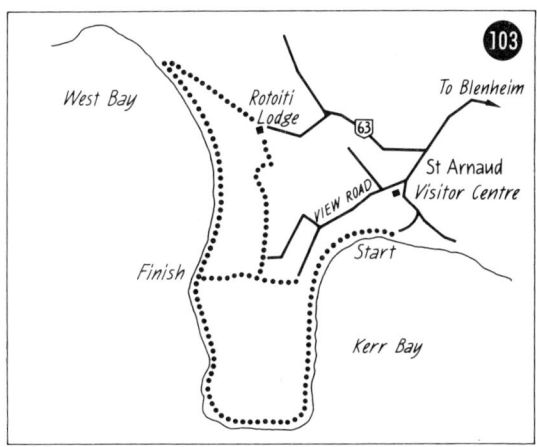

Six Mile Walk

Length: 3 kilometres
Time taken: 1–1½ hours return

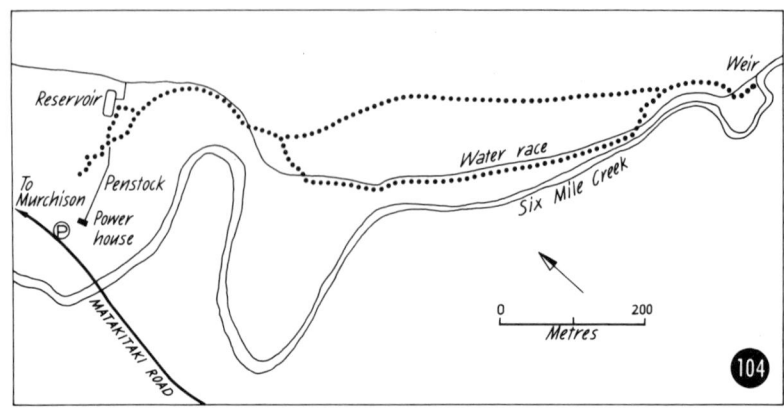

Grading: Easy to moderate
Apparel: Casual
Code: Year-round, trees, birds, history

Points of note: The Six Mile hydro station, opened in 1922, is believed to be the oldest power station still in existence in New Zealand. The operation was closed in 1975. The track follows the old water race to the weir, through an attractive remnant of mixed beech-podocarp forest.

Access: The walk is 10 kilometres south of Murchison on the Matakitaki Road, which turns off State Highway 6 in the town. It starts and finishes at the power station by the Six Mile Creek bridge.

Starting at the power station, the track zigzags up beside the penstock to the intake and then follows alongside the water race. After a short distance it crosses the race and climbs on to a forested terrace. The main canopy trees are red and silver beech, with some mountain beech, kahikatea, matai and totara. A smaller water race to the left of the track was constructed by early Chinese gold prospectors. After about 20 minutes the track descends back to the main race and continues to the weir, below which a waterfall tumbles through a narrow granite gorge.

The return walk heads back the same way for a short distance to a track junction, where an alternative route descends to follow the water race. It rejoins the main track and returns to the start. Fuchsia trees grow alongside the weir, and the tree-daisy *Senecio hectori*, found only between North-West Nelson and Greymouth, is also present. Bellbirds, tui, robins, fantails, silvereyes and kingfishers are found in the forest.

WEST COAST

Truman Track

Length: 1 kilometre
Time taken: 30 minutes return
Grading: Easy
Apparel: Casual
Code: Year-round, trees, birds, plants, coastal views, blowholes

Points of note: An easy forest walk, this leads to an interesting coastline of rocky cliffs, small blowholes, caves and beaches.

Access: The walk is well signposted 3 kilometres north of Punakaiki. A carpark is provided on the opposite side of the road.

The track plunges downwards from the side of the road into a profuse growth of nikau palms and a confused tangle of ponga, supplejack and kiekie. Tall trees of the forest are still standing here – rimu, rata and kahikatea, many with parasites and epiphytes: one enormous matai tree is encircled by the massive roots of a northern rata vine. You can hear bellbird and tui and the rustling of pigeons' wings, and see fantails, tomtits, grey warblers and silvereyes.

The forest soon gives way to coprosmas and kamahi, and then the track winds through flax and gorse as it descends to the rocky coast. Take care with small children here, as the rocky shelf is some height above sea level. The view to the south is splendid, but do not venture onto the rocks – they are extremely slippery, even when dry, and have claimed lives. The blowholes, best seen at high tide, can be easily experienced from the safety of the track.

Follow the steps and descend along the wooden staircase down to the beach, where you will see gulls, oystercatchers and shags. At low tide you can explore the surrounding rocks and coastline, but watch the tide at all times. You can follow the coastline further north and reach a sea cave, but this may prove a difficult scramble for some people.

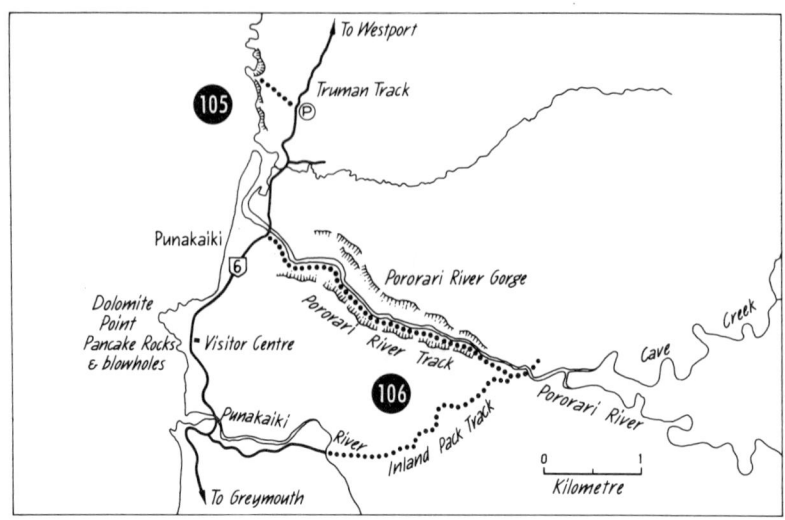

Pororari River

Length: 3 kilometres
Time taken: 3 hours round trip
Grading: Easy to moderate
Apparel: Casual
Code: Year-round, trees, birds, plants, orchids, swimming, canoeing

Points of note: The Pororari River flows through untouched native forest from a rugged and inaccessible hinterland. Towering limestone cliffs on either side of the river make the scenery spectacular.

Access: The walk is reached from State Highway 6, at the south end of the bridge across the Pororari River.

The lower reaches of the Pororari River are lined with kowhai trees, and when these are flowering in September there are an unbelievable number of songbirds present. The walk follows the river upstream, through a profuse growth of nikau, ponga, cabbage trees, flax, macropiper, whiteywood, coprosma, wineberry and kamahi, while kiekie, creepers and supplejacks festoon everything. Many parasites and epiphytes grow on the tall rata trees that line both sides of the river, and there are occasional banks of white rata. Orchids border the walk, as do many different types of grasses.

There are several small sandy beaches along the river; the best one is reached within 15 minutes. The river is shallow, and bathing and canoeing are pleasant in summer, though some deep pools further upstream demand care be taken with small children. The track has been recently widened and shingled, and there are commanding views of the river. The bird life is abundant and includes pigeons, tui, bellbirds, grey warblers, tomtits, robins, Australasian harriers, pied and black fantails, blackbirds, thrushes, silver-eyes and finches.

The track continues to climb, giving lovely views of the river, with its deep pools and clear bright water. Towering bluffs reach up on either side. A great deal of work has been done on this track with bridges and boardwalks, so that it is now a pleasant riverside walk. Beyond the point where the canyon appears to close in, however, the track is no longer corduroyed or shingled, though it is still well defined and easy to follow. After about an hour or so, the path turns away from the river and meets the old Inland Pack Track. Following the signposts, take this track down towards the Pororari River, which is reached within 5 minutes. With its mossy banks, shingle beach, sparkling river and tall beech trees, this is a delightful spot for a picnic lunch or just a rest. A pair of kaka is often seen and heard here.

Retracing your steps south towards the Punakaiki River, you can observe the change that has occurred in the vegetation, which is now more open, with beech, kamahi and toro trees, while the ground is carpeted with mosses and ferns. The well-graded Pack Track, which was used by the early miners, winds up to a ridge about 150 metres high. A gap in the bush reveals some of the peaks of the Paparoa Range, and the track now descends through a denser type of broadleaf vegetation.

The old road and the Punakaiki River are soon reached. The original ford over the river has washed out, and the safest crossing point is about 50 metres upstream. This is normally less than knee-deep, but care must be taken in wet weather, as West Coast rivers rise quickly and dangerously. Follow the road to the main road and continue back to the starting point.

Point Elizabeth Walkway

Length: 5 kilometres
Time taken: 3 hours
Grading: Moderate

Apparel: According to weather; boots recommended
Code: Year-round, trees, birds, plants, views, water race, dam

Points of note: The Point Elizabeth Walkway is situated at the northern end of the Twelve Apostles Range, largely within the Rapahoe Range Scenic Reserve. There is a marked difference in vegetation on either side of the high ridge. This might be because of a difference in climate – exposed to the sea on the west – but it could also result from the clearing on the west side of the bush in the early days. At one time the track was used by gold miners, and evidence of their activities can be seen in the water races still existing and the dam at Darkies Terrace.

Access: The walkway can be reached from either Cobden or Rapahoe. Follow the signposts at the far end of the Cobden Bridge for the Cobden end. The distance from Greymouth to the Cobden end is 7 kilometres, while it is 11 kilometres to the Rapahoe end on a sealed road. At Rapahoe, follow the signs at Seven Mile Creek bridge. Go through the gate along the road, where there is plenty of room for parking.

From the Cobden end, the walkway rises from the shingle beach through grass, scrub and regenerating second growth until a height of about 60 metres is attained. Here there are good views of the beach and coastline, the Grey River tip head and the distant hills, and on fine days Mt Cook and Mt Tasman can be seen. The windswept coastal scrub consists of ponga, coprosma, flax and whiteywood, but as the track winds away from the windblown cliffs the vegetation becomes more profuse, with nikau, macropiper, cordyline and kiekie, and many parasite ferns and orchids.

Eventually the track emerges from the bush to give fine views of the sea. There is a seat in a sheltered spot for those wishing to rest. The track then descends towards Darkies Terrace, the scene of gold mining in the early days. The old dam site is now overgrown with flax, and from here the track turns and winds through flax and grass towards the point. There is a railed-off rest area at Point Elizabeth. Take care with young children all along this area. From the point there are fine views of the coastline looking north and reaching as far as Punakaiki, with the Paparoas in the background. Looking seawards, you can see the Needle, Big Rock and Shag Rock, and southwards, the Grey River tip head and the distant Alps.

Retrace your steps to the main track, where the turn-off to Rapahoe is well marked, and continue through the flax around the terrace edge to an old mining road. On either side of the track there is a tangled mass of kiekie, whiteywood, macropiper and the occasional cabbage tree. After an avenue of ponga, the track soon enters the bush with its taller trees – miro, kahikatea, rimu and kamahi – giving shelter to ponga, kiekie, ferns, vines and creepers, marbleleaf and wineberry, toro and lancewood. Some very tall rata trees may be observed, with profuse growth of parasites, epiphytes and kiekie. The water race made by the early miners can be seen along much of the way, and there is a seat about halfway along. You may see grey warblers, bellbirds, chaffinches, yellow-breasted tits, pied and black fantails, pigeons, redpolls, house sparrows and Australasian harriers.

The end of the reserve is marked by a fence with a stile. Now the track winds down the open hillsides, with splendid views of the coastline and the surrounding hills. On this section you can hear the skylark and the pipit, and see weka and pukeko in the nearby paddocks.

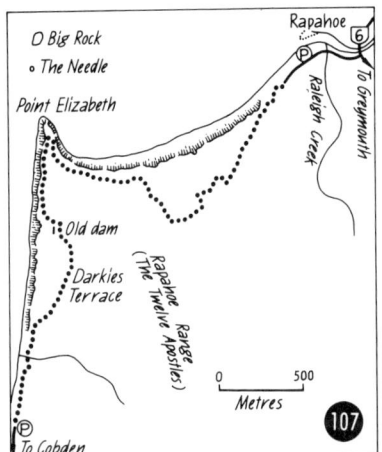

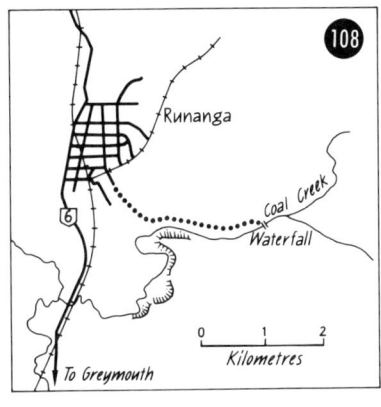

Coal Creek Falls

Length: 2 kilometres
Time taken: 1 hour return
Grading: Easy
Apparel: Casual
Code: Year-round, trees, birds, ferns, waterfall

Points of note: Coal Creek Falls used to be a popular picnic spot in the days before the advent of the car, but for many years afterward the track lay overgrown and muddy. However, a great deal of work has been done recently – the track widened, shingled and corduroyed, and boardwalks laid over small creeks – and many elderly people are now able to walk to the falls.

Access: Take the road from Greymouth to Runanga. Follow the signs from the

Seddon Street corner opposite Erskine Motoring Services. Turn right at McGowan Street, cross the railway line and continue up Ballance Street to the end of the road.

The track starts at the end of the street, goes through a short stretch of scrub and then follows the edge of the terrace overlooking Coal Creek Valley and the distant hills. The valley below is covered with beech trees, which look very beautiful in the morning sun. After a short time the track enters the bush and descends from the terrace at an easy grade to Coal Creek. There are tall trees here and many birds can be heard and observed – bellbirds, blackbirds, chaffinches, silvereyes, grey warblers, grey ducks, brown creepers, pied fantails, pigeons and redpolls. The track winds alongside Coal Creek through beeches, rimu, kamahi and an undergrowth of wineberry, broadleaf, toro, pepper trees and many ferns. Here and there the smell of sulphur is apparent from abandoned coal drives. As the track nears the falls, it rises slightly and winds away from the creek. A waterfall on the left cascades down a mossy bank and is seen at its best in rain. There is a comfortable seat here and steps lead down to the edge of the water. In summer it is pleasant to paddle in the water or swim in the creek.

Lake Kaniere Walkway

Length: 11 kilometres
Time taken: 4 hours
Grading: Easy to moderate
Apparel: Casual

Points of note: Lake Kaniere is part of the Kaniere Scenic Reserve, which protects twenty distinct types of forest. There are a total of seven walks in the reserve, ranging from a 5-minute stroll to the spectacular Dorothy Falls to the more challenging climb up Mt Tuhua for views of the Southern Alps and coastline.

Access: Turn off State Highway 6 south of Hokitika at Kaniere. The walk begins just south of Slip Bay, at the southern end of the lake.

Following the western shores of Lake Kaniere, the track starts with a short steep climb over a low saddle on the side of Mt Upright. The hillside along this track was once covered by a glacier and is in a stage of regeneration. Trees to look out for are mahoe, wineberry and coprosma.

At the foot of Mt Upright is Lawyers Delight Beach – a popular spot for

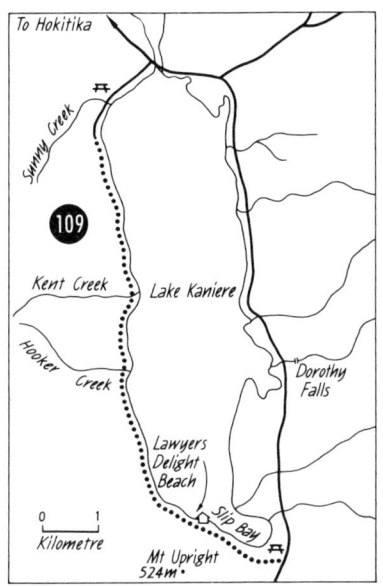

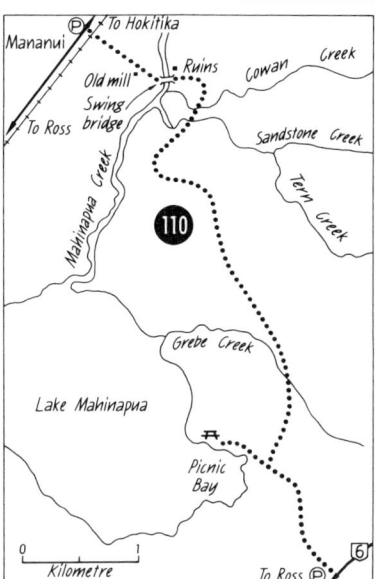

locals in the 1920s and visitors in the 1990s. Just along from this beach is a two-bunk shelter.

Other plants that can be seen along the walkway are umbrella fern (tapuwae kotuku – the footprints of the white heron), tree-ferns, broadleaf, toro, quintinia, hinau and kiekie.

Mahinapua Walkway

Length: 6 kilometres
Time taken: 4 hours return
Grading: Easy to moderate
Apparel: Casual
Code: Year-round, trees, birds

Points of note: There is a marked difference in the quality of the sections of this walk. The first part, from State Highway 6 (the eastern end), passes through the Mahinapua Scenic Reserve, containing tall rimu, while the western end goes through an area of scrub, swamps and regenerating forest.

Access: From State Highway 6 at the eastern end, 14 kilometres south of Hokitika, the entrance to the walkway is well signposted. To reach Mananui, at the western end, take the road to Ruatapu through Arthurstown, turning right just past the bridge over the Hokitika River. The distance to Mananui from Hokitika is 14 kilometres on a sealed road.

From the highway entrance the track winds through very tall rimu and kamahi, with an understorey of quintinia, coprosma, broadleaf, lancewood, ponga and the occasional miro and celery pine. You can see and hear bellbirds, tui, pigeons, fantails, grey warbler, yellow-breasted tit and brown creeper. After about 20 minutes' walk, there is a branch off the track to Picnic Bay on the Lake Mahinapua foreshore. This track, which completes the better end of the walk, takes 30 minutes return and winds through pleasant bush, climbing to about 50 metres above the level of the lake before descending to a small bay. Shags and herons may be seen near the lake.

Returning to the main track, you soon reach the end of the Lake Mahinapua Scenic Reserve, and the walkway emerges into an open logged area, now planted with small eucalyptus trees. To the left, in the distance, you can see the tall native trees of the scenic reserve, while on the far right are plantings of Japanese cedar. In these open parts pukeko, weka, blackbirds and thrushes may be seen.

Eventually you come to a swamp with a boardwalk, about 200 metres long, built across it. A wire swingbridge then crosses Mahinapua Creek and the track continues on an old tramline to its western entrance.

Harihari Coastal Walkway

Length: 7.5 kilometres
Time taken: 3 hours return
Grading: Easy
Apparel: Casual
Code: Year-round, coastal forest, history

Points of note: Originally called the Wanganui Coastal Pack Track, this walkway follows an old tramline used for transporting logs to Houston sawmill, which was built in 1935 but was closed a year later when the scow carrying machinery for the mill was wrecked on the Wanganui bar. Houstons took over the mill in 1937 and transported timber to the railhead at Ross. By 1958 the forest was almost cut out. While logs were brought in from other places, the mill became uneconomic and finally closed in 1963.

Access: Leaving State Highway 6 at the southern end of Harihari, La Fontaine Road crosses farmed river flats and ends in a carpark.

The first section of the track follows a logging tramway through regenerating bush in logged kahikatea forest. The track leaves the tramline at the site of the bridge across Black Creek, where only the piles remain, and joins up with the old pack track. It then opens out onto the Poerua River flats, where those once using the track caught the ferry south.

Walking towards the sea, there is an alternative track over the Oneone Ridge if access along the coast is not possible. The coastal forest has been sculptured by the prevailing salt-laden winds, and penguin tracks and New Zealand fur seals are often seen.

At the northern end of the beach is The Doughboy, a moraine remnant that was stranded when the Wanganui River changed its course. A climb up this provides magnificent views of the Wanganui River flats and Southern Alps.

The track then crosses unmodified wetland and follows the Wanganui River to the carpark.

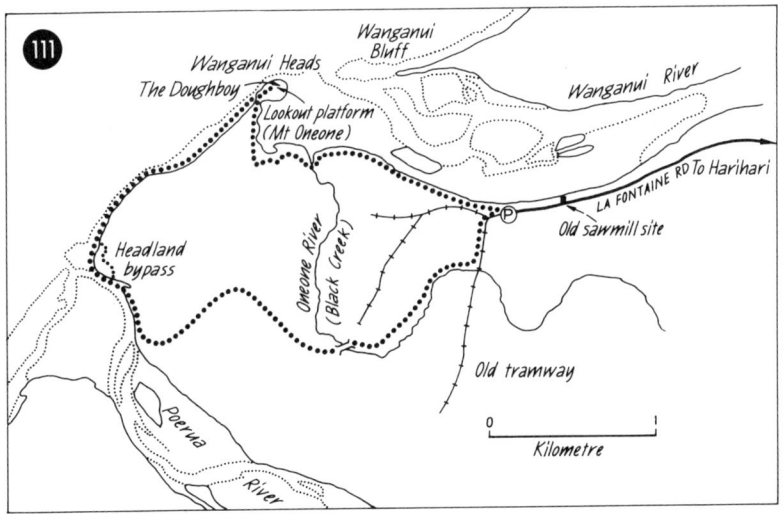

Monro Track

Length: 1.5 kilometres
Time taken: 1½ hours return
Grading: Easy
Apparel: Casual
Code: Year-round, rainforest and coastline

Points of note: Monro Beach was named after an early gold miner. Supplies for gold diggings were carried on horseback along this route, which was built as a pack track in 1884 to link the Haast–Paringa cattle track, then the main South Westland route, with the coast.

Do not take dogs along the track to the beach – their presence and scent alarms birds and threatens penguins.

Access: Turn off State Highway 6 just north of the Moeraki River bridge. Drive 1 kilometre to the carpark.

A gently graded forest track takes you through lush and diverse lowland and coastal forest, with kotukutuku and tree-fern glades, and finishes at the coast. Fiordland crested penguins are often seen on Monro Beach, which is protected by rocky headlands in the north and south. It is possible to climb over the north headland and travel further up the coast, but beware of rising tides and rough seas when walking around headlands.

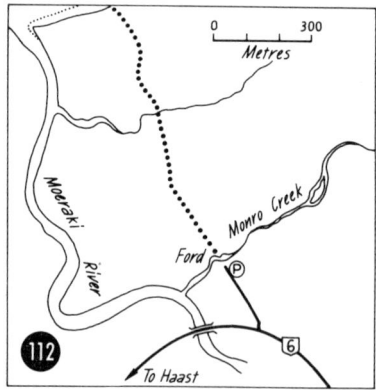

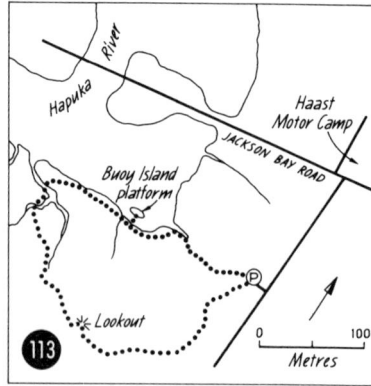

Hapuka Walk

Length: 1 kilometre
Time taken: 30 minutes return
Grading: Easy
Apparel: Casual
Code: Estuary, kowhai and coastal podocarp forest

Points of note: A recent addition to walks on the West Coast, the Hapuka Walk was developed under DOC's South Westland Recreation and Tourism Strategy.

Access: Take the Jackson Bay Road off State Highway 6 to the Haast Motor Camp. The walk starts at the carpark sited off Turnbull River Road and is approximately 5 minutes from the motor camp.

A well-formed track leads through a transition zone from kowhai forest and cabbage-tree-dominated shrubland to tidal mudflat. The mudflats, rushlands and swamp are traversed by a boardwalk with interpretation panels telling the story of whitebait, an important feature of South Westland culture.

The Hapuka estuary and surrounding forest are home to many species of seabirds, waders and forest birds. There is also an abundance of aquatic species living in the estuary, which is a whitebait reserve.

The track leaves the rush wetland and enters jungle-like coastal podocarp forest covered in kiekie. A lookout on this section of the walk offers views to the Open Bay islands and the coast.

CANTERBURY

Port Robinson Walkway

Length: 7 kilometres
Time taken: 3½–4 hours
Grading: Easy
Apparel: Casual; warm clothing
Code: Year-round, trees, views, geology

Points of note: This walk follows the coastline from Gore Bay to the Hurunui River mouth, with a variety of vegetation and topography along the hillsides and shoreline. The section around the Bluff can only be negotiated about 2 hours either side of the low tide, so check tide tables when planning your walk. Alternative access can be gained to Port Robinson by a foot track further south on the Gore Bay Road when the tide is too high to pass the Bluff. Part of the walk passes through the Manuka Bay Scenic Reserve, which is a remnant of coastal forest. If you are planning to do the full walk, transport should be organised either end.

Access: To reach the northern end of the walk, turn off State Highway 1 at Cheviot, 85 kilometres north-east of Christchurch. It is about 8 kilometres down the Gore Bay Road. The Hurunui Mouth Road turns off State Highway 1 about 5 kilometres south-west of Cheviot.

From the start at Gore Bay the walkway heads south along the beach to the stratified rock outcrop called the Bluff and the boulder beach beyond. Just before the boat ramp the walk heads up to join the old road. This leads past the site of the port, which operated between the 1880s and 1907.

The track then proceeds around the headland, passing the lighthouse and an interesting area of 'badland' erosion, similar to the Cathedrals further north. A sweeping view down the coast of Manuka Bay and the limestone cliffs of Napenape can be seen once around the point. There is a picnic area at the road end at Manuka Bay (1½ hours from Gore Bay). Beyond here a track enters the dense vegetation as it heads up through the reserve to emerge on open paddocks.

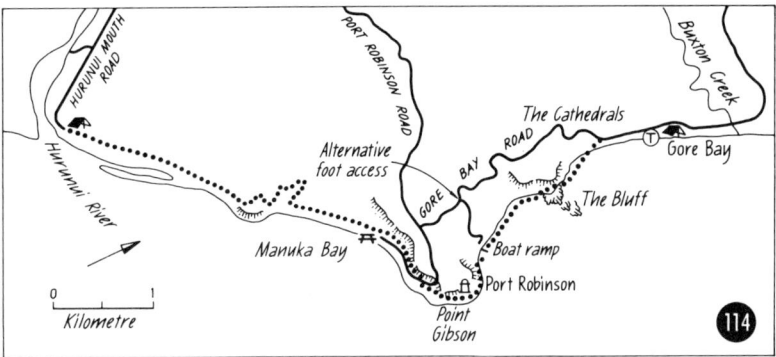

The walk continues across farmland and into scrub before entering another area of coastal forest. It follows the hillside and gullies, with attractive views of the coast, and finally ends by a grassed terrace above the Hurunui River mouth.

Napenape

Length: Various
Time taken: Up to 1½ hours
Grading: Easy
Apparel: Casual
Code: Year-round (except after heavy rain), trees, birds, plants, seals

Points of note: A remarkable enclave in the form of a semi-circular amphitheatre in limestone contains a residual patch of largely broadleaf native forest, with its own special plant species. The area is bounded on the south side by a spectacular cliff, and on the south-east by a steep rim wall of magnificent eroded buttresses, below some of which are rare limestone screes.

Access: Napenape is about 1½ hours' drive north from Christchurch, on the coast. Access is by an unsealed road on the right bank of the Blythe River (just south of the Hurunui River), reached either by Blythe Road, just south of the drop into the Great Valley, or from Cheviot.

The circular walk through the reserve takes about 45 minutes. You can carry on further south to a small seal colony, this round trip taking 1½ hours.

175

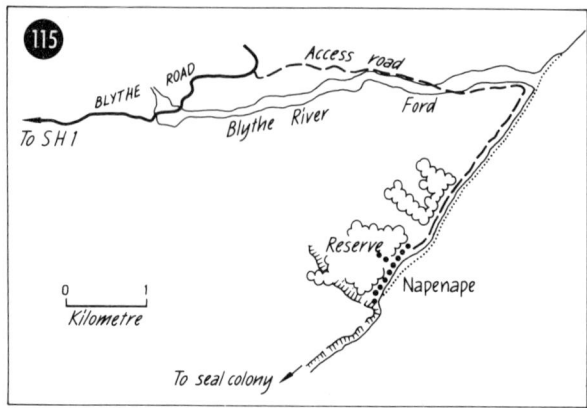

Mt Thomas Forest

Length: Various
Time taken: Up to 6 hours
Grading: Easy to moderate
Apparel: Good footwear and warm clothing if going to the top of Mt Thomas
Code: Year-round, trees, views, waterfalls, birds

Points of note: Mt Thomas Forest is close to Christchurch and makes an ideal destination for a day's outing, with picnic facilities, various bush walks and panoramic views from the summit of Mt Thomas, a moderate walk away. The forest covers an area of 10,800 hectares on the Canterbury foothills, between the Ashley and Okuku Rivers.

Access: Turn off State Highway 1, either passing through Rangiora and Loburn or Oxford and the Ashley Gorge. The forest is about 31 kilometres from Rangiora and 23 kilometres from Oxford. There are two points of access that turn off from the Oxford–Loburn Road. The Glentui picnic area is reached via Glentui Bush Road, and the Wooded Gully picnic and camping area is reached on Hayland Road.

Wooded Gully Track (2–3 hours): A track leads up through mountain beech forest to the saddle west of the Mt Thomas summit. From here it is possible to continue to the open summit at 1,023 metres, and descend via the south-west face of the mountain through privately owned pine forest, back to the start (Track 1), or to return down the forested ridge west of the Wooded Gully (Track 2). Both these tracks take about 2–3 hours.

176

Loop 1 (1 hour): The track starts a short distance up on the west side of the Wooded Gully Track.

Loop 2 (2 hours): This loop, which is steep in places, branches off the Wooded Gully Track a little further up on the right and crosses to join Track 1.

Red Pine Track (1½ hours): Starting at the Wooded Gully picnic area, this climbs through mountain beech forest, with scattered podocarps, including rimu (red pine), to meet the Wooded Gully Track.

Glentui Loop Track (1–2 hours return): The track descends from the picnic area to the Glentui River and then climbs a ridge on the other side. It passes the Bypass Track, which leads off to the right, and joins the Richardson Track to return to the start.

Glentui Waterfall Track (20 minutes return): This easy walk starts at the picnic area and is suitable for family groups.

Richardson Track (3–4 hours one way): This track was once an old stock route. It starts at the Glentui picnic area, is moderate to steep and climbs through mountain beech forest to open tussock and dracophyllum scrub on the summit of Mt Richardson (1,047 metres). Either return the same way or

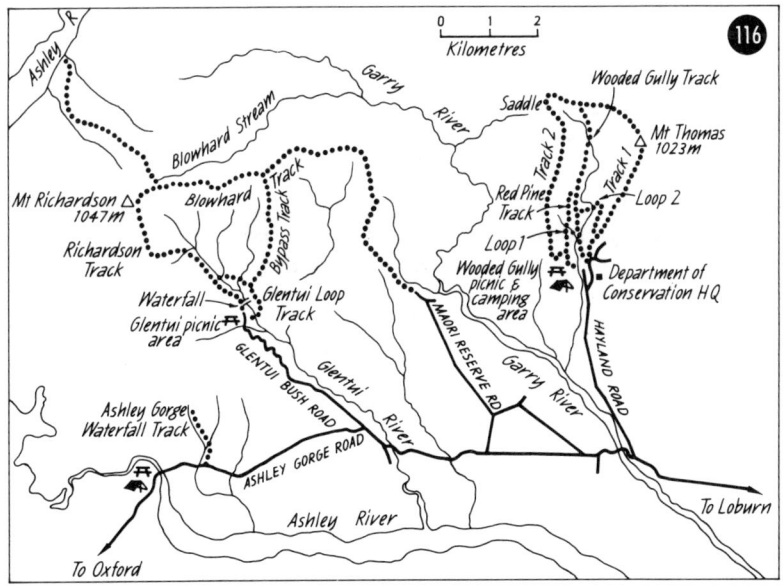

make a round trip via the Blowhard Track and the Bypass Track (about 7 hours round trip, suitable for fit trampers).

Bypass Track (1–2 hours one way): Branches off the Blowhard Track about halfway along and heads down to join the Glentui Loop Track.

Blowhard Track (5–6 hours): This track was also a stock route. It starts at the end of Maori Reserve Road near the Boys Brigade camp and continues to the Lees Valley. It takes 3–4 hours to reach the summit of Mt Richardson, passing through forest along the ridge and heading out onto the open top near the summit.

Ashley Gorge Waterfall Track (1 hour to the waterfall): This track starts 1 kilometre east of the Ashley Gorge bridge on the road between Oxford and Loburn. A moderate track leads up through beech forest, with some emergent podocarps, to the head of the gully and the 12-metre waterfall, amid an area of fuchsia trees.

Crater Rim Walkway

Length: Various
Time taken: Up to 7 hours
Grading: Easy to moderate
Apparel: Good footwear and warm clothing
Code: Interesting volcanic rock formations, views, plants, history

Points of note: The Port Hills form part of the rim of an ancient volcano that became active about 12 million years ago and reached a height of more than 1,500 metres above sea level. Erosion and changing sea levels have led to the drowning of the crater, or caldera, to form Lyttelton Harbour. The hills rise abruptly from the plains of Christchurch, and consequently are exposed in bad weather and prone to changeable conditions. Walkers are advised to carry drinking water if planning to walk the full length.

Access: The walkway runs along the Port Hills of Christchurch, adjacent to Dyers Pass Road and the Summit Road. There are a number of side tracks that join the walkway, one of which starts from the Sign of the Takahe, on the Dyers Pass Road. Christchurch city buses run from the Square to the Sign of the Takahe.

Sign of the Takahe to Sign of the Kiwi (1 hour): The track starts south-east of the Sign of the Takahe above Dyers Pass Road and follows the H. G. Ell Track, named after the major force behind the creation of the Summit Road. It skirts three reserves (Elizabeth, Victoria and Thomson Parks), and passes through open tussock land and areas of native and exotic trees to join the Summit Road just above its intersection with Dyers Pass Road and the Sign of the Kiwi. The Crater Rim Walkway heads east from here to the Bridle Path and west to Coopers Knob.

Sign of the Kiwi to Bridle Path (3 hours): Two tracks lead east from the stile opposite the Sign of the Kiwi and cross the Sugar Loaf Scenic Reserve. Mitchells Track takes the lower route, passing through some of the best native forest of the walkway, with mahoe, broadleaf, tarata, lancewood and coprosma. Gilpins Track heads up through open tussock and around the summit of Sugar Loaf with its 120-metre television mast. Both tracks rejoin after a little over 500 metres, making a good round trip of about 30 minutes (then back to the Sign of the Kiwi for refreshments). The walkway continues across pasture to the Scott Recreation Reserve, then zigzags around the slopes of Mt Vernon to the Witch Hill Scenic Reserve. Here it skirts the rocky knob of Witch Hill, flanked by a bluff popular with climbers, and heads on through private land to the Tors Scenic Reserve. The Tors and Castle Rock, across the road, are both volcanic dykes with well-developed columnar jointing, making them popular with climbers. The track climbs steeply to the trig of the Tors. A native scrub present on these slopes, *Hebe lavaudiana*, is found only on Banks Peninsula. From the trig the track descends to the Bridle Path, which was built in 1850 to provide a route from Lyttelton to the Heathcote Valley.

Motu-Kauati-Rahi Walkway (1 hour): The Motu-Kauati-Rahi Walkway joins the Crater Rim Track with Cass Bay, via an open ridge with views of the harbour. It is signposted at either end, takes about an hour, and is suitable for anyone of reasonable fitness. The track crosses private land and may be subject to closure for lambing or in periods of high fire risk. A round trip can be made via the Crater Rim Walkway, Bridle Path and the Lyttelton–Cass Bay foreshore walk.

Sign of the Kiwi to Coopers Knob (3 hours): The track begins by the Sign of the Kiwi and heads through private land. It crosses the road and continues for a short distance on that side before recrossing to enter the Hoon Hay Park Scenic Reserve. Here the track moves up the hill for a while, through grassland and bracken, and gives a good view of the Canterbury Plains. Returning to the road, it passes the Kennedys Bush Scenic Reserve then skirts around the side of Mt Ada. A more interesting track heads around the harbour side through private land and passes through bush of mahoe, fuchsia, lancewood and ferns. The two tracks rejoin near the Sign of the Bellbird. From here the track heads to Cass Peak, with its impressive red cliff, and the nearby scenic reserve, which contains the only remnant of montane forest left on the Port Hills. The ridge trends south from here to the highest point at Coopers Knob (573 metres).

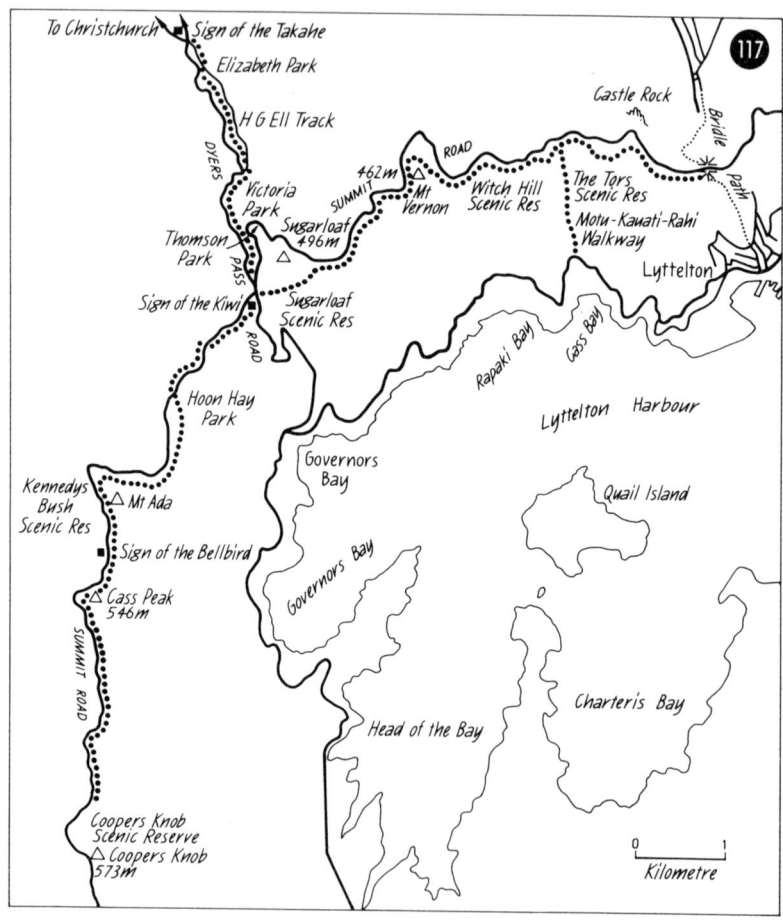

Otepatotu Reserve

Length: 2 kilometres
Time taken: 1 hour
Grading: Easy to moderate
Apparel: Casual; good footwear
Code: Year-round (track may be wet in winter), trees, plants, birds, views

Points of note: Banks Peninsula is a wide promontory, deeply indented with inlets and bays and backed by steep cliffs rising to high ground inland. Before European occupation much of the peninsula was forested, but now only small bush patches remain, mainly in reserves. One of the better remnants, mainly totara, is Otepatotu Reserve, where there is a parking area, picnic tables and a well-marked track leading up a rocky spur to Lavericks Peak.

Access: The reserve is 87 kilometres from Christchurch. Take the Akaroa Road until you reach the Hilltop Hotel. Turn left along the Summit Road to the Eastern Bays and proceed for 19 kilometres. The road winds around the steep hillsides, with fine views of Akaroa Harbour on the right, and Pigeon Bay, Little Akaloa Bay and Okains Bay on the left. The Otepatotu Reserve is signposted.

Lavericks Peak Track starts from just above the parking and picnic area, and ascends through forest that is predominantly five-finger, fuchsia, horopito and fern. A short detour to the left leads to a basalt outcrop, affording a panoramic view of Akaroa Harbour.

Return to the track and continue climbing toward the peak. Here you can find hebes, including *H. salicifolia,* and there is more forest containing a few broadleaf, marbleleaf and totara, with epiphytes, hen and chicken fern and mosses. The understorey, badly damaged in the past through grazing, is regenerating well. Pate is in evidence, and near the peak there is an abundance of hanging mosses. The song of the grey warbler can be heard, and tomtits often appear. The peak offers inspiring views of the peninsula's bays, farmed valleys and volcanic high points.

On the descent you will notice that the trees are stunted and bent by the south-westerly gales that lash the peninsula in winter. Re-enter the forest and proceed downhill for 10 minutes until the main path (an old cattle track) is reached. Turn left and follow the fenceline. Ahead are stumps of ancient totara, testifying to the size some of these majestic trees attained before being felled. Below are Okains and Lavericks Bays. Head toward the larger bay, Okains, climb a fence and proceed through an area of tree stumps until you

181

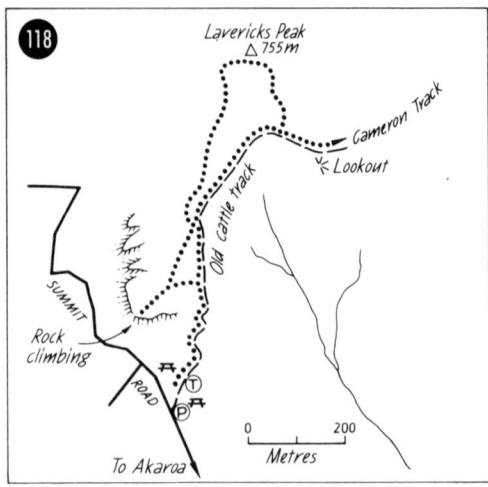

reach the next fence. Then turn right and follow the fenceline. Go through a gate and continue along the same fenceline until you see a track on the left, about 400 metres away. Head for this and turn right on to Cameron Track.

Follow this as far as time permits; views of the bays are spectacular from here. Make your way back to the reserve and proceed down the cattle track through the forest. You can see the mountain tree-fern *Cyathea colensoi* and tiny filmy ferns, and a search may find a libertia, a plant of the iris family, as well as fern epiphytes. There are fantails here and, if you are lucky, a rifleman or two.

Hinewai Reserve

Length: Various
Time taken: 2–4 hours
Grading: Moderate (some climbing)
Apparel: Good footwear
Code: Year-round (track can be slippery in places, in winter there may be snow but this does not stay long on the ground), trees, plants, birds, geckos, waterfalls, views

Points of note: Hinewai Reserve (109 hectares) is the focus of a major regeneration project, undertaken by a private trust and managed by Hugh Wilson, a botanist of some renown. The project is being scientifically monitored and depends on voluntary labour, so donations towards continuing this work are welcome. Prior notice of a visit to the reserve would be appreciated. Contact: Hugh Wilson, Eastern Bays, RD 3 Akaroa, Ph: (03) 304 8501 or Christchurch (03) 797 433.

Access: Hinewai is 91 kilometres from Christchurch on Banks Peninsula, via the Summit Road from Hilltop. Turn off onto Long Bay Road to the carpark a few hundred metres down on the right.

The reserve is in the head of a valley on the outer flank of the extinct Akaroa Volcano. The land is quite steep, with several permanent streams and over twenty waterfalls, and affords a spectacular view down to Otanerito Bay and the ocean beyond. The four-day Banks Peninsula Track runs through the southern area of the reserve. The most popular walk is a loop that takes in Fuchsia Falls, a big totara (about 600 years old) and the ridge of red beech on the West Track. These mature trees are extremely rare elsewhere on Banks Peninsula. From the West Track, either head down Knoll Flat Track or Pokaka Track through Toi Clearing, along South Track briefly and back up the Big Kanuka Track and return to the start. The round trip takes about 2 hours.

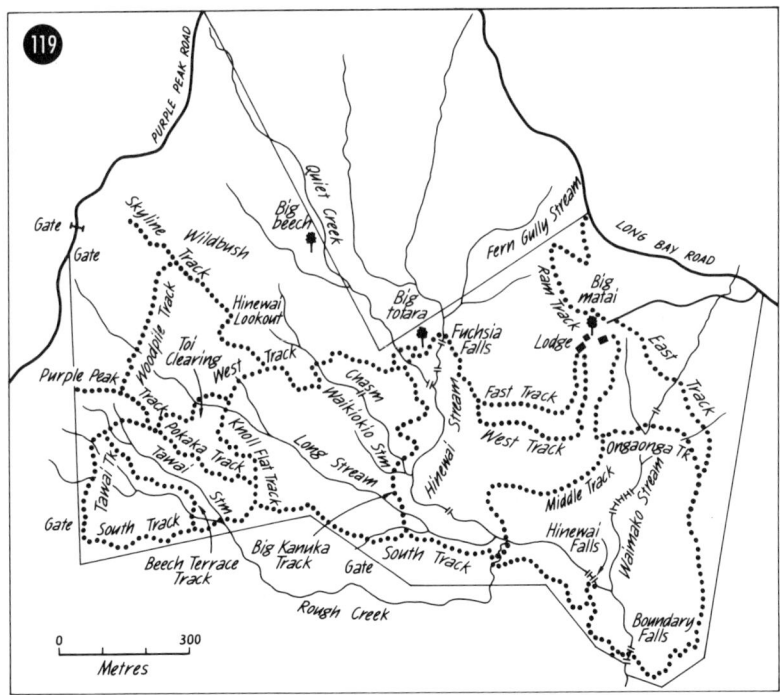

Awa Awa Rata Reserve

Length: 4 kilometres
Time taken: 1¾ hours
Grading: Average, some steep sections
Apparel: Good footwear, parka or jacket
Code: Year-round, trees, flowers, birds, views

Points of note: This bush walk from an attractive picnic spot is not recommended during or after heavy rain. The Awa Awa Rata Reserve has fireplaces, barbecues, toilets and shelter. It has extensive plantings of rhododendrons and a 10–15 minute walk through native bush.

Access: The reserve is about 26 kilometres from Methven. Turn left north of the town off State Highway 77 along Waimarama Road, across Highway 72 and then along McLennans Bush Road past the turn-off to the Mt Hutt skifield.

This loop track is clearly signposted. Take the right-hand track, which leads immediately into fuchsia, five-finger, broadleaf, putaputaweta, makomako and hoheria. Deer and opossum have been almost eliminated from this area, and the regeneration is most noticeable and heartening.

The track becomes fairly steep and ferns dominate the scene; the umbrella species is very attractive. As you ascend, lancewoods are more frequent and about three-quarters of the way to the top of the ridge there is a

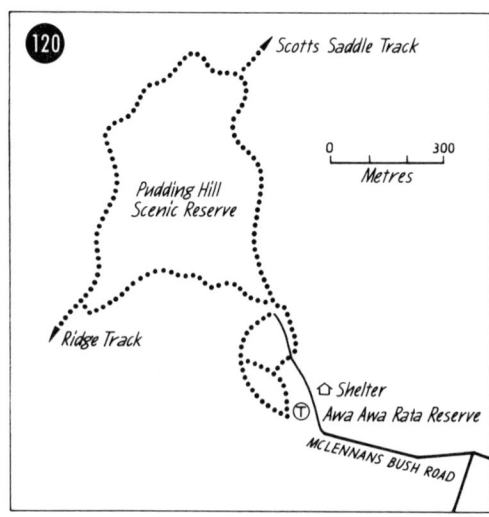

mature specimen of the 'ferocious' lancewood (*Pseudopanax ferox*).

After nearly an hour you reach the top of the ridge, where a track leads off to the right, taking the more hardy climber over to Scotts Saddle through alpine rocks and vegetation to the Mt Hutt skifield access road – a 2-hour journey.

The loop track continues to the left. The deep moss covering the forest floor has a scattering of orchids, of which there are five varieties here. There is a welcome seat for a rest at this point. On the right-hand (northern) slope of the track there are many beech seedlings, while on a slight southern slope ferns again crowd the way. There are glimpses of the north branch of the Ashburton River well below.

Soon you enter a larch plantation, which gives way to native bush as you descend. There are attractive views of the picnic area and the plains beyond. In season, the flowers of clematis, bush lawyer and a few rata brighten the prevailing green, and the koromiko are splendid. Dense sedge with its hooked seeds can be a nuisance on the track in late summer.

Apart from bellbirds, the bird life is not prolific, but wood pigeons, grey warblers, tomtits and fantails may be seen, as well as finches and larks in the open.

Snow and wind damage to the beech is visible from the picnic area. At one time rata were profuse here, but the early settlers of the area found the wood made excellent fuel for their fires and stoves.

Sharplin Falls Scenic Reserve

Length: 3 kilometres
Time taken: 1½ hours
Grading: Average to steep
Apparel: Good footwear
Code: Year-round, trees, birds, waterfalls

Points of note: A well-signposted walk through delightful bush with many birds. It is not, however, recommended immediately after heavy rain. Sharplin Falls is the finishing point for the Mt Somers Subalpine Walkway. There is a parking area, with water available, and toilets.

Access: Turn west off State Highway 72 at Staveley, north of Mt Somers township. Across the bridge turn right into Flynns Road and drive 3 kilometres to a carpark.

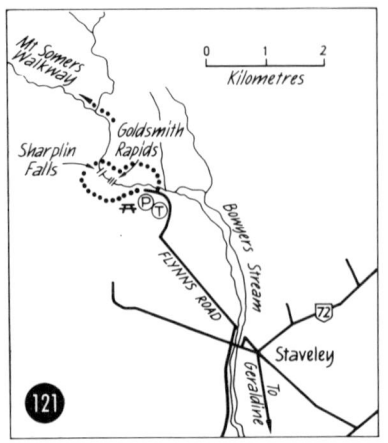

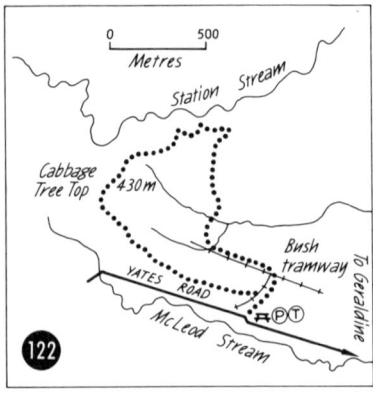

Many people are satisfied with just the area around the carpark, where open mountain beech forest reveals the tumbling Bowyers Stream, with its many-coloured rocks, and an unspoiled bush-covered hill across the water. A chorus of bellbirds is almost a certainty here.

In the bush there is an interesting combination of mainly mountain beech and rata. Also found here are some black beech. From the sooty fungus on their trunks honey dew, excreted by a scale insect feeding on the sap under the bark, can be extracted.

The bush also contains some totara, matai and kahikatea, with broadleaf (papauma) common and sometimes quite large. Marbleleaf (putaputaweta), notable for its masses of small white flowers in January, is also common, and there is lancewood, five-finger, wineberry and pate. Numerous ferns and rice grass grow in the area, and very striking near the stream is kahaha, a bush lily that produces a spike of reddish orange berries.

For the walk to the Goldsmith Rapids and Sharplin Falls, cross the swingbridge and follow a reasonably good track through handsome banks of ferns. After a stiff pull to the ridge, where the rata is at its best, the track descends to the rapids, where the boulders are of enormous size and a variety of colours. The falls are a short distance beyond the rapids.

You can return by following the streambed, if the stream is not in flood. After about 200 metres a sign directs you back to the track. This area abounds in bellbirds, and their call may be heard all day long. They are also easily seen, as are fantails, tomtits and grey warblers. There are also thrushes and goldfinches.

Cattle, deer and possums were once rife in the area, but now the numbers are down and regeneration is taking place. Near the entrance to the carpark, on private land, is the Staveley skating rink, which operates in the winter months when the frosts are sufficient to freeze the ponds.

Orari Gorge Scenic Reserve

Length: 5.5 kilometres
Time taken: 2–2½ hours return
Grading: Moderate
Apparel: Casual
Code: Year-round, birds, trees, plants

Points of note: Established in 1911, the reserve contains 272 hectares of cut-over regenerating native bush, with fine examples of mature kanuka and the best kahikatea regeneration in Canterbury. A few surviving matai and totara are scattered throughout.

Access: The Orari Gorge is 16 kilometres north of Geraldine. Three kilometres from Geraldine along State Highway 72, turn left into Tripp Settlement Road, and 7 kilometres further on turn left into Yates Road. The reserve is on the right opposite the Glenburn Youth Camp.

The track follows the line of an old bush tramway into a valley where you can see regenerating kahikatea and nursery kanuka. Soon the track begins to rise through areas containing broadleaf, konini, lemonwood, lancewood, mahoe and five-finger. Later it emerges on to a grassy knoll with prominent cabbage trees and views of bushy valleys. From there the track descends steadily to the picnic area.

Peel Forest Park

Length: Various
Time taken: Up to 6 hours
Grading: Easy to moderate
Apparel: Short walks, casual; longer, tramping gear
Code: Year-round, trees, flowers, birds

Points of note: Peel Forest is one of South Canterbury's most enjoyable areas of native bush. The entire area of 773 hectares is a forest park and scenic reserve, first established in 1909. The park is dominated by Little Mt Peel (1,311 metres). Much of the bush has been cut over, but the 16.2-hectare Mills Bush area, conserved by the visiting English MP Arthur Mills in 1884, remains untouched. The Rangitata River runs close by and excellent camping facilities are available.

Access: Peel Forest is 135 kilometres from Christchurch and 55 kilometres from Timaru. Access is via Hinds and Arundel when approaching from the north, and via Winchester and Geraldine from the south. The roads are clearly signposted. Near Arundel follow Coopers Creek Road and then Rangitata Gorge Road to the Peel Forest visitor centre, in the village, where pamphlets are available for further information.

Big Tree Walk: One of the easiest and most popular walks, this is of an easy grade suitable for all ages. Begin this track at the stone bridge near Te Wanahu or from two other entrances near the shelter in the picnic area. The track passes through Mills Bush, an area of virgin forest with fine examples of totara, matai and kahikatea. The track ends at a huge totara 9 metres in circumference and thought to be a thousand years old.

Other plant life includes lemonwood, wineberry, pokaka, five-finger, matipo, ribbonwood, mahoe, kowhai, konini, supplejack, clematis and parsonsia.

Aerobatic displays by native pigeons are a great feature of the area. Other bird life includes bellbirds, fantails, tomtits, riflemen, grey warblers and silvereyes.

Interpretation Walk: In the Clarke Flat area, this is of easy grade and takes under an hour return. Features are remnants of swamp forest and early sawpit sites. This walk can be entered by the picnic area adjoining the camp, the roadside at Te Wanahu Flat and from the lower part of Clarke Flat.

Acland Falls: Also of easy grade, this walk takes 45 minutes return. Beginning opposite the camp, the track leads off to the 14-metre-high waterfall. Access can also be gained off Allans Track (45 minutes one way).

Fern Walk: With an easy grade and taking 3 hours return, this walk begins at the stone bridge near Te Wanahu and continues through to Blandswood. There are sixty-eight different species of fern in the park.

Allans Track: Of moderate grade, the track on this 2–3-hour round trip climbs from Te Wanahu Flat, traverses the head of Mills Stream and joins the Deer Spur Track where it drops steeply to join the Fern Walk. A feature on this loop is the great range of botanical communities.

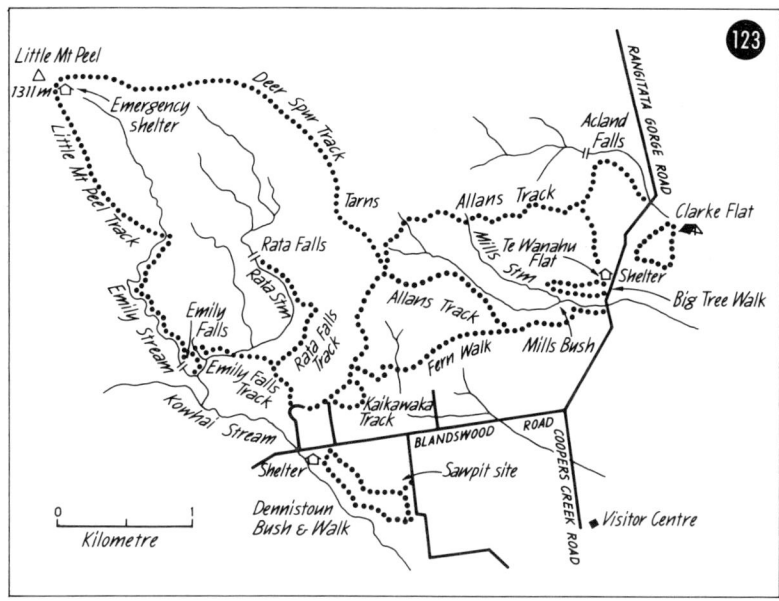

Dennistoun Bush: Providing a 1½-hour round trip, this well-formed, flat track with easy grade provides a real nature ramble. Remnant podocarps and an old sawpit site are special features.

Emily Falls: The return trip on this moderate grade track takes 1½ hours. It begins from the road to Blandswood Lookout and climbs up to the Rata Stream. It soon reaches a track junction; the falls are 5 minutes from this fork. The main track climbs above the falls and continues to Little Mt Peel.

Rata Falls: For this moderate grade track (2 hours return), begin on the same track as Emily Falls, but branch off to the right. The waterfall has recently been destroyed by collapsing rocks. There is a fine display of flowering rata from December to early January.

Kaikawaka Track: Beginning close to the Blandswood Lookout, this track is of easy grade and the round trip takes 20 minutes. Notice the mountain cedar, *Librocedrus bidwilii*, after which this track is named.

189

124

Opihi River Walkway

Length: 13 kilometres
Time taken: 5–6 hours
Grading: Moderate to strenuous
Apparel: Tramping gear
Code: Year-round (although there may be some snow in winter), views, swimming, fishing, geology

Points of note: The Opihi Gorge is prone to flooding and should be avoided after or when heavy rain is likely. The Department of Conservation grade this walkway as a route, suitable for experienced and fit walkers.

Access: The northern entrance starts at the end of Opihi Gorge Road, 4 kilometres from Fairlie. The southern entrance is at the Rockwood Bridge, reached either on the Rockwood Road, which turns off State Highway 8 south of Fairlie, or from Pleasant Point via Raincliff and Spur Roads.

From the Fairlie end, the track follows the true right bank of the Opihi River for about 1 kilometre before crossing a bridge to the left of the gorge. It then climbs through forest, crosses two stable screes and sidles to a spur well above the river. The spur offers a good view of the steep-sided gorge before the route

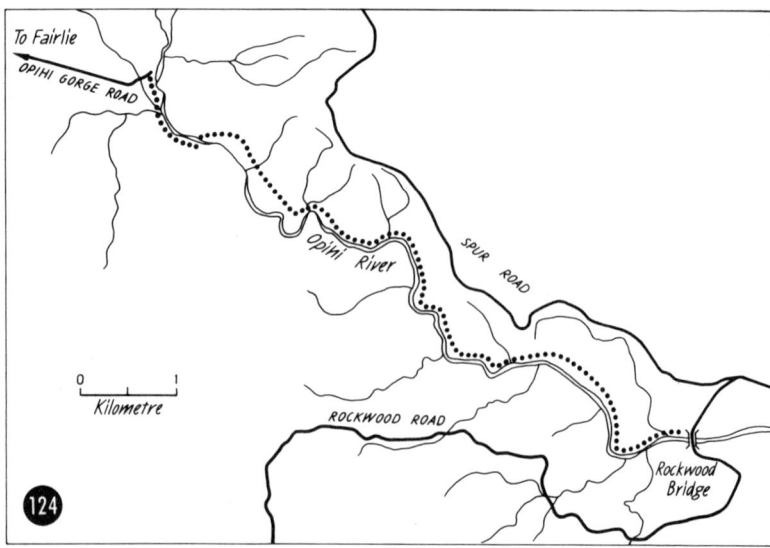

descends through the forest back to the water. It stays close to the river for the next 3 hours or so, following rapids and enticing pools. Finally it climbs to avoid a bluff and remains high for a couple of kilometres, until the gorge widens to grassy flats. The Rockwood Bridge is about 1 kilometre downstream.

The forest is a broadleaf-hardwood association, mainly of secondary growth following past fires in the area, and the canopy consists of mahoe, broadleaf and fuchsia with some matai and totara. Various shrubs and the tree daisy *Olearia fragrantissima* are also present, with a number of ferns. Watch out for ongaonga, the stinging tree-nettle.

Pioneer Park

Length: Various
Time taken: Up to 2 hours
Grading: Easy to moderate
Apparel: Casual
Code: Year-round, birds, trees, plants

Points of note: One of the most interesting preserved forests in South Canterbury, Pioneer Park was presented to the nation by Major P. H. Johnson of Raincliff Station in 1940. The area is a memorial to the pioneers, and the remains of a slab hut built by Michael John Burke, who took up the Raincliff run in 1840, have been preserved for their historical interest. Burke Pass in the Mackenzie Country is named after him.

Access: The park is 24 kilometres from Pleasant Point, via Raincliff Road and then Middle Valley Road. The attractive boulder gateway is 8 kilometres from Raincliff Bridge.

Track 1 (30 minutes): Beginning near the remains of Burke Hut, this rises steadily, passing groups of tall kahikatea and occasional big matai trees. From the track you can see mountain beech, introduced from the Arthur's Pass area, and two extremely large totara. The slope becomes more gradual near the top, and you descend through many juvenile totara and kahikatea to the Loder Stream picnic area. This area and the roadsides have been planted with many deciduous exotics, including large aspen poplars, mountain ash, maples and oaks, which are a blaze of colour in autumn.

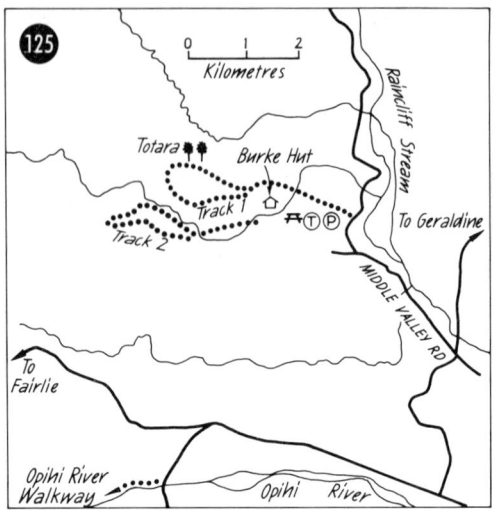

Track 2 (2 hours): This loop begins at a stile on the far side of the picnic area. The outer fringe of bush contains much manuka and kanuka, which act as nursery trees to regenerating native seedlings and saplings. The right fork of the track follows the stream, passing good examples of kowhai, matai, kahikatea, totara and smaller trees. It then turns back along short sections of vehicle track before descending along a bush-covered ridge to the picnic area.

Native birds abound in the bush and include pigeons, riflemen, grey warblers, tomtits and bellbirds.

Mt Nimrod Scenic Reserve

Length: 8.5 kilometres
Time taken: 3–4 hours return
Grading: Moderate to steep
Apparel: Good footwear
Code: Year-round, trees, plants, birds, waterfall, panoramas

Points of note: The reserve, classified in 1898, is at the base of Mt Nimrod (1,500 metres). There are many interesting streams and gorges in the area, and a spectacular waterfall on the Nimrod Stream emerges through a natural arch. Wallabies inhabit this area of the Hunters Hills.

Access: The reserve is 20 kilometres south-west of Timaru, from Cave. Follow Cannington Road and then Back Line Road for 10 kilometres to Mt Nimrod Station. Enter the station road and take the right fork, which follows the stream across paddocks to the picnic area.

There are three short easy walks in the vicinity of the picnic area, but the main circular track has some steeper sections and requires fitness and suitable footwear. This track begins at the footbridge near the picnic area and passes through bush thick with mosses and vines. It soon zigzags uphill through lemonwood, mahoe and fuchsia to a small saddle. From here there are good views of the bush and valleys. The track then sidles through gullies on the bushline before dropping down through tussock and dracophyllum to a ford in the Nimrod Stream. From here a short scramble up the streambed soon brings a waterfall into view.

The track zigzags very steeply out of the streambed. Care is needed and trampers should sight the marker pegs. The high point, some 300 metres above the picnic area, offers panoramic views of Mt Nimrod, the White Rock River Valley, Mt Studholme and the Hunters Hills. From here the track descends steeply through broadleaf and mahoe forest to the valley floor.

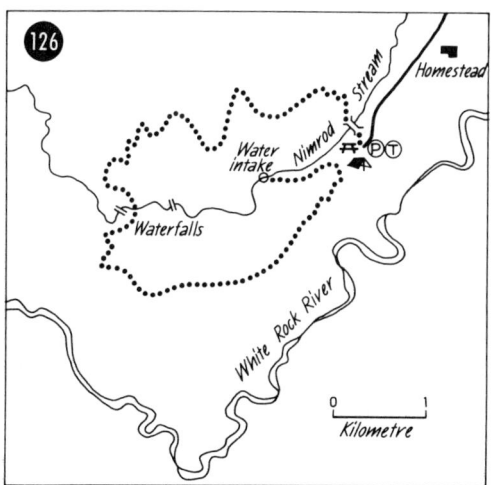

OTAGO

Herbert Forest

Length: Various
Time taken: Up to 6 hours
Grading: Easy to average
Apparel: Short walks, casual; longer, some tramping gear
Code: Year-round (except during fire risk), trees, birds, plants, waterfalls, caves

Points of note: There are three tracks in Herbert Forest, all of easy to average grading, mainly through gullies that escaped earlier milling, conversion to farmland and later planting of the then-gorse-infested grazing lands with *Pinus radiata* plus small stands of oregon, Corsican pine and larch. There are attractive grassed picnic areas, with shelter and barbecues, near the forest headquarters and at Glencoe, with swimming available in the Waianakarua River only a short stroll away.

Access: Herbert Forest is 25 kilometres south-west of Oamaru and 90 kilometres north of Dunedin. The forest headquarters is about 2 kilometres from State Highway 1, the turn-off being just north of the Waianakarua Bridge and south of Herbert township.

Cars can be taken to both ends of the Podocarp Track – Queens Road and Diamond Hill Road – from forest headquarters, and there is parking at both entrances.

An all-day forest walk takes in the three main tracks (Swallows Walk, Podocarp Track and Hoods Creek Track). The Podocarp Track is described here. Access to, and the layout of, the tracks can be checked on a map in a display case outside the forest headquarters. The track takes about an hour from Queens Road and a little less back via the Glenburnie Loop.

From the carpark the track is well formed, as it is most of the way, and after 5 minutes' walk through oregon plantation, you reach the native forest. There is a good mixture of podocarps all along the track, with rimu and totara especially plentiful. On the valley floor there are ribbonwoods and some exceptionally large pokaka, with ferns and moss-trails from tree and shrub

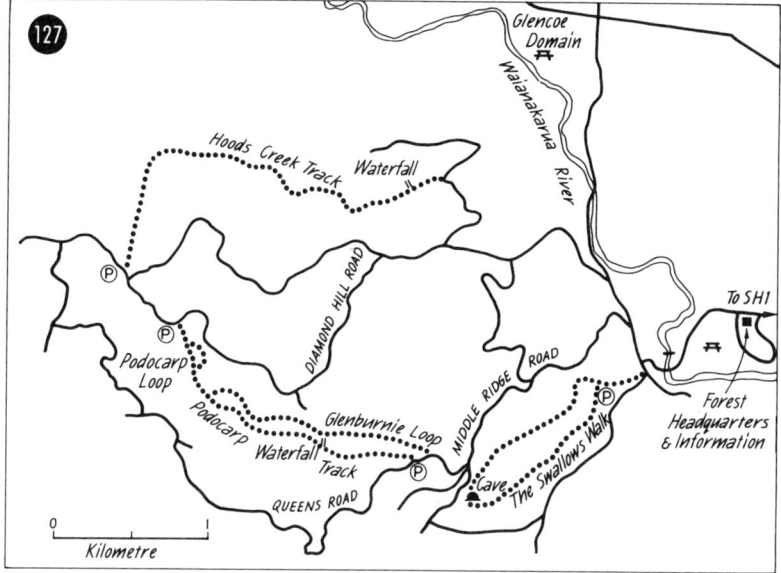

branches. Broadleaf and lemonwood are plentiful. Rimu, totara and miro are regenerating. Bellbirds and fantails are among the birds to be seen.

About 25 minutes from the start, the track climbs (just past a small waterfall) to the left through silver tree-ferns. Forty-five minutes from the start, the track branches. The left branch continues on as Podocarp Track to Diamond Hill Road. The right branch is the Glenburnie Loop, which returns you to the road about 100 metres away from the carpark on Queens Road. For those who only want a short bush walk, the Podocarp Loop takes about 30 minutes return from Diamond Hill Road.

The Forest Walk (6 hours) is the combined walk from the carpark at the bottom of Swallows to the end of Hoods Creek Track, with transport required at each end of the walk. At the time of writing, the Hoods Creek Track was closed but it was planned to reopen this in 1992.

Trotters Gorge Scenic Reserve

Length: 1.5–2 kilometres
Time taken: 30 minutes

Grading: Easy to average
Apparel: Good footwear
Code: Year-round, trees, birds, plants

Points of note: Trotters Gorge is a beautiful scenic reserve and picnic area with spectacular cliffs and bluffs of greywacke and breccia.

Access: You reach the reserve by turning off State Highway 1 about 8 kilometres south of Hampden on to Horse Range Road. When coming from the south, take Horse Range Road at the northern exit from Palmerston.

The picnic area is beyond the cattle stop and is reached either by crossing the ford or walking along the track that leads off to the right just before reaching the ford. From this track a footbridge crosses Trotters Creek into the picnic area. The track continues beside the creek and through a natural tunnel to join up with a stock-access route. It meanders up the gorge, crossing and recrossing the sheltered creekbed (usually ankle-deep) of the main branch of Trotters Creek. It is 1.5 kilometres to a hut, owned by the University of Otago, but a track goes on up the valley.

A short track up the south-west branch commences on the west branch of Trotters Creek (without crossing it) at the far end of the picnic area and leads up the side stream to several overhangs inhabited by cave wetas.

Kanuka is the dominant tree in the reserve. Kowhai grows near the creek and up the slopes. Mahoe is common, as are marbleleaf, broadleaf, *Fuchsia excorticata*, wineberry, lemonwood and kohuhu. At least eight species of coprosma are present. *Celmisia hookeri*, one of the largest and most handsome of New Zealand's mountain daisies, is found only in north-east Otago around

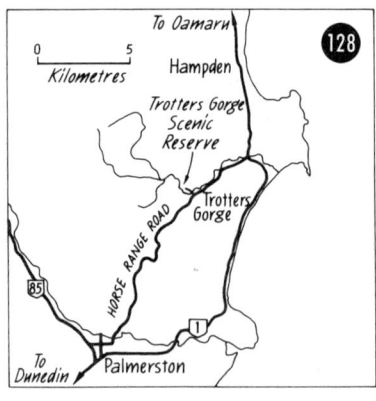

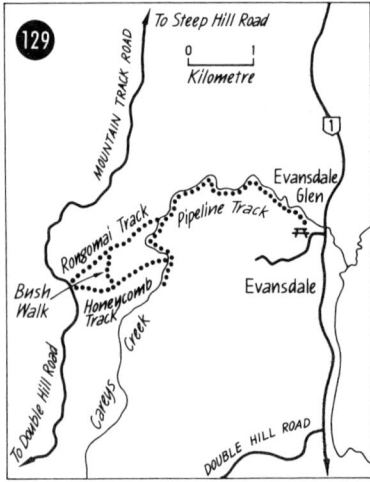

the Horse Range and is common on ledges and crevices of the rock faces of the gorge, particularly the shady areas beyond the hut and reserve boundary sign.

There is an interesting variety of both native and introduced birds in the reserve, including bellbirds and South Island tomtits and fantails.

Silver Peaks Forest

Length: Various
Time taken: Up to 3½ hours
Grading: Easy to moderate
Apparel: Casual; good footwear
Code: Year-round (except during fire risk), trees, birds, flowers, plants, waterfall

Points of note: Three tracks in this forest are linked and can form one walk. The start is from a well-sheltered picnic ground. Careys Creek is suitable for paddling, with a few swimming holes. The main track follows the stream toward its source through bush-clad slopes, mainly under a manuka canopy.

Access: From Evansdale township, 20 kilometres north from Dunedin on State Highway 1, go 200 metres north along the highway and turn left at the signpost 'Evansdale Glen'. About 200 metres down the side road there is a small parking area before a ford, which can be crossed in most weather, taking cars to the perimeter of the picnic ground from which the track system starts.

Pipeline Track: The main track leading upstream, this takes about 3½ hours from the lower end and about 2½ hours from the top. The first crossing of the stream at the picnic ground has a footbridge, but there are at least seven other fordings, which become progressively drier higher up the stream.

Rongomai Track: This starts 35 minutes up the Pipeline Track and leads up a steep, bushy ridge between Careys Creek and Whaitiripaka Stream, 5 minutes up which is a waterfall. After following the track for 45 minutes through bush and scrub, there are views of the valleys of Careys Creek and its tributaries, all bush-clad with occasional rock outcrops and bluffs. The bush in the valleys is mainly manuka with areas of more leafy evergreens like broadleaf, lemonwood and kowhai. Three-quarters of the way up, the track is joined by the Bush Walk. The last stage leads to Mountain Track Road.

Honeycomb Track: This turns off to the right from the Pipeline Track 20 minutes beyond the junction with the Whaitiripaka Stream, after passing through an area in which fern is abundant. It climbs steeply and steps are cut in parts. About 45 minutes from the start, you reach the junction of the Bush Walk. Honeycomb Track climbs up on the ridge again, with well-cut steps, and reaches Mountain Track Road about an hour from the bottom.

Bush Walk: Skirting the ridges rather than climbing, this is very well formed, with wired log bridges. The bush contains more variety, including a pepper tree, tree-ferns and young black pine.

Organ Pipes Track

Length: Mt Cargill summit return, 5 kilometres; Organ Pipes return, 2 kilometres
Time taken: Mt Cargill summit return, 1½ hours; Organ Pipes return, 1 hour
Grading: Easy to average
Apparel: Good footwear, parka
Code: Year-round (except in extreme winter weather or heavy fog), rock formations, trees, plants, birds

Points of note: The main point of interest is the rock formation near one end of the track. Volcanic in origin, the rocks look like huge 'pipes', fused together. They are in the open with a large area of debris lying at the base of a high battlement of rock.

Access: The track can be reached from the Mt Cargill end (Cowan Road) of the Bethunes Gully–Mt Cargill Walk. After leaving the carpark near the television transmitter, walk along the A. H. Reed Track (left off the roadway). Branch off to the left before reaching the trig station and follow the Bethunes Walk to a point on a saddle between the high point of Mt Cargill and the next highest point, Buttars Peak. Turn left here on to the Organ Pipes Track.

There is also access from the Mt Cargill Road, which leads up the hill from the suburb of Normanby, skirting Mt Cargill until you reach the site of Mt Zion Quarry. Just beyond here is a carpark.

From the Mt Cargill end, after leaving the Bethunes Gully Walk, cross a small flat and, climbing again towards Buttars Peak, you will reach a fork in the track. The right branch is a loop track that takes in the peak and then rejoins the main track at the foot of a sharp ridge. There are excellent views from this peak of Dunedin City, the harbour and surrounding hills. To the north of the track is a fine area of podocarp forest with mountain cedar prominent.

The main track skirts Buttars Peak and then drops down to cross a swampy area. The vegetation varies from alpine scrub such as dracophyllum, cassinia and senecio to five-finger and kanuka with occasional celery pine, *Dacrydium biforme* and *Neopanax simplex*. There is a short steep climb after the boggy area. Follow a ridge to the Organ Pipes.

From the Mt Zion carpark on Mt Cargill Road, a flight of steps, followed by a short uphill climb, lead to the podocarp bush remnant. As you walk round the hill where the Organ Pipes are situated (Mt Holmes), you can see some of the fallen pipes on the side of the track, and there is a good view of the main outcrops to the left. The track soon turns to the left to reach a junction with the other access track near a viewing platform. From here you can see that the original outcrop must have been very massive when formed.

Birds seen on the walks include bellbirds, tui, fantails, tomtits and wood pigeons.

Pineapple Flagstaff Walk

Length: 5 kilometres
Time taken: 2 hours
Grading: Average
Apparel: Casual in lower reaches with strong shoes, but some tramping gear (parka, etc.) needed for climb over summit
Code: Year-round (although restricted in some winter months), plants, trees, birds

Points of note: Although originally called the Ross Track after a local settler, this

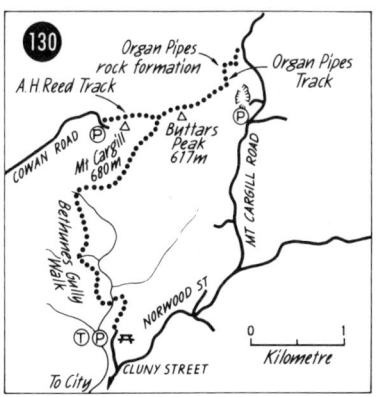

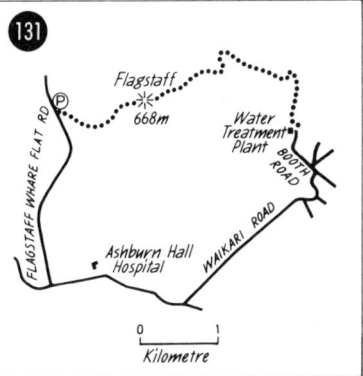

later became the Pineapple Track because of the 'signature' of an empty can of the fruit left by Otago Tramping Club parties in the 1920s. The track is now a walkway, deviating a little from the earlier route to provide more scenic attractions, including views of Dunedin and its surroundings and of inland plains and ranges.

Part of this track passes over open tussock country prone to quick weather changes and, although the track is well marked, care should therefore be taken.

Access: The two ends of the track can be reached by car via Taieri Road, Three Mile Hill Road and Flagstaff Whare Flat Road; or by Malvern Street, Fulton Road and Booth Road. Alternatively, you can take a bus to Ashburn Hall Hospital, walk up Three Mile Hill and Flagstaff Whare Hill (1½ hours) to the carpark at the end of the walk and, after walking the track, catch a Glenleith bus back to the city.

You are recommended to start from the carpark in Flagstaff Whare Flat Road. The track climbs gradually, levelling out in an area of mainly tussock, flax, hebe species, some wild spaniard, snowberry and a few subalpine species. You reach the highest point (668 metres), with its wide views, in about 30 minutes.

The track crosses a shallow gully, gradually ascends the second highest hill (from which Swampy Hill and the Silver Peaks area can be clearly seen) and shortly after takes a right turn and starts to descend more rapidly through scrub. (The left turn is the track to Swampy Hill.) The scrub gets taller (coprosmas, pepper trees, dracophyllum, cottonwood, fuchsia) and you enter the bush (totara, broadleaf, lemonwood, wineberry) until the track finally emerges at the Booth Road water-treatment plant. Follow the road through the pine plantations, but carry straight ahead when the road turns left. The track meets Booth Road again just above the Fulton Road junction, where there is room for parking.

Skylarks are seen in the higher areas, and pigeons, bellbirds, fantails, tomtits, tui and brown creepers frequent the bush.

Ross Creek

Length: 4.5 kilometres
Time taken: 1¾–2 hours
Grading: Easy to average
Apparel: Casual; good footwear
Code: Year-round, birds, trees, plants

Points of note: There is a notable stand of rimu in a section of this bush, reputed to be between 700 and 800 years old. One of Dunedin City's reservoirs is another feature of the walk. Ross Creek, which supplies the reservoir, is named after an early settler.

Access: The track can be reached from Dunedin's main street, George Street, where it crosses Duke Street. Turn left up Duke Street and pass Woodhaugh Gardens, when the street becomes Malvern Street. After 20 minutes' walk, turn left and cross a bridge to Rockside Road. Fifty metres past the bridge you will see the entrance to the track on the left. Access can also be gained from the corner of Tanner and Wakari Roads. A Glenleith bus will take you to either entrance.

Starting in Rockside Road, cross a small area of grass, walk through some exotics and second-growth native bush and proceed upstream with the stream on your left. The cliffs at right have glow-worms. Past School Creek Track, which branches off to the left, the path climbs up the valley with a canopy of mixed native trees and banks clothed in ferns.

A left turn takes the track over a bridge spanning a concrete spillway, and where it forks in a clearing, take the right fork up a steep climb up the dammed section of the reservoir. From another bridge over the spillway, there is a good view of mixed forest across the reservoir with Mt Flagstaff in the background. Turn left over the bridge, follow around the reservoir, keeping left, to Wakari Road. A short distance to the right along the road you will see the fine stand of rimu.

Back along the track about 30 metres, a track to the left passes through an area of tree-ferns and climbing rata, with the remains of an old stone stable and settler's cottage, and through the Craigieburn Native Plant Reserve to the corner of Tanner and Wakari Roads. If walking back the whole route, keep to the left-hand track back and above the dam before descending to Rockside Road.

School Creek

Length: 2 kilometres
Time taken: 1½ hours
Grading: Easy to average
Apparel: Casual; good footwear
Code: Year-round, trees, birds, plants

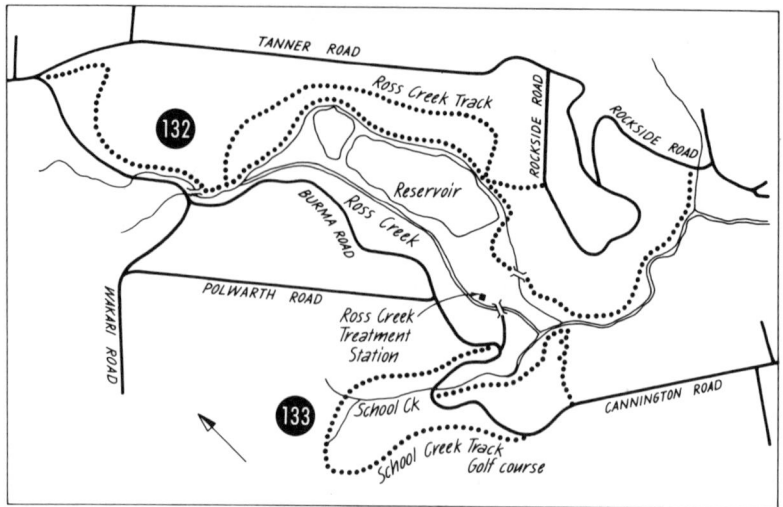

Points of note: A Dunedin track suitable for walkers at all levels of fitness, School Creek is handy to the city. Long popular, the track was formed about eighty years ago. Several local groups have given considerable financial assistance and many hours of labour to bring the track back to a good standard.

Access: Immediately past the last house in Cannington Road, opposite the Otago Golf Course, a cycle barrier marks the track entrance. Access may also be obtained from Burma Road at the Ross Creek treatment station end, and from the Ross Creek Track.

From Cannington Road the track follows a steep downhill zigzag through mixed native shrubs and small trees such as red matipo and mahoe beneath a manuka canopy. The track then follows School Creek upstream through ferns and flax-like astelia, past deep pools and cascades. The track emerges on to Burma Road; follow this across a bridge to the right for 200 metres, where the track recommences at a left bend in the road. The track passes through a wetter type of bush with greater variety to a clearing. Cross the footbridge and climb the steps, avoiding a track leading off to the left downstream. The track re-emerges on Burma Road.

Dunedin City No. 3 Walk

Length: 3 kilometres
Time taken: 1 hour
Grading: Easy
Apparel: Casual
Code: Year-round, trees, birds, plants

Points of note: A Dunedin City nature walk, this takes in a remnant of native bush within the inner-city area. A fine viewing point at Prospect Park offers a panorama of the northern part of the city, from Leith Valley across to Pinehill, Dalmore, North-East Valley, Opoho and the Botanic Gardens, with rolling grass- and bush-covered hills in the background, and the Woodhaugh Gardens in the foreground.

Access: The starting point is seven blocks along George Street from the Octagon, at the corner of Regent Road and George Street.

Walk up Regent Road until you reach Cosy Dell Road. Here the bush starts, noted in this part for ferns (*Asplenium* and *Blechnum* sp.) and astelia. After you turn right into Queens Drive, the bush consists of kanuka canopy, with marbleleaf, lemonwood, fuchsia and five-finger. Circle Prospect Park and, in approaching the viewing point, look out for two varieties of mistletoe growing in the bush.

Turn right into Cannington Road, and then right again into Stonelaw

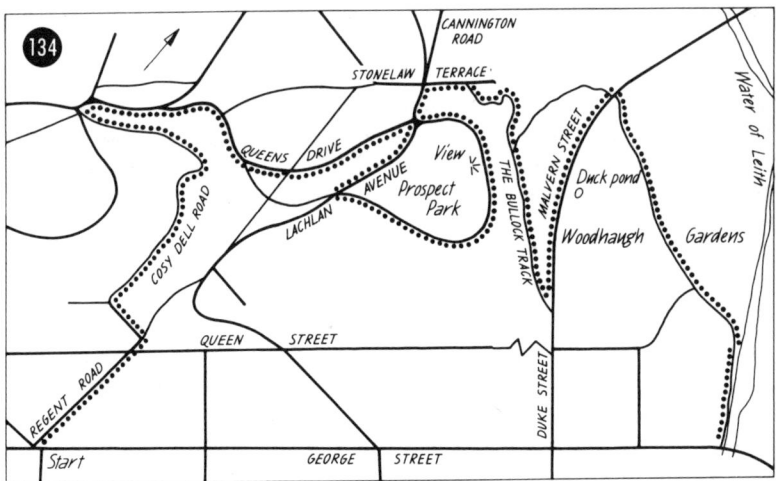

Terrace. The Bullock Track, a footpath, continues down from here to Duke Street, past kowhai, ngaio and whiteywood trees. The Bullock Track is so called because it was used in the early days to drive cattle from North-East Valley to the Burnside abattoir. Turn left from Duke Street past the duckpond in the Woodhaugh Gardens and, just before the end of the gardens, turn right, following either of the two walks through the bush. There are exotic trees on the outskirts of the remnant of native bush, and in the gardens ribbonwood, lacebark, totara, pokaka, rimu and other native trees can be seen. There are excellent picnic areas here. Birds in the area range from wood pigeons and bellbirds to fantails, finches and others.

The bush paths eventually lead back to George Street, where there is a regular bus service.

Lovers Leap and The Chasm

Length: Various
Time taken: Up to 1 hour return
Grading: Easy
Apparel: Casual
Code: Year-round, rock features, seabirds, coastal scenery

Points of note: This coastal walk offers two outstanding natural features, close together in a beautiful area. Keep children under firm control because of the steep cliffs. Colonies of native stinging nettles thrive near the carpark, and children especially should take care to avoid contact with these plants.

Access: The carpark from which the walk starts is 21 kilometres from Dunedin. Follow Andersons Bay Road, Musselburgh Rise, Silverton Street and then Highcliff Road to the Lanach's Castle turn-off, where you proceed straight ahead downhill. Turn second right into Sandymount Road and carry on straight ahead to the end of the road and the carpark.

The track starts through private property, so please keep to the path. It is well signposted and leads from an old farmyard straight ahead toward the cliffs through open farmland. After about 5 minutes' walk the track forks, with a sign posting to the left to The Chasm – the lookout can be seen from here – and to the right to Lovers Leap. From anywhere in this area there are excellent views of Allans Beach, Hoopers Inlet, the steep-sided Mt Charles and up and down the picturesque coast.

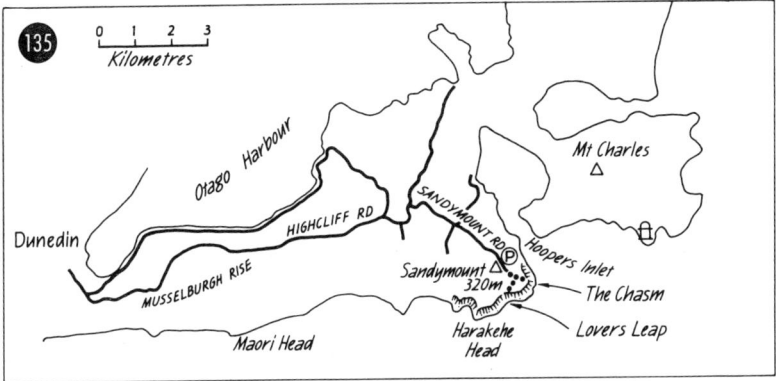

The Chasm is the nearer of the two features and can be reached in 10 minutes. The track to Lovers Leap is a little longer, following the cliff top. From the lookout there is a sheer drop of 180 metres to the rocks and sea, spanned by a natural bridge. You can see how the walls of the inlet were built up by successive layers of cindery ash (tuff) and basalt lava flows. One of these flows has cooled to form organ pipes, and a fissure has been eroded out by the sea, first as a cave and then, as the roof collapsed, to form the long inlet with the natural rock bridge.

Another track leads further on to a bush remnant and the summit of Sandymount. Some interesting native shrubs and trees can be seen clinging to the cliffs out of reach of browsing animals. Seabirds are the main bird life.

Waipori Gorge

Length: 8 kilometres
Time taken: 2½–3 hours
Grading: Average
Apparel: Good footwear, some tramping gear
Code: Year-round, trees, birds, plants

Points of note: The track leads for the most part through a scenic reserve under the control of the Dunedin City Council. As it was apparently a route to the Waipori goldfields, it must be at least a hundred years old. On a surveyed roadline most of the way, the track is usually 2–3 metres wide, rising on an easy even grade. The area is noted for its fishing and picnic spots (further up the valley), but the public are warned by notices to watch for a rise in the river caused by hydro-electric works upstream.

Access: On State Highway 1, travelling south 33 kilometres from Dunedin, turn right to Berwick 200 metres south of Henley Station. Berwick is reached after 6 kilometres. Turn right at the crossroads, and 100 metres later turn left to Waipori Falls township via Waipori Gorge. Just before entering the gorge you will see a sign describing the scenic reserve. About 300 metres past this the track begins.

The bush on the first part of the track is podocarp type, with totara and black pine plentiful and regenerating, and an association of ribbonwood and lacebark. Broadleaf is abundant, some trees of considerable size, together with kowhai. The main beech forest is not entered until almost an hour along the track. Clematis blooms in the spring (both the snow-white and greenish-cream varieties), as does bush lawyer. Ferns include the filmy fern and *Polystichium richardii*.

At about the 50-minute mark the track emerges into open scrub of coprosma and *Helichrysum glomeratum*, and shortly you reach an open grass slope with the track showing as a groove around the ridge. There is a good view here of the Waipori Valley, bush-clad on both sides with a tussock ridge on the south-west skyline, and the river winding through picnic spots.

The bush ahead is mainly silver or southern beech, the track leading into it with the same even rise. Some very large beech trees are seen. Just after 2 hours the track passes through lower manuka, and then into the open, joining a rough road. Anyone wishing to retrace the track should note carefully where the unmarked track enters the bush. The road leads downhill to the left to the Waipori Falls township (with the falls visible near the end in a deep ravine).

Birds you will see on a typical walk of the track are pigeons, brown creepers, fantails, tomtits, bellbirds and rosellas.

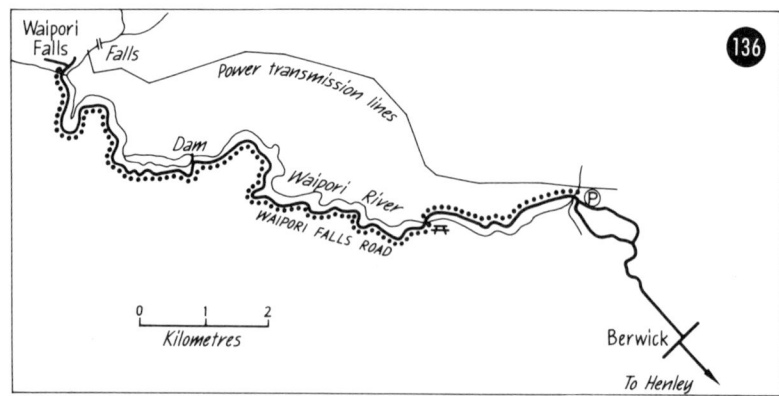

Akatore Bush

Length: Various
Time taken: Up to 1 hour
Grading: Easy to average
Apparel: Good footwear
Code: Year-round, trees, birds, plants

Points of note: Several bush walks through 95 hectares of forest, with a pleasant stream and bush clearings. This is the northern limit of podocarp-kamahi-rata forest association.

Access: Take the coast road south of Dunedin via Brighton and Taieri Mouth. The Otago Coast Forest Headquarters is at the southern end of the Taieri Mouth area.

To reach the walks, follow the coast road south from the forest headquarters, with farmland on the left and pine trees on the right. The turn-off into the forest is signposted and the road passes through pine plantations until you reach a delightful picnic area. Water and fireplaces are available.

The walks start opposite the picnic area and, on entering the trees, you have two choices. The left-hand Kamahi Track is timed for 30 minutes return, and the right-hand Rata Ridge Track for 45 minutes return, but you should allow more time to enjoy the bush and discover its great variety of indigenous

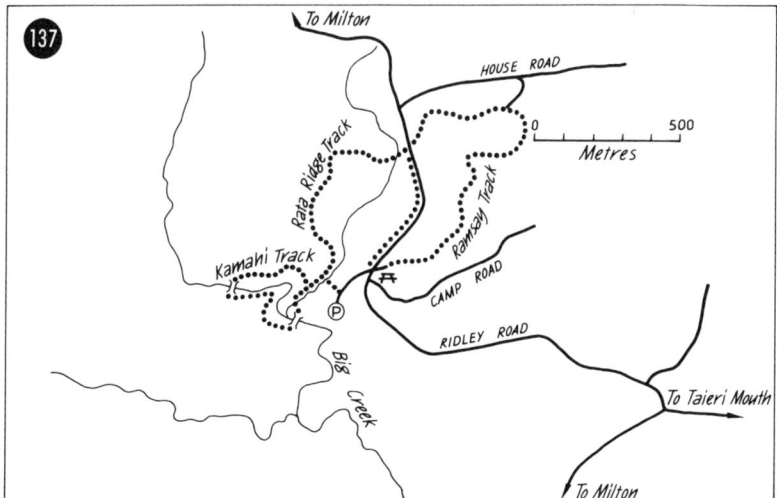

plants. Both tracks provide easy to medium footing, although good walking shoes are necessary if the ground is wet.

Considering that logging was at one time carried out in this area, there are some good specimen plants close to the track and many trees including broadleaf, totara, pokaka and southern rata (a blaze of colour in late January). Lancewood, kamahi, rimu and miro are plentiful.

Ramsay Track, a 1-hour loop, is a mixture of native bush, scrub and pine forest.

The trip back to Dunedin is best made by the coast for the view of white-sand beaches and numerous headlands.

Catlins River Valley

Length: Various
Time taken: Up to 5 hours
Grading: Average
Apparel: Good footwear
Code: Year-round, trees, birds, fishing

Points of note: The Catlins River walks form a continuous well-marked track (divided into three sections) that follows the river down from The Wisp to Tawanui. The track can be walked in sections, as there are two exits to forestry roads. You are advised to obtain a map at the Department of Conservation visitor centre in Owaka before setting out. If you use forestry roads from Tawanui, a drop-off and pick-up system can be organised by car if you do not want to walk back. There is a short (1 hour) loop track at The Wisp picnic area.

Access: You reach The Wisp picnic area at the upstream end of the track by taking Owaka Valley Road, turning off on Chloris Pass Road, and continuing down to the Catlins River. The Tawanui camping and picnic area, at the downstream end, is 13 kilometres from Owaka. Take State Highway 92 south of Owaka, and turn off to Tawanui at Houipapa. This side road follows the Catlins River.

If you start from The Wisp roadside area, there is first a loop track taking about an hour — the Anglers Track — which follows a loop in the river. Cross the river by swingbridge and walk down the river to another bridge back across the river to the Wallis Stream picnic area. A short track leads to a roadside parking area (with an exit to forestry road).

The next stage, to Frank Stream, takes 1½ hours and is mainly alongside

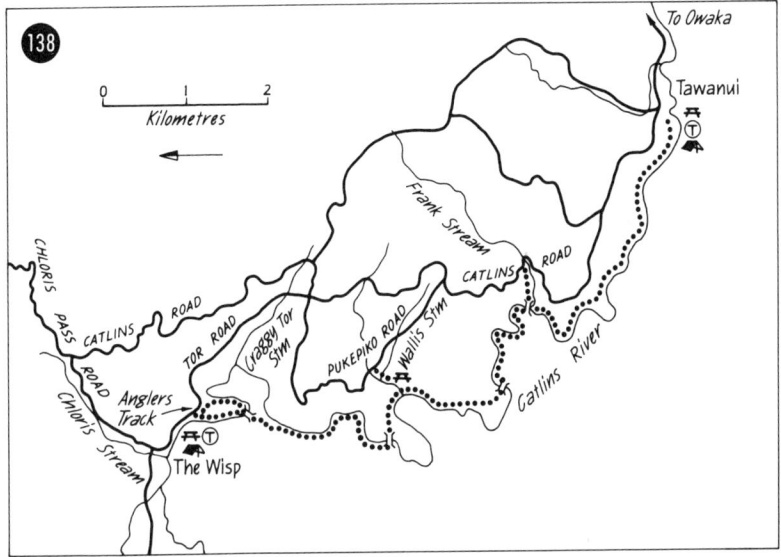

the river, which has many small rapids. It again bridges the river twice. There is a side track to Catlins Road through silver beech trees, which are a feature of this section.

The final section of the walk, all on one side of the river, ends up through exotic forest, and takes 2½ hours to reach the Tawanui picnic area.

The walk, mainly through native bush, is the only track system in the northern area of Catlins Forest Park. The four crossings of the river are all via swingbridges.

Purakaunui Falls

Length: 1 kilometre
Time taken: 30 minutes return
Grading: Easy, with steep steps and handrail to falls (suitable for wheelchairs to the top viewing point)
Apparel: Casual
Code: Year-round, trees, birds, waterfall

Points of note: A feature of this walk is a stand of silver beech on the roadside, with mixed podocarp forest on the track, which is well signposted, with a parking area

209

and toilets at the entrance. There is a viewing platform at the top of the waterfall and another at the bottom.

Access: Follow State Highway 92 south of Owaka, cross the Catlins River Bridge, turn left and take the next turn to the right.

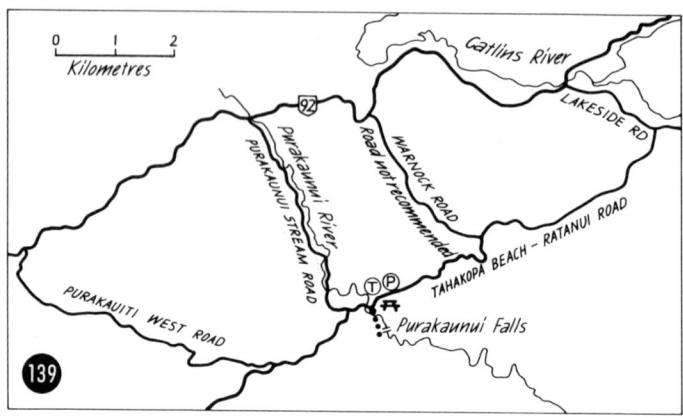

Picnic Point

Length: 0.75 kilometre
Time taken: 20 minutes
Grading: Easy
Apparel: Casual
Code: Year-round, trees, birds

Points of note: A delightfully easy walk on a well-kept pathway, Picnic Point offers plenty of variety in forest and coast and takes 20 minutes each way, whether you return by the same route or via the beach.

Access: The entrance is at the lower end of a loop road through the Papatowai settlement from State Highway 92, about 30 kilometres south of Owaka.

A sign and rimu seat mark the entrance to the path, which is through a podocarp and kamahi mixture to coastal rata-totara-mixed broadleaf forest. It emerges to the sound of waves breaking on a rocky coast. The view is across the mouth of the Tahakopa River to a long sandy bay of the same name. Behind this bay is an important reserve of young and maturing rimu and a swamp forest. At the far end of the beach, the old coach road emerged, before the cliffs became too high, and, after travelling along the sand, the coaches forded the Tahakopa River near the mouth at low tide.

Turn left to return via the beach and enjoy the rock pools when the tide is out. You will find colourful paua and many shells here. Several large rata trees near the water's edge give a striking display about Christmas time. There are usually waders, gulls and terns about. Around the point is a picnic area with toilets near the loop road.

A branch track from the bush path will lead south to Kings Rocks, a favourite rock-fishing spot for blue cod, butterfish and trumpeter. From here a climb up a cleared and farmed hill face leads to State Highway 92 and Florence Hill above Papatowai.

Tautuku Bay

Length: 1 kilometre
Time taken: 15 minutes to the beach
Grading: Easy
Apparel: Casual
Code: Year-round, birds, trees, plants, flowers

Points of note: A well-formed bush track, this features trees labelled for students who attend the nearby outdoor education centre, and has a beach walk back to the highway.

Access: On State Highway 92, 2 kilometres north of Tautuku Lodge, the walk begins opposite the Tautuku Outdoor Education Centre, where booklets on the walk can be obtained at a small cost.

The walk traverses a good cross-section of coastal forest trees and plants, giving a brief impression of a primeval forest. The track emerges on to a high sand dune with a view out over a long, curved, sandy beach suitable for bathing.

An excursion to the right leads to the Tautuku Peninsula, with its rugged cliffs and sandy bays. Once a whaling station, it is now grazed and favoured by holiday fishermen and their families. To reach the peninsula, the tide must be out, as the Tautuku River has to be forded. At the other end of the beach is the wildlife sanctuary of Rainbow Isles.

Rata fringes this bay and, in a good flowering season, makes a blaze of

211

colour. The dune is covered mainly with marram grass, but the native sand-binder pingao is still to be found.

Lake Wilkie

Length: 0.5 kilometre
Time taken: 20 minutes return
Grading: Easy (suitable for wheelchairs to the top viewing point)
Apparel: Casual
Code: Year-round, trees, view, lake

Points of note: The walk passes through the Tautuku Bay Scenic Reserve and shows an unusual forest sequence around the shore of the lake.

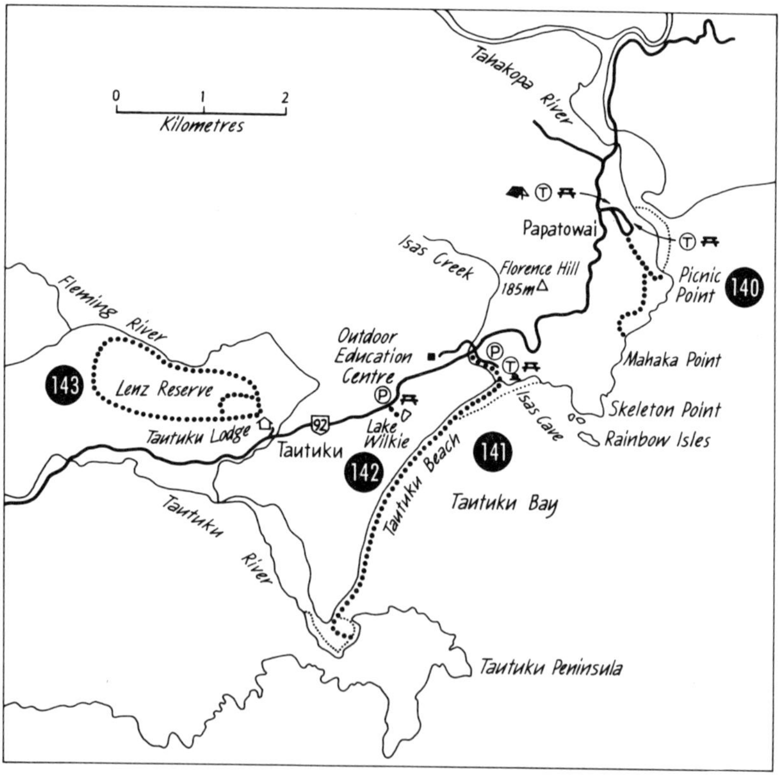

Access: This signposted walk starts at a parking area off State Highway 92, just south of the Tautuku Outdoor Education Centre.

The walk leads through the bush to a viewing point and descends to the lake shore, where a boardwalk leads out around the water's edge, giving a close view of the sequence of dune and swamp forest, with dense rimu, totara and matai present. The lake is very sheltered and often mirrorlike.

Lenz Reserve

Length: Various
Time taken: Up to 4 hours
Grading: Easy to moderate
Apparel: Tramping gear
Code: Year-round, trees, birds, plants

Points of note: This walk is in the Tautuku Forest Lenz Reserve of the Forest and Bird Society. Although it can be traversed in 4 hours, it is best not rushed over and is most enjoyed with a break for lunch at the Fleming River.

Access: The track starts in a clearing by the society's Tautuku Lodge, which is reached from State Highway 92, 33 kilometres south-west of Owaka.

Near the start are relics of timber-milling days, and from there the track follows the route of an old tramline up the hill through cut-over bush. There are views across to Florence Hill and Longpoint on the coast before the track descends, fairly steeply in one or two places, to Fleming River. The track at this point loops and twists through a fairly flat and sometimes swampy area, following and crossing the river twice before climbing back up the hill to the lodge. Walkers should not deviate from the well-blazed and cut track.

Where milling has not taken place, there are tall stands of rimu, miro and kahikatea; elsewhere there are second-growth trees of these species, plus rata, kamahi and broadleaf.

Signs of birds are plentiful, from the swish of the wood pigeon to the quick flick of the fantail. The bellbird and tui call, along with the shining cuckoo in summer.

A short nature walk branches off the main track and makes a circuit near the lodge, providing a 30-minute walk for those short of time or energy.

SOUTHLAND

Croydon Bush

Length: Various
Time taken: Up to 2½ hours
Grading: Moderate
Apparel: Good footwear and parka
Code: Fair weather, trees, birds, views, waterfall

Points of note: The Croydon Bush Scenic Reserve of 960 hectares on the Hokonui Hills came into being in 1893 on the instigation of D. L. Popplewell, later Mayor of Gore. It covers easy to steep country, rising from 180 to 520 metres. The open tussock tops rise from the bushline to 630 metres at East Peak.

Sawmillers operated through most of the area followed by post-cutters, but some magnificent old rimu, matai and miro, especially on steeper slopes, escaped the axe. An area of bush to the west of, and upstream from, Dolamore Park remains untouched and can be viewed in its natural state.

Access: Dolamore Park is 11 kilometres from Gore via State Highway 94 and Reaby Road to Retreat Croydon Road. The domain area has a tea kiosk.

Dolamore Loop: (1 hour return): Signposted, this enters the bush at the northern end of Dolamore Park. After crossing the footbridge over the Waimumu Stream, follow the well-defined walk to the left, passing through a portion of the only unmilled bush within the reserve. Many of the trees have been labelled. At the highest point on the track, a track leads to an observation point over the surrounding area. The walk then leads down to the banks of the Waimumu Stream and back to the park.

Whisky Creek Falls: (2 hours): This also enters the bush at the northern end of Dolamore Park. Cross the footbridge over the Waimumu Stream and follow the left bank. After crossing the second footbridge (just before this, glow-worms light the streambank by night), the walk leads up and over a ridge through the bush, passes the side track to Popplewells Viewpoint and

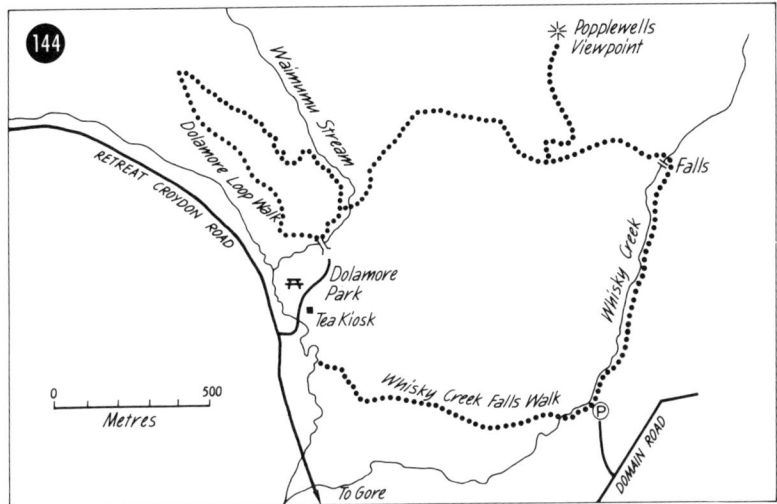

descends to the Whisky Creek Falls. A short side track descends to the foot of the falls, which are well worth viewing after rain.

The walk continues on a well-benched track through open bush, with views down the valley to the Whisky Creek carpark. From the downstream end of the carpark clearing, the walk crosses Whisky Creek and leads through regenerating bush to come out at the lower picnic area at Dolamore Park.

Popplewells Viewpoint Track: The walk to this viewpoint is 30 minutes return from the Whisky Creek Track. It climbs gradually to the clearing, which has a magnificent panoramic view, extending as far as Stewart Island on a clear day.

Seaward Downs

Length: 1½ kilometres
Time taken: 30 minutes return
Grading: Easy
Apparel: Casual
Code: Year-round, trees, birds

215

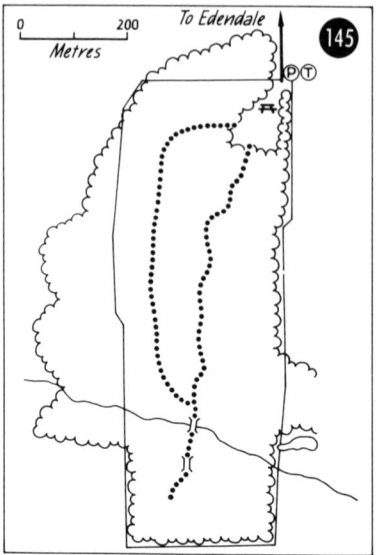

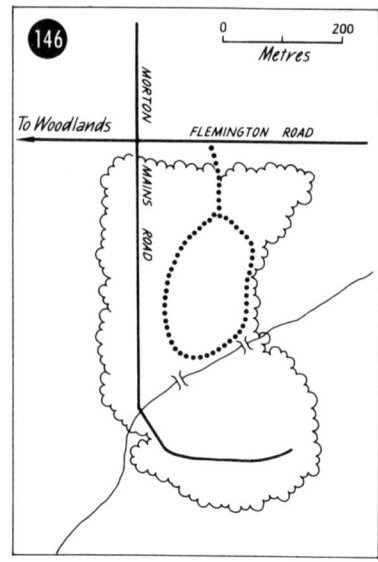

Points of note: This short walk in the 26-hectare Seaward Downs Scenic Reserve contains a good example of the native bush of the area, surrounded by Southland farmlands. The main tree species are rimu, miro, totara, broadleaf, tarata, matai and kahikatea.

Access: About 40 kilometres north-east of Invercargill along State Highway 1, turn right at Edendale toward Seaward Downs and then right again down Tramway Road West. The reserve is about 4 kilometres down this road on the left.

The track leads from a picnic ground ringed by native trees and shrubs, and passes through pleasant bush in which specimens of some individual trees have been labelled. You should take the main route (with markers) out into the reserve; an alternative, sometimes muddy, route is available for the return walk. There is a variety of native birds in the reserve, which is a favoured habitat for native pigeons.

Kingswood Bush

Length: 0.5 kilometre
Time taken: 20 minutes return

Grading: Easy
Apparel: Casual
Code: Year-round, trees, plants, birds

Points of note: This walk is in an 8-hectare scenic reserve on Woodlands Research Station.

Access: The area lies about 2 kilometres east of Woodlands on the road to Morton Mains, 5 minutes from State Highway 1, via a turn-off 26 kilometres north of Invercargill.

The loop walk enters the bush just before the sealed road passes over the first gully, and although not signposted, it is easy to find. The track is maintained by voluntary labour and may become overgrown from time to time.

The area, also known as Flemington Bush, is an example of the original heavy forest of the Southland plain. The main trees are rimu (some 700 years old), kahikatea, totara and miro, with many fuchsias and ferns. Birds abound in the bush.

Hokonui Forest

Length: 4 kilometres
Time taken: Up to 1½ hours return
Grading: Easy
Apparel: Good footwear and warm clothing in winter
Code: Year-round, trees, plants, birds, waterfall

Points of note: An excellent bush walk beside a stream, not too far from Invercargill (35 kilometres), this sheltered, all-weather track is usable most of the way by wheelchair, although it is damp in places. The excellent picnic area has tables and fireplaces; there are toilets and parking bays.

Access: Turn off Highway 96 between Hedgehope and Waitane, north into Dunsdale Valley Road. Then turn right along a metalled side road to the picnic area.

Cross the bridge from the picnic area and follow an easy, well-formed track through low bush to a larger swingbridge and return down the other side of the stream, where there are good specimens of large trees and less undergrowth.

The many varieties of trees and plants on the outward track include

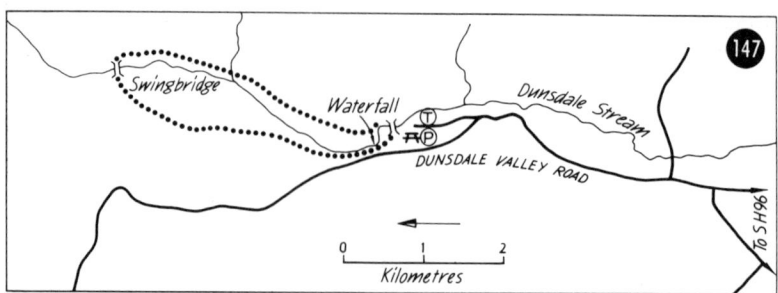

coprosma, lancewood, fuchsia, pepper tree, putaputaweta, pittosporum, small broadleaf, native broom, olearia, ferns and lichens. On the other, more shady, side there are some excellent rimu, totara, kahikatea and kamahi. There are views of the stream and waterfall, and of the Hokonui Hills. The bush has a large number of bellbirds, pigeons, silvereyes and a few grey warblers.

Forest Hill

Length: Various
Time taken: Up to 3 hours
Grading: Easy to moderate
Apparel: Good footwear and warm clothing in winter
Code: Year-round, trees, plants, birds

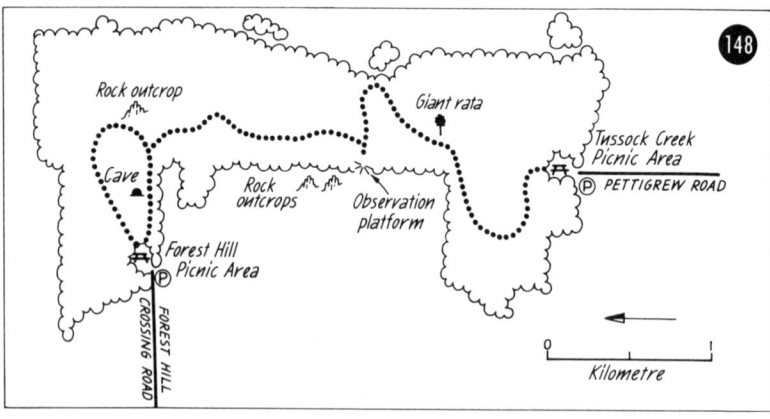

Points of note: The Forest Hill Scenic Reserve, of about 580 hectares, shows evidence of milling that occurred until the 1930s, but in areas least disturbed there are large matai, kahikatea, miro, broadleaf, rata, totara, kaikomako and ribbonwood. It is probably the best place to see brown creepers in Southland. Other birds found in the area include grey warblers, tomtits, bellbirds, wood pigeons, fantails and tui.

Access: The reserve is about 26 kilometres north of Invercargill and can be reached from State Highway 6. There are two access points to the reserve, at the Tussock Creek and Forest Hill picnic areas respectively. The first, and most popular, is reached by turning off the highway about 15 kilometres from Invercargill, onto Wilsons Crossing Road. About 7 kilometres along is Pettigrew Road, which leads to the picnic area. For the Forest Hill picnic area, turn off the highway about 22 kilometres north of Invercargill and follow the Forest Hill Crossing Road to its end.

From the Tussock Creek picnic area a track leads off through the forest, reaching a giant rata after about 30–45 minutes. After another 30–45 minutes there is an observation platform, giving an extensive view over the Southland plains. This makes a good 2–3-hour return trip. The track does, however, continue to the Forest Hill picnic area, taking about 2 hours in total and passing a limestone cave about 15 minutes from the end.

From the Forest Hill picnic area there is also a loop track, which is not as well-formed as the other walks in the area. This takes about 1½ hours to complete and can be muddy in places. For those wanting a shorter walk, a return walk to the cave, which is inhabited by weta, takes about 30 minutes.

Foveaux Walkway

Length: 3–4 kilometres
Time taken: 1 hour return
Grading: Fairly easy
Apparel: Good footwear and warm clothing in winter
Code: Year-round, variety of vegetation, birds, views

Points of note: This walk around The Bluff offers panoramic views of Foveaux Strait, with Stewart, Dog and Ruapuke Islands visible.

Access: The walk begins and ends at the Stirling Point carpark, at the termination of State Highway 1, about 2 kilometres from the centre of Bluff township.

From the carpark a track leads up the hill, through private land, about 5–10 minutes to the gunpits and the start of the Glory Track. This leads down through mixed podocarp-hardwood forest, with the main canopy species being rimu, totara, miro, rata and kamahi. The sailing vessel *England's Glory* was wrecked on the rocks in 1881, and this track is said to be the route taken by the crew on their way to Bluff.

On the coast the track meets the Foveaux Walkway. To the left it is about 1.5 kilometres back to the carpark on a wide and relatively flat track. To the right the walkway continues about 5 kilometres to Ocean Beach. About 300 metres along is the old beacon. It is worth continuing along the coast for some distance before returning to the carpark. The coastal vegetation includes five-finger, olearia, manuka, fuchsia and hebe, along with flax, ferns and astelias. The coast is very exposed to southerly winds, and visitors should be prepared for sudden changes in weather.

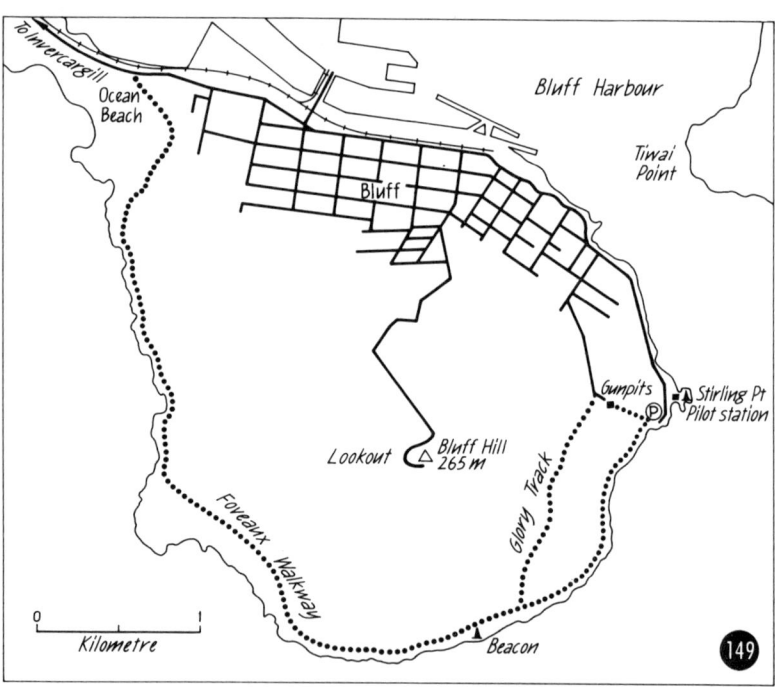

Observation Rock

Length: 0.5 kilometre
Time taken: 15 minutes
Grading: Easy to average
Apparel: Casual
Code: Year-round, birds, views

Points of note: Observation Rock, above Stewart Island's Halfmoon Bay, provides a vantage point for views of Paterson Inlet and its islands, of Mt Rakaehua and Pryse Peak, and, to the north-east, Stewart Island's highest point, Mt Anglem (980 metres). It is also a popular place to observe the island's often spectacular sunsets. A diorama indicates the points of interest within viewing range.

Access: Leave from the Halfmoon Bay Post Office by way of either Golden Bay Road or Excelsior Road (the steeper of the two).

Among the native plants and trees in the area of Observation Rock are rimu, red matipo, muttonbird scrub, fuchsia, kamahi, coprosma and many interesting ground plants.

Bird life is plentiful, and in the summer there is considerable activity from bellbirds, tui, pigeons, parakeets, kaka, fantails, grey warblers and cuckoos.

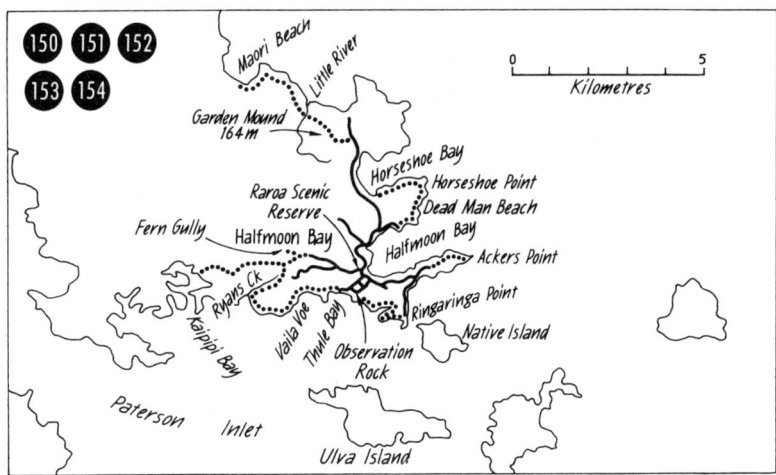

Raroa Scenic Reserve

Length: 1 kilometre
Time taken: 20 minutes return
Grading: Easy
Apparel: Casual
Code: Year-round, bush, birds

Points of note: The Raroa Scenic Reserve, gifted to the Crown by G. M. Turner, has a luxuriant understorey of ferns and mosses and is one of the few forested areas around Halfmoon Bay unspoiled by early milling.

Access: From the western end of Traill Park, the reserve is 10 minutes from the post office.

The track descends very gradually to Watercress Beach in Paterson Inlet, through native bush including some fine stands of mature rimu. The return to Halfmoon Bay can be either through the reserve, by way of Rankin Street, or past Golden Bay, all pleasant walks.

Tui, bellbirds, kaka, parakeets and pigeons are usually seen and heard in good numbers.

Ackers Point

Length: 4 kilometres
Time taken: 1½–2 hours
Grading: Easy
Apparel: Good footwear, parka
Code: Year-round, birds, views

Points of note: Blue penguins, muttonbirds and blue shags nest along this coast. At the end of a summer evening, the muttonbirds can be seen coming in to land at Ackers Point to feed their young. At Harrold Bay stands the oldest dwelling on the island, the stone cottage built by Lewis Acker in about 1835. Along with the nearby Travellers Rest, it has been gazetted as a historic house.

Access: The point is on the south side of Halfmoon Bay.

From the signpost beyond Lonnekers Beach the track follows the coast past Leask, Jensen and Harrold Bays, mainly through coastal vegetation, to Ackers Point. Open areas along the coast afford good views of Foveaux Strait and the north side of the bay.

Ringaringa Point

Length: 3 kilometres
Time taken: 1–1½ hours return
Grading: Easy to average
Apparel: Good footwear and parka
Code: Year-round, trees, birds, views

Points of note: Ringaringa Beach is noted for its shells and seaweeds, and for the many interesting rock pools exposed at low tide. The place is believed to be named after Ringa Ringa Moses, who also has Moses Corner in Paterson Inlet and Moses Nugget on Ringaringa Beach named after him. A first-class boatman, Moses more than once pulled his 3.3 metre dinghy to Bluff.

Access: Access is on the north side of Paterson Inlet, by the road that turns right at the signpost beyond Lonnekers Beach.

Beyond the beach, and where the road becomes a track leading past the old Traill homestead, is a monument to the Reverend Johann Wohlers, a German who arrived at Ruapuke in 1844 and, with his wife, is remembered for missionary work among the southern Maori.

To the east of the promontory, and separated from Ringaringa by a narrow passage, is Native Island, a place of early Maori occupation. To the west is Traill Bay, from the north end of which a track leads around the coast to Deep Bay and then climbs up to the top of Peterson Hill overlooking Halfmoon Bay.

Horseshoe Bay

Length: 4 kilometres
Time taken: 2½ hours
Grading: Easy to average

223

Apparel: Good footwear, warm and waterproof clothing

Code: Year-round, trees, plants, views

Points of note: The track passes through some fine bush. At the open grassed area of Horseshoe Point, there are splendid views of Ackers Point and The Neck to the east, Garden Mound and Mt Anglem to the north, and across Foveaux Strait to Southland, where snow-capped mountains are visible on a clear day.

Access: Beyond Butterfield Beach in Halfmoon Bay the road turns right and skirts Moturau Moana down to Bragg Bay. The track to Horseshoe Bay begins at a marked gate.

From Halfmoon Bay to Bragg Bay takes 1 hour, and from Bragg Bay to Horseshoe Bay 1½ hours. The track crosses private land and descends to the secluded Dead Man Beach, continuing on around Horseshoe Point to the southern end of Horseshoe Bay, a curving beach some 2 kilometres in length. At the north end there is a wharf and a fish-packing shed, and on the hill above, the Department of Conservation Outdoor Education Centre, overlooking Frenchmans Beach.

Beyond Horseshoe Bay to the north lie Garden Mound, Little River and Maori Beach for those who wish to extend their walk.